SEARCH AND RESCUE
A Wilderness Doctor's Life-and-Death
Tales of Risk and Reward

CHRISTOPHER VAN TILBURG, MD

FALCONGUIDES

GUILFORD, CONNECTICUT
HELENA, MONTANA

FALCONGUIDES®

An imprint of Globe Pequot
Falcon, FalconGuides, and Make Adventure Your Story are registered trademarks
of Rowman & Littlefield.

Distributed by NATIONAL BOOK NETWORK

Copyright © 2017 by Christopher Van Tilburg

Photos by Christopher Van Tilburg

British Library Cataloguing in Publication Information available

Library of Congress Cataloging-in-Publication Data available

ISBN 978-1-4930-2735-4 (paperback)
ISBN 978-1-4930-2736-1 (e-book)

∞™ The paper used in this publication meets the minimum requirements of American National
Standard for Information Sciences—Permanence of Paper for Printed Library Materials, ANSI/
NISO Z39.48-1992.

Printed in the United States of America

CONTENTS

Author's Note

A DECADE HAS PASSED SINCE PUBLICATION OF MY MEMOIR *Mountain Rescue Doctor, Wilderness Medicine in the Extremes of Nature*. I've been collecting mountain rescue experiences ever since. Unfortunately, I also was involved as a patient in a near-death accident on Mount Hood, after which I had newfound interest in risk and reward. In particular, I became intrigued with balance between the two: How do we take positive risks to achieve great reward yet minimize consequences? My curiosity was not solely focused in my volunteering with the legendary Crag Rats mountain rescue team of Hood River, Oregon. But my intrigue regarding risk seeped into various aspects of my life as an outdoor athlete, as a writer, as a doctor, and as a father. I became fascinated by why risk is such an important characteristic in all aspects of a healthy, fulfilling life.

Thus, herein lies a collection of stories of mountain rescues during my second decade of volunteering with Crag Rats in the small, beautiful, rugged, and remote mountains, canyons, and forests of Hood River. The stories are bound together by a universal theme of risk: why it's important, how we mitigate it, and how we deal with accidents once they occur. Part One is a collection of stories that occurred on gigantic, ominous Mount Hood, an active, glacier-clad stratovolcano punching 11,249 feet above the endless Douglas fir forests. With these stories, I explain what risk is and how we mitigate risk as individuals and as a team. Part Two is a collection of stories from the second dominant and distinct geographic feature of Hood River County, the gargantuan Columbia Gorge, shaped by the 1,243-mile-long Columbia River and the 4,000-foot-high basalt and andesite walls that encase the 25-mile section in our county. In these rescues, I dive deeper into risk: why it's important for everyone, kids and adults alike, and how risk is influenced by modernization, technology, and responsibility.

This nonfiction book has limitations. Identifying characteristics of patients and victims, as well as certain locations, dates, times, group size, and other details, have been changed for confidentiality. In a few stories, I created composite characters, composite rescues, and fictitious locations. The sections of dialog are based on my personal recollections; the exchanges are included to provide a general idea of how we communicate during missions but are not exactly verbatim. And the stories are recounted from my memory after the rescues were completed. Thus, portions of this book are not 100 percent accurate, given the stress generated from and the focus required by a mountain rescue mission, the inability to record or document activities during the rescues, the need to disguise individuals for privacy, and the limitations of my memory.

In addition, search-and-rescue missions are much more complicated than my singular role in these stories. This is my perspective only—opinions, musings, and observations—and in no way represents anyone's perspective other than mine.

I thank many for direct and indirect support for production of this book. Joelle Delbourgo, my agent, is a stalwart believer in my work and the cause about which I'm writing. John Paine, my editor, helped me shape the early outline of this book. The crew at Falcon has been fabulous including David Costello, Erin Turner, Courtney Oppel, Lauren Szalkiewicz, and Jessie Shiers.

My daughters Skylar and Avrie Van Tilburg and my parents Wayne and Eleanor Van Tilburg have been supporters for the duration. I thank my many, many family and friends who came to my aid when I was injured, including Jennifer Sato, Peter Van Tilburg, Suzy Rylander, and Jo Guralnick, and especially Jon and Adrienne Davies and Andrew and Melissa McElderry.

I thank my colleagues, too numerous to name: mountain rescuers, firefighters, paramedics, doctors, nurses, sheriffs, sheriff's deputies, dispatchers, and search-and-rescue personnel, including those in the field, in the office, and behind the computers and phones of dispatch centers. Only those folks can truly know the stress, camaraderie, risk, and reward when the call comes in at 10:00 p.m., and we climb all night into the dank, dark, foreboding mountains.

And most of all, I owe thanks to my team, Crag Rats, a ninety-year-old volunteer group with which I have had the privilege of serving for two decades.

I hope these stories offer a glimpse of the daunting task of mountain rescue and encourages everyone to endure a bit of risk, albeit cautiously, to achieve great reward.

—Christopher Van Tilburg, Cloud Cap Inn, Mount Hood, August 2016

PROLOGUE

Shock Trauma

CARRYING A BRIGHT GREEN WRISTBAND IN HER HAND, MY NURSE WALKS into the lone trauma bay in the Providence Hood River Memorial Hospital Emergency Department. At that instant, I know I am gravely injured, but I have no idea how close I am to the brink of death. The iridescent emerald plastic Oregon Trauma System bracelet unfurls like a streamer, appearing much larger than it is, lashing out toward me like a snake tongue in a 3D movie. I recognize the nurse, but I can't place her name. My head is foggy. My left chest and shoulder ache: not sharp and stabbing, but throbbing in an angry, annoying manner. All I can focus on is the neon green talisman coming to zap me.

The room had been eerily silent ten seconds before, like in a movie when everything pauses in slow motion before the action explodes on the screen. Then, like an electric shock, the nurse clicks the bracelet onto my wrist and the room erupts with activity. The band reminds me of the ones my daughters and I wore at Great Wolf Lodge waterpark. However, this band is the farthest possible reach from fun and family adventure. I know exactly what the green band represents, having placed it multiple times on my own patients, in that very emergency department, where I work as a doctor and now surrender as a patient.

I am about to die.

That January day began as I sat in my home office, watching the mountain dawn overcome darkness, as I am wont to do, with a cappuccino of Hood River Roaster's Abruzzo dark and an hour of work already behind me (yes, I'm one of those annoying morning people). While wading through a ream of legal documents on a heatstroke consulting case, I paused to spy a sunrise sky filled with fuchsia, tangerine, and violet streaks overtaking darkness, for just few seconds. Then the morning colors quickly subsided to pale shades of sunup, azure turned a robin's-egg blue.

I knew it was going to be a good day on Mount Hood, Oregon's iconic snow-clad volcano, towering 11,239 feet above a massive ocean of forest-green Douglas fir foothills. New snow coated the big peak and the sky cleared for the first time in weeks. I paused work for the morning, because at precisely 6:30 a.m. the morning cacophony began as my two teen daughters tumbled out of bed. Sleepy-eyed, Skylar and Avrie appeared downstairs. I orchestrated breakfast as they packed school backpacks with homework and soccer kits. In a flurry of text messages, I made plans to ski with my new friend Margaret, an athletic, cheery, blonde work-at-home corporate tax lawyer transplanted to Oregon from Minnesota.

The mountain was set up for a powder day, what we skiers and snowboarders bide our time for and drop everything to score. The weekend before, a Pineapple Express—a thick, warm, wet marine weather system from the South Pacific—had unleashed torrents of rain on the mountain. Six inches of liquid sunshine, aka rain, fell in 24 hours, a record deluge even for waterlogged Oregon. The snowpack was soaked with water and the runoff carved deep troughs in the snow called *rain runnels*. Newton Creek flooded one of the county's main arteries, Highway 35, which connects the town of Hood River to Portland and Bend, Oregon, via the east and south sides of Mount Hood. The Hood River, the chocolaty creek that is the town's namesake, breached the train bridge with turbulent, muddy water and dumped massive quantities of silt into its confluence with the Columbia River.

Monday, the day after the rain stopped, temperatures dropped and rain-soaked snowpack froze solid into rock-hard ice.

Tuesday, the day after the ice froze solid, the air cooled, the freezing elevation fell to 2,000 feet, and the Pineapple Express turned from rain to snow: eight inches of creamy powder fell on Mount Hood.

Wednesday morning, as if on cue, the sun came out. This sort of day occurs regularly, but not frequently, in the Pacific Northwest: clear sky, cold temperature, and fresh powder snow. When it does, if we can, we'll drop what we're doing and head to Mount Hood Meadows resort, aka *the mountain*, because this is the largest ski resort in close proximity to Hood River and Portland.

On the mountain, the sun and snow were spectacular. Margaret and I cruised the whole mountain, catching runs of silky smooth, untracked powder snow. But after two hours, the brilliant, hot sun began to warm the snowpack and the temperatures rose again. *The snow is getting heavy*, I remember thinking. As the sun beat down, the powder snow slowly metamorphosed to thick gooey slush, first the consistency of apple sauce and then of mashed potatoes. When we ventured higher on the mountain, we occasionally carved through the soft snow and broke through to the rock-hard layer of ice. Something should have clicked in my head, like a yellow roadside caution sign that said, BURIED ICE: DANGER.

Nearing the end of the morning, I separated from Margaret when I popped down a run called Cry Baby, one of my favorite short and steep gullies, hidden from most skiers. I was making fast, wide, smooth turns in the soft snow. I was feeling elated, and my mind wandered a bit. I had an upcoming trip to Haiti, a new job, and decent reviews for my latest book. I was spending a lot of time with my daughters, traveling the world. And I was skiing creamy powder snow in the sun, with Margaret nonetheless.

Then, I crashed. And I crashed hard. Something that heretofore had never happened to me. I was skiing fast, but not out of control. I was making big wide turns, wall-to-wall, in the gully, but not hucking a cliff or spinning a 360 or skiing recklessly. I wasn't being careless.

Skiing, as in backcountry skiing and ski mountaineering, by the way, is one of my great passions in life—topping a list that includes mountain biking, road cycling, mountain running, kite surfing, stand-up paddle surfing, and global adventuring. I grew up on Mount Hood, learned to ski here at age seven, and spend fifty days a year carving the slopes, both inbound runs and the backcountry. I have climbed to and skied off the summit of Mount Hood, spent hundreds of hours on mountain rescue missions on the mountain, and written a backcountry ski and snowboard guidebook for Oregon, not once but twice. I have given scores of lectures on wilderness medicine focusing often on backcountry skiing, avalanche safety, and ski mountaineering. I've skied all over the world: Portillo,

Chile; the Haute Route ski tour from Chamonix, France, to Zermatt, Switzerland; the famed powder of Hokkaido, Japan; the Ortler Circuit in Northern Italy.

After four decades of skiing, ski mountaineering, climbing, and rescuing people, I crashed.

It was like those crash-test dummies ramming a cement wall, full speed to stop in one microsecond. One second, I was cruising along in soft snow making big, wide, fast turns. The next second, both of my skis slammed head-on into a buried block of ice, stopped in place, and stayed perfectly aligned; meanwhile I was ejected from the bindings instantly. My body catapulted head over heels. I accelerated in the air the way you do when you flip on a trampoline: you spin instantly, abruptly, and violently. The blue sky, the white snow, the big green conifers zoomed by so fast that it wasn't even a blur, it simply did not register.

Then, *bam!* I landed with a sickening thud, after a 270-degree rotation. My back impacted directly on another block of ice, this one a sharply pointed pyramidal chunk the size of a bowling ball. A sudden, severe, piercing pain rammed my left back and flank as if I had been jousted off a horse with a lance. Gasping for breath, with my brain foggy and dizzy, I was stunned. Lying in the snow, I wondered if I was alive, right there, on the mountain, on *my* mountain, the great, dominant feature in my life and work: Mount Hood.

I tried to suck in a lungful of air, but drew in a shallow, weak breath as an intense sharp stab shot through my left chest, like a knife jammed in my lung. When I exhaled, the pain morphed to an ominous, more worrisome ache—a deep pressure that squeezed my lung.

I had a flash of what might be called anxiety, not panic: I stood up immediately, because I wanted to make sure my legs worked and I wasn't paralyzed. (That moment, by the way, was the single most fearful one.) I got dizzy, so I sat back down. I was immensely relieved that my legs worked but when I put my hand under my jacket, I could feel that my chest was crackly and spongy, a condition called *crepitus*, from fluid leaking into the skin and surrounding tissue. *Probably broken ribs, hopefully not a collapsed lung*, I thought.

I was alone in a remote, little-visited gully. And then I was consumed by one idea, an instinct that certainly saved my life: *get down the mountain.* It wasn't a panicky thought but a matter-of-fact one. Had I sat there waiting for help, which may have been a long while, I might just have died.

So after a few seconds, I stood up again, stepped gingerly into my skis, and schussed tentatively, slowly out of the gulley, unaware of my ruptured, bleeding spleen, which would over the next two hours pump at least liter of blood into my abdomen, a fifth of my total blood volume. I found Margaret waiting at the bottom of the run.

"I crashed. I have to go to medical," I said with my head foggy and never imagining I would need help. I knew I had to get down the mountain. Margaret escorted me slowly to the resort's Mountain Clinic, the ski resort clinic where I work as a doctor but was off duty that day. Unbeknownst to me or the clinic nurse or Margaret, I was critical.

An hour later, I am lying in the gurney in Providence Hood River Memorial Hospital, where I also work as a doctor, with the fangs of the green trauma band searing through the skin on my wrist. I am near death and about to embark on the biggest emergency surgeries ever done at the small hospital in the small town where I live. In fact, I would end up with the year's highest Trauma Index for Providence Hood River Memorial Hospital, the most critically ill patient.

Internal hemorrhage from trauma is one the most ominous lethal conditions because doctors can't readily see it, can't gauge the severity, and can't often determine exactly where the leak is coming from. Usually, blood loss is noticed only when a patient succumbs to shock, a lethal or near-lethal shutdown of the body's vital functions. Although shock is a commonly misused word to describe general difficulty with vital functions or emotional distress, it really means one thing: inadequate blood flow to vital organs—heart, lungs, and brain being the most essential. When blood cannot deliver vital oxygen and dispose of toxic carbon dioxide, cells start to die, organs start to fail, and life begins a precipitous spiral to cessation. If not treated, shock leads quickly—in minutes or hours—to one outcome: death.

Shock is usually determined in an emergency setting initially by physical exam and not some expensive, high-tech test: low blood pressure, high heart rate, high respiratory rate, pale and cool skin with slow capillary refill (when skin blanches briefly with pressure, then returns back to normal color), low urine output, and mental status changes like confusion and slurred speech. Bleeding to death is called hypovolemic shock because the blood volume is diminished. I was in hypovolemic shock—shock from trauma. The exact cause of my shock was later confirmed by CT scan: ruptured spleen (along with four broken ribs, two chipped lumbar vertebrae spinous processes, and a lacerated kidney).

Other types of shock can occur as well. Neurogenic shock, such as with a concussion or spinal injury, occurs when the nerves of the brain malfunction and tell the blood vessels to divert blood away from vital organs. Cardiogenic shock occurs when the heart stops pumping blood to vital organs, as with a heart attack or congestive heart failure. Septic shock is a massive blood infection. Anaphylactic shock is a life-threatening immune response to an allergen. All types of shock result in the same ultimate outcome: inadequate blood flow to vital organs. One of the most lethal, most difficult to detect, and the most difficult to treat, is hypovolemic shock, or blood loss due to trauma. That was me. Shock trauma.

Initially, I had no signs of shock. When the body goes into defense mode to counteract shock, fit athletes have the profound ability to stave off shock, called *compensation*. In fact, athletes compensate so well that it's often difficult to detect signs of shock until the situation is dire.

First, blood sensors detect toxic levels of carbon dioxide and lactic acid, which build up from decreased blood flow to tissues. So the lungs increase respiratory rate to clear toxins—breathing hard and fast is something athletes do all the time. Then nerve sensors detect a drop in blood pressure and react by excreting a powerful hormone called epinephrine, aka adrenaline. Epinephrine increases the heart rate and blood pressure to circulate the blood more efficiently—something athletes are also acctustomed to—to deliver more life-sustaining blood. In addition, tiny muscles in blood vessels constrict to shut down blood flow to less crucial organs like the kidneys and intestinal tract. Vessels dilate in essential areas—heart, lungs, brain—to maximize blood flow with less volume. And the heart, being a muscle, is fit in athletes so it can circulate blood more efficiently.

Compensation is efficient in athletes because we are accustomed to training at maximum requirements. We are conditioned to drive as much oxygen and glucose to the tissues as possible, and clear out as much toxic carbon dioxide and lactic acid as possible. Only when athletes are at the brink of death does the blood loss outpace the compensation.

So, no one knew I was bleeding until seconds before the green band attacked me.

I just about died.

Powerful questions rattle around in my brain during the months that follow as I recuperate from emergency surgery. I never wonder, "*Why me?*" but rather, "*I'm surprised this didn't happen earlier in my life!*"

The first underlying query—*Why is risk so important in life?*—neither haunts nor perplexes me. Rather, my study of risk is academic: I become fascinated with risk in outdoor recreation, adventure travel, and extreme sports. I want to investigate why risk is so important. I am not interested in negative aspects—those are all around me in my life as a physician and mountain rescuer. I am not interested at all in avoiding risk altogether, because I have a deep love for playing outside, adventuring around the world, and trying new sports. Rather, I am interested in risk's contribution to success and safety in my endeavors in the world's mountains, forests, rivers, and oceans.

We all know that some level of risk is vital for success. We need to take risks to improve skills, go to new places, have fun, and, in the case of mountain rescue, help people in trouble and save lives. In the outdoors, we take risks to help us excel. We become skilled at an activity, physically fit, and mentally sharpened by taking risks. The more subtle but equally important benefit of risk is that we gain self-confidence and self-respect by taking positive risks. In short, taking risks builds character.

But it turns out, risk is very difficult to quantify and qualify, especially with regards to outdoor adventure.

So then a secondary question becomes my real focus: *How do we reap great rewards, yet mitigate dire consequences?* How do we take *positive risks,* those that give us a high likelihood of benefit and yet minimize chance of mishap? Athletes call this "the fun factor." How much fun (or insert any benefit here) can you have while taking reasonable risk?

The more I investigate my two quandaries—*Why is risk important?* and *How do we balance risk with reward?*—I realize that these lessons so vital to my life in mountain rescue, outdoor recreation, and adventure travel are applicable to every stanchion in my life. Thus the natural sequela of my studies became the most intriguing of all: *How do I apply these important lessons to the rest of my life?*

I begin to understand how risk permeates every component of our lives and is essential in a productive, positive, happy life. Risk isn't just a phenomenon of the outdoors: it infiltrates and extends its wiry fingers into every nook and cranny of our lives, well beyond slicing fresh powder on the most deadly mountain in North America. We need risk to start a new romance, build new friendships, construct a business, advance in our career, build financial wealth, mentor our colleagues, and teach our children. Risk helps us achieve great feats of technology, art, science, and design.

It is this focus—analyzing risk, mitigating consequences, and reaping great rewards—that then becomes my ultimate quest as a mountain rescue doctor, a father, and an adventurer.

With the green band's assault on my body, the silence of the room cracks suddenly, like a shaken can of soda that's just been opened with a pull tab, and pops. The din of the emergency room explodes—nurses scuttling about, the doc speaking on the phone in a hushed tone, footsteps echoing in the hall, the neighboring patient's chit-chatting, the faint pump of the blood pressure cuff inflating, the beeping of the pulse oximeter that measures the life-sustaining oxygen percentage in my blood, and the ambulance doors opening and closing. Lying in the gurney, I know I took a big hit; I was speared—nearly impaled—in the left chest wall by a pointed bowling-ball-size ice block. My doctor, who is also a friend and colleague, tells me, "You didn't just crush your spleen; you pulverized it into a thousand pieces."

I am not mad, frustrated, worried, or angry: I had almost expected eventually getting hurt. *It finally happened,* I think. Inevitable. Even though I'm cautious in the mountains. After four decades of mountain adventuring—skiing, biking, climbing, hiking, and running—something is bound to happen.

Everything I know to be normal changes in one sudden moment. I mean everything: family, work, recreation, romance. Mental, physical, and spiritual. I fully metamorphose in one instant from a mountain rescue doctor to a shock trauma patient on the brink of the crevasse that could lead to the end of my days. I am an outdoor adventure athlete turned critically injured patient, so far from my normal reality.

I am, in fact, on the brink of mortality.

I have collided with the earth.

At that moment, I become, forevermore, Oregon Trauma System #236439.

PART ONE

TRUTH OR DARE
ON MOUNT HOOD

CHAPTER ONE

Zero Dark Storm

ON A BITTER COLD, MIDDLE-OF-WINTER, MIDDLE-OF-THE-NIGHT, MID-dle-of-the-storm Sunday, no one hears the call for help.

While a beefy, dark storm pulverizes Mount Hood, a mountain rescue page zings to four dozen cell phones in the Hood River Valley, a quaint, picturesque fruit-growing and outdoor recreation community in north central Oregon.

But no one hears the page. No one responds to the call for help. It is deathly quiet.

The 911 call comes sometime after midnight. A backcountry skier is in distress at the Tilly Jane Guard Station, a rustic shelter tucked in a thick forest on the remote north flank of Mount Hood.

Mount Hood, I'll remind readers, is a gargantuan, ice-clad, rocky, snow-covered volcano that sticks up in the middle of the vast Mount Hood National Forest, which has miles and miles and acres and acres of evergreen conifers: the stands are mainly Douglas fir, but are spiced with western hemlock, western red cedar, larch, and lodgepole and ponderosa pine. The thick understory is hearty crop of every imaginable shade of greenery—vine maple, big leaf maple, Oregon grape, white oak, broadleaf ferns, Old Man's Beard lichen—and rocks—basalt and andesite boulders, crags, cliffs, and promontories deposited by volcanic eruptions eons ago.

And Mount Hood is a big mountain towering over the land. The peak has several purported heights. In 1867 Lt. Col. Robert Williamson calculated the elevation at 11,225 feet. In 1980, the US Geodetic Survey measured 11,239 feet using the National Geodetic Vertical Datum of

1929. A 1986 US National Geodetic Survey measurement was adjusted in 1991 to 11,249 feet using the North American Vertical Datum of 1988. A group of surveyors unofficially measured 11,240 feet in 1993 using Global Positioning System from the summit. But mountaineers and cartographers and geologists are funny, in the way they need to know the exact height. When you climb to the summit, soak in the panoramic view, and ski down on creamy smooth snow, in my opinion, the actual height really doesn't matter. It's just one gigantic, ominous mountain.

Mount Hood—named after British Admiral Lord Samuel Hood by Lt. William Broughton when he spied it from the Columbia River in 1792, but originally called Wy'East by the indigenous people—has four general regions. The south has Timberline Lodge and Summit ski areas and the bustling year-round ski and snowboard community of Government Camp. The east has Mount Hood Meadows Mountain Resort, one of the busiest ski and snowboard areas in the Western United States. The west is much less visited, accessible by only one potholed road. The north has the one-chairlift Cooper Spur Mountain Resort and the Cloud Cap–Tilly Jane Historic District.

It is here, in the Cloud Cap–Tilly Jane Historic District, where a collection of antique buildings are clustered at 6,000 feet. The US Forest Service Tilly Jane Guard Station was built in 1934 by the Civilian Conservation Corps as a backcountry cabin for snow surveys and fire protection. Long since defunct for government operations, it's a popular hut for backcountry skiers to rent in the winter. This area is accessible in the winter by skis or showshoes via the 2-mile Tilly Jane Trail, which was hewn from the forest during 1938–39 by Hood River mountaineers Percy Bucklin, Bill Cochran, Harold Wells, and Walter Applegren.

Other antique buildings of the same era still remain in the heavily wooded Tilly Jane area. The relatively dilapidated, but still functional, A-frame is another winter backcountry ski hut available for rent. The American Legion Cookhouse, currently with a collapsing roof, was also built around the same time; it was used by Legionnaires who held annual cookouts and summit climbs from 1927 to 1948.

A mile through the woods from these three Tilly Jane cabins are two other buildings at Cloud Cap Saddle, a prominent outcropping of basalt and andesite. To the south, this saddle overlooks the Hood River Valley and, on a clear day, Mount St. Helens, Mount Adams, and Mount Rainier. To the north stands the giant north face of Mount Hood. The Cloud Cap Saddle buildings predate the Tilly Jane structures by a good four decades. The Snowshoe Club Hut is a century-old private hut perched in a clearing on the saddle. And in a sparse collection of lodgepole pines sits our historic mountain rescue cabin, 130-year-old Cloud Cap Inn, where currently two dozen members of our ninety-year-old volunteer mountain rescue team, the Crag Rats, are sleeping after a day of powder skiing and avalanche-rescue training.

Earlier that day, the victim, her husband, and another couple had rented the Tilly Jane Guard Station for a weekend outing of backcountry skiing. The skiing that day had been excellent: light, dry, deep powder snow. The weather was blustery: windy, spatters of snow, and intermittent clouds, which moved eerily and rapidly across Ghost Ridge so that occasional sunbreaks lit up the forest in sparkly sunlight. After skiing all day, the woman jolted awake after midnight with excruciating back pain, so debilitating that she was only able to alleviate the pain by resting on her side, curled up in a ball, on the floor of the Guard Station.

Fortunately, the husband found cell reception—despite the thick trees, thick storm clouds, and being many miles distant from a cell tower—and called 911. The Hood River County dispatcher, after checking with the sheriff's deputy on duty, dispatched the Crag Rats by using our cell phone text messaging system.

But none of us hears the callout text.

Our mountain rescue group is in deep.

We Crag Rats are deeply sleeping in the middle of a deep, dark storm after skiing deep powder all day. We are exhausted and hunkered in our sleeping bags in the bunks of our cabin, Cloud Cap Inn, or for us, *the cabin*. This old structure was constructed in 1889, a mile from the Tilly Jane buildings, on this outcropping of rock at 6,000 feet with a spectacular in-your-face view of Mount Hood's north side. The sight of Mount Hood's north face includes Cooper Spur ridge on the left horizon, the giant serac- and crevasse-filled Eliot Glacier and steep, sheer Eliot Glacier Headwall (a 2,500-foot nearly sheer cliff) in the center, and

Cathedral Ridge on the right skyline. The cabin was originally built as a private bed-and-breakfast in 1889, well before the Civilian Conservation Corps erected the other buildings in the historic district. Several owners ran the inn intermittently and with limited success, considering guests came from Hood River 35 miles away, via horse and buggy. Often they came up the Columbia River via ferry from The Dalles, 20 miles to the east, or from Portland, 60 miles to the west. After a short trial and failure as a B&B, the cabin was sold to the Forest Service in 1942 for a few thousand dollars. After the Forest Service took it over, the lodge eventually succumbed to weather and vandalism. It fell into a state of disrepair. It was in danger of being razed by 1954: the Forest Service was set to burn it. When the Crag Rats heard about the plan to destroy Cloud Cap Inn, our group, with support from Hood River County Historical Society, struck a deal with the Forest Service. The Crag Rats would repair and maintain the building in exchange for using it as a base for snow surveys and mountain rescue. That was six decades ago. Although we call it *our* cabin, it is owned by the Forest Service and we lease it under a special-use permit. We've maintained the cabin ever since—putting thousands and thousands of hours and dollars into maintenance and repair—as our mountain rescue base for missions and training on the north side of Mount Hood. Originally, the cabin was also used as a base for snow surveys, in which Crag Rats would take manual measurements of the depth of the snowpack to gauge the summer water supply. Those surveys have long been discontinued with the advent of modern electronic devices.

We ski this mountain year-round, all seasons, every month, due to the permanent glaciers and snowfields. Every winter we take a long weekend to train, ski, and foster general camaraderie. We affectionately still call this weekend *The Winter Outing*. The Winter Outing begins on a Wednesday in the third week of February with a group of self-described old-timers who open up the cabin, fire up the woodstoves, tell stories, and pack in food via snowcat. The outing ramps up on Friday and Saturday when other members ski up the mountain, after being released from household, work, and family duties. If the snow is excellent, we mostly ski, and do a bit of training such as avalanche-rescue simulation, snow cave building, crevasse rescue training, or *cabineering*, hanging out in the cabin. The Winter Outing culminates with a big dinner on Saturday night.

This particular year, the snow quality is superb. We ski deep powder all day on Friday and Saturday: the wind and intermittent spats of snow showers keep filling in our track so nearly every run we have fresh, untracked snow. Because the storm brings wind and poor visibility above timberline, which is for the most part at 6,000 feet on Mount Hood, we choose to ski the thick trees below the cabin, Ghost Ridge, which is a slope often too low in elevation to maintain good snow. Bernie Wells, long-term member and probably the Crag Rat who knows the most about the cabin, drives our snowcat up and down Ghost Ridge, shuttling skiers back uphill.

That afternoon, since later in the year we have a mountain rescue recertification coming up, we run avalanche-rescue simulations. Our parent organization is the national Mountain Rescue Association. We belong to a subsection, Oregon Mountain Rescue Council, which includes all five mountain rescue teams in our state: Corvallis Mountain Rescue, Eugene Mountain Rescue, Portland Mountain Rescue, Deschutes County Sheriff's Office Search and Rescue Team, and us. As a council, we are responsible for certifying each other in high angle (cliffs), avalanche, crevasse, and ground search-and-rescue techniques. This year, we're up for avalanche-rescue recertification, so we take the time to drill on a rescue scenario on the Back Lawn, a wide, smooth, low-angle snow-covered slope just below the cabin.

After the rescue simulation Bernie and his son Todd set up the rope tow. A generator attached to a pulley is set up at the back door of the cabin. A 1,000-foot rope tied in a loop is stretched out down the back lawn and threaded into a pulley attached to a 15-foot-high steel water survey tower. We fire up the generator, which pulls the loop rope, and we have a backwoods rope tow.

About the time we all hunker down in the cabin for dinner, the sky darkens and the storm thickens. We share a giant vat of chili that Joe McCulloch brewed up. By bedtime, we are all exhausted. The sky is a full-on storm: the windows of the old cabin rattle and the rafters creak as wind finds every nook to pierce the century-old log walls. The temperature drops. Sometime after 10:00 p.m., we crawl deep into our sleeping bags. I find space in a back room in the east wing: the air is stale and bitter cold. I'm several rooms removed from the fireplace and woodstoves that keep the main room of the cabin toasty.

So, when the text message pings our phones, no one hears the text message, even though our crew sleeps 1 mile away from the Guard Station, where the woman is curled up in a ball on the floor and the husband is pacing around waiting for dispatch to call him back.

Fortunately, someone at dispatch in our small county gets ahold of a Crag Rat down in the valley by phone, perhaps Bill Pattison, an octogenarian who has been a member for six decades. He's calm and collected: he's been doing this rescue business a long time. A dispatcher learns that the Crag Rats are at The Winter Outing and starts old-school communication: phone calls.

"Try calling Don," says Bill to dispatch.

Somehow, Don Pattison, son of Bill, hears his phone ring. Don bolts awake, answers the phone, and quickly musters key players. He first jostles Rick Ragan to fire up our snowcat. Rick is a soft-spoken, level-headed, bearded, senior member of our group. He was an original snow ranger on Mount Hood and later became a Forest Service wildland firefighter. Now retired from the Forest Service, he brings a calm sense of expertise to our crew, both with rescues and the challenging task of navigating multiple agencies we work with: sheriff's office, Forest Service, and fire department.

A few other Crag Rats tumble out of bed to help organize the rescue, including Scott Hukari and Dale Crockett. Don wades from the front room, warmed still by smoldering fires in the cast-iron stove and the fireplace, to the frigid east wing of the cabin, where boards creak loudly underfoot. He's apparently looking for me. I'm deep in my sleeping bag, in a back room.

"Doc, we have a callout. Guard Station. Ragan is firing up the snowcat," he says in staccato due to bitter cold as he walks into the small room in the east wing—it's the size of a dorm room, with two bunks and a stack of Rubbermaid bins. The bins, one for each Crag Rat, are where we store our personal sleeping bags, toothbrushes, and extra clothes, so we can ski up in the winter with just a small day pack.

"Now? Seriously?" My brain is fuzzy for a second as I am staring into the white light of Don's headlamp, which lights up his face in the pitch black room, like the scene from a low-budget horror film. Then, a second later, I jolt awake, sit up, and get pulverized by the bitter cold when my sleeping bag falls off my shoulders. Accustomed to being called in the middle of the night after two decades of working as an emergency physician, I wake up instantly.

My brain clears; the bitter cold helps. It's cold. Really cold.

Paul Crowley, a retired circuit court judge, is in the bunk across the room and also sits up.

"I'll come," he says matter-of-factly. He immediately turns on a headlamp and starts searching for ski clothing.

"What's the story?" I ask.

"Someone at the Guard Station," says Don again. "Rick's warming up the cat."

"Ok, let me get dressed," I say. I click on my headlamp and watch vapor pouring out of my mouth. I'm breathing hard just from the frigid air temperature. I had slept in my long underwear and ski socks, so I just need to pull on ski pants, layers of fleece and down, and my parka. I wiggle into ski clothing while still in my sleeping bag. I have a headache. I'm thirsty. I'm cold. I'm tired.

When I snake out of bed, sit up, and crowbar my feet into foam-and-plastic backcountry ski boots, I am greeted with another shock: the boots are freezing cold. Usually I leave them warming by the fire in the front room, but with the big crowd in the cabin, I'd brought them into the tiny back room in the east wing. Cold ski boots: good way to get frostbite.

Paul and I grab our ski packs and bumble through the cabin, bumping into bunks of sleeping Crag Rats, prospective members, and friends of Crag Rats. In the front room, I find a bustle of activity and bright lights from the propane and solar systems we have at the cabin. Ragan is outside with the snowcat, which is growling laboriously, trying to warm up in the cold. Others ready their gear: Portland firefighter and Crag Rat Tim Mortenson and Don join us as we quickly organize our ski gear and retrieve our clothing, which had been hung in the rafters of the main room above the fire to dry after skiing. Scott and Dale don't come on the rescue but get out of their bunks, pull on clothing, and help us get out the door. The cabin is more than a hundred years old, dusty, and creaky. We've got two woodstoves and a fireplace. Either Dale or Scott has just refueled the fires from our stash of fruitwood from the Hood River Valley, world-renowned for pear, apple, and cherry orchards.

In full winter ski regalia—helmet, goggles, parka, layers of fleece and down, skis, boots, and backpack full of avalanche-rescue and winter-survival gear—I step outside in the middle of the night, in the middle of the storm.

This will, as readers will come to learn, become a recurring scenario: night rescue. Often cold, sometimes stormy, and always dark. Outside, I get chilled to my core. And visibility is horrible because the storm has reached full potential. The sky is *puking*, big flakes of snow falling from the night. The wind blows the snow in all directions in whirlwinds. I put on goggles just to walk 20 feet from the cabin to the snowcat. I squeeze through the back door of the metal box wearing my backpack. Inside the back of the snowcat, we have a bit of respite from the weather, but the wind still finds a way to leak through the cracks of the walls and send a deep chill. The metal compartment smells of gasoline. Miscellaneous ropes and bungee cords litter the floor, as we had used the snowcat earlier that day to shuttle skiers up Ghost Ridge. The rudimentary bench has no padding, so as I plop down, the metal conducts heat and sucks the energy out of me through my thin ski pants.

It's cold. It's dark. We are tired. We are hungry. And I have a small, nagging headache. Nothing like starting out a rescue feeling lousy. It's the middle of the night, in the middle of a storm. If it sounds like I'm being repetitious, it's because this is exactly the way it seems at the time. Cold, then more cold, then colder. Wind, then more wind. Darkness, and more darkness. It is everywhere in repeated and larger doses.

This is a mountain rescue mission. This is what we do, the Crag Rats. We are the nine-decades-old, all-volunteer mountain rescue team for Hood River County. Even though we specialize in high-angle cliff, crevasse, avalanche, and snow rescue, we function as the all-purpose, all-terrain search-and-rescue team for the entire county. When we get called for rescues, we operate under the authority and direction of the Hood River County Sheriff's Office. This will be one of thirty missions for the average year—many of which are in foul weather, half of which are on the mountain, and a third of which are at night.

We pile into the snowcat and shut the back door with a slam, as Ragan guns the throttle. Ragan navigates the trusty 1988 LMC 1800 snowcat as we lumber out of the Cloud Cap Inn parking area, squeeze though a tight gap where the road goes between the cabin and a 50-foot cliff, and plow down the snow-drifted road, as all the while the machine is belching and burping, tossing us around in the back. Although the ski trail to the Tilly Jane Guard Station is about a half-mile from Cloud Cap directly through the woods, we have to take a wider path with the snowcat: the road. Rick drives a mile from Cloud Cap Saddle on the snow-covered road to a fork, and then a mile back up another road to the Tilly Jane area. As the heavy machine plows through the drifts, the snowcat struggles with a deep guttural moan like a growling dog about to pick a fight.

The Crag Rats have had many snowcats over the years; currently we have a second-hand Logan Manufacturing Company machine. The LMCs were made from 1978 to 2000, originally owned by the Thiokol snowcat division but later renamed LMC when the company was bought by John DeLorean, the same guy who made the car that bears his last name that appeared in the film *Back to the Future*.

Ragan can barely see through the storm. The windshield wipers are full speed, a defrost fan is on high power, and the headlights are on max. Every few minutes he wipes condensation from the front window with a rag. But the night is dark and the snow is blowing wildly. Visibility is 20 feet or less. We careen through the blackness a half-mile to the Tilly Jane Guard Station. It takes twenty minutes of expert driving.

When we arrive, Ragan aims the snowcat lights on the Guard Station and we wade through the deep snow, like walking through thick mud, to the front door. Inside, we find the woman curled up in a ball on the floor.

"We're search and rescue," I say, matter-of-fact. "I'm the doc, Van Tilburg," I introduce myself. I almost always use my first and last name, but in the middle of the night, in the middle of the storm, I'm going to be as brief as possible. Staccato. Get to the point quickly. The first task, which I try to complete within about twenty seconds of entering the room, is to determine whether this is a critical situation.

"What happened?" I ask. At the same time, I see the woman is flushed and sweating from pain, but her color is good, she's breathing okay, and she's alert. All good signs.

"I have pain in my stomach, started out of the blue," she says. I kneel down and do three things at once: I look to see if she's breathing normally, I check her pulse, which is ninety beats per minute and strong at the wrist, and feel her skin, which is cool and sweaty. I check her abdomen: she winces in pain.

In mountain rescue, patients are usually stable, since it takes so long for us to reach them, or dead, unfortunately. Rarely are we able to respond immediately. Normally, the Crag Rats respond from home and our response takes some time. Several things happen before we're even dispatched. The 911 center gets the call, gathers information, and calls a sheriff's deputy, usually one of three trained in search and rescue. The sheriff's deputy then needs to figure out three key things, which sometimes takes five minutes and sometimes several hours: What is the emergency? Where is the victim? What resources do we need?

In this case, a 911 call via phone answered the questions quite quickly. Woman in trouble. At Tilly Jane Guard Station. Need Crag Rats to evacuate. Fortunately, we were already on the mountain, which eliminated the second major time suck that occurs after someone calls 911: the Crag Rats' response. For most missions, we are at home or work. So we need to gather our gear from home, muster at the county yard where we store our truck, drive up the mountain, organize ourselves at the staging area, receive an assignment from the sheriff's deputy running the rescue, and then climb up the mountain.

Lucky for the woman, Bill answered the phone and then Don answered the phone.

My job, as medical lead for this rescue, is to determine in the first few minutes if the patient is critical and needs an immediate response, or if the patient is non-critical and we can take a bit of time. A critical patient in the backcountry, with no medical gear and no chance of a helicopter evacuation due to the storm, would be a dire situation.

This woman, however, is not about to die. First, she is talking, although obviously struggling due to the pain. She's got a steady, strong pulse at ninety beats per minute in her wrist, which means her blood pressure is at least 90 mm Hg systolic (the top number, systolic, is responsible for pumping blood to the vital organs and tissue to deliver vital oxygen and pick up toxic carbon dioxide. The bottom number, diastolic, is when the heart relaxes, rests, rejuvenates). I don't carry a blood-pressure cuff in the field because space and weight in my medical pack are limited and the actual number isn't as critical as the clinical assessment.

"No injury?"

"No," gasp.

"Sudden onset?"

"Yes," gasp, wince.

Abdominal pain is a difficult symptom to diagnose in the ER, more so in the backcountry with no medical supplies or equipment. I should know—my accident is still quite fresh and I have a zipper scar down the center of my abdomen as a perpetual, indelible reminder. The abdomen is packed with many organs from several organ systems. The nerves are jumbled so that pain in one area may signify an injury in that area, or the pain can be referred from another area. My spleen injury presented as left shoulder pain, lower-lung pneumonia can show up as belly pain, and appendicitis can show up as left-side pain, even though the appendix is on the right side. The digestive system alone could have multiple life-threatening conditions: gallstones blocking the exit ducts, gallbladder infection, liver inflammation, stomach ulcer that's bleeding or ruptured, twisted intestine, blocked intestine, appendicitis, or injury from trauma such as a liver or bowel laceration. The urinary system could have any number of issues: a blocked duct from a stone, a lacerated kidney, or an infection. In females, there's a host of problems that can occur specific to female parts: twisted ovary, ovarian cyst, gynecologic infection. Men can have abdominal pain from acute prostate infection or twisted testicle. Abdominal pain is one of the most difficult *differential diagnoses*, the list of all possible problems.

"Any medical problems?" I ask.

"Two babies. And a hysterectomy but they left one ovary. Feels like it twisted. It happened once before." It is always good to talk to patients and always good when they know what the problem is. "I think I have another twisted ovary."

The woman is not in shock, even though general popular usage of the term sometimes refers to severe pain. She is breathing, mentating, and pumping blood to her tissues. But at any time she could turn critical.

At this point, all we can do is evacuate the patient. I have no medical gear suitable to fix this woman: IV fluids and pain medication would be useful.

So, four of us rescuers bend over the woman, lift her up by the arms and legs, and carry her in a seated position. It is not a gentle process but a rough one: we have no choice. We have to squeeze out the tiny door of the cabin, wade through knee-deep snow, lift the patient up and over the transom of the snowcat, and wiggle her into the back of the LMC. We are trying to be gentle and concerned for her pain and well-being. But it's not easy. Did I mention it's also in the middle of the night, in the middle of a storm? Darkness pierced only by tiny headlamps and the old LMC lights, with snow falling, wind blowing, deep snow drifting. Coldness and blackness. And we are fatigued.

Once inside the snowcat, we rescuers pile in. The woman curls in the position of comfort: on her side in the fetal position on the floor. We make room for the husband and backpacks.

When we are all in the snowcat, Ragan pauses. He doesn't like something about the way the snowcat sounds. It idles at a low hum that perks up to a growl when Ragan juices the throttle. Sounds okay to me, but I'm a medical guy, not a mechanical one. Regan gets on the radio.

"Ragan to Cloud Cap," he says.

"Cloud Cap," answers Scott Hukari, staffing the radio all night.

"Can you have someone warm up the sheriff's snowcat?" Since we have been training at the winter outing, we'd had both our LMC snowcat and the sheriff's snowcat up at Cloud Cap. Ragan, thinking ahead, wants a backup plan. "The LMC sounds funny."

"Will do," says Scott, who then clambers into the storm to warm up the second snowcat, parked outside the cabin.

Then, with Ragan at the controls, we start the long, harrowing descent down the mountain.

One might picture a snowcat at a ski resort, grooming the runs. These tend to be state-of-the-art snowcats with hi-fi sound systems, warm heaters, and plush seats. And often in ski resorts, even if visibility is limited, the ski runs are well defined. The LMC, however, is a different animal: a sturdy backcountry work machine, purchased secondhand. It is simple, small, and burly. But driving the beast is no easy task—it's physically strenuous. Ragan has a throttle to control speed. Steering is rudimentary: Ragan grips handles like joysticks that activate brakes: one lever for each of the tracks. Pull the right lever, activate the right track brake, and the snowcat turns right, for example. Top speed is maybe 15 miles an hour on firm, smooth, flat snow. We're moving much slower due partly to lack of visibility and partly to the deep, thick drifts of snow. Maybe 4 miles per hour. If we didn't have the snowcat, the only other option would be to put the woman in a specialized toboggan called an Akja (ah-key-uh). The Akja is a fiberglass toboggan that has two 4-foot-long aluminum handles at each end. These handles allow rescuers to ski down the Tilly Jane trail while carrying and sliding the toboggan, with one rescuer in front and one in back.

Luckily, we've got the snowcat. And luckily, we are already on the mountain.

In addition to the rigors of driving, navigating is a problem in the storm. The 9-mile-long Cloud Cap Road, which allows access to the Cloud Cap–Tilly Jane Historic District, is closed to car travel for most of the year. It is gated from the first snow in November until late spring when the snow melts and the road dries out. In winter, the snow-covered road is used by snowmobilers and cross-country skiers. The road begins at Tilly Jane Trailhead, and starts out heading west, meandering around corners and bends, mostly on the 4,000-foot contour. After 4 miles, the road turns south up the mountain. But here, the road is not straight. The road ascends via a dozen steep, rocky, narrow switchbacks, and gains

2,000 vertical feet in another 4 miles, a 22 percent grade. Near the top, the road forks. The right-hand fork heads a mile to Cloud Cap Saddle Campground, Cloud Cap Inn, and the Snowshoe Club Hut. The left-hand fork heads to Tilly Jane Campground and the A-Frame, Guard Station, and American Legion Cookhouse. In the winter with the snow-cat, we take a shortcut, the Wagon Road Trail #642, which is the original path to Cloud Cap Inn used when guests would come down the Columbia River on a ferry and then take a horse and buggy 30 miles from the Columbia River to the cabin. This old road cuts directly to Cloud Cap Inn, bypassing most of the switchbacks. In summer, it is steep, narrow, and full of downed timber: pretty much impassable. But in winter, it's still steep and narrow, but the gully fills with snow and gives us a more direct route to the cabin via snowcat.

But we have a visibility problem due to the storm as well as the Gnarl Ridge forest fire in 2008. The Wagon Road is difficult to find. The burned snags that look like silver spears poking from the snow, the thick drifts, and the zero-dark-thirty storm make everything look the same. The Wagon Road is not marked like the usual cross-country trails, which have blue diamond trail markers, called blazes, hammered into the trees every 100 feet.

The snowcat snarls as Ragan navigates it down the mountain. Every ten minutes he stops, gets out of the cab, stands on the track, and peers through the blinding snow to get his bearings. He tries to find the Wagon Road, or at least confirm he's on the right path. Even if we miss the Wagon Road, heading due north, down the mountain, we will eventually reach the flat east-west section of Cloud Cap Road. There, we need to take an abrupt right-hand turn to the east to head back to the Tilly Jane Trailhead and an awaiting ambulance. Yet, that is a potential problem too: we are at risk for missing the Cloud Cap Road altogether by driving right across it. If we miss the road we will end up driving north, down the mountain, into thick, steep drainages of Crystal Spring Creek. That would get us basically nowhere but into a thick forest.

Then the snowcat gets stuck. As Ragan revs the motor, the tracks spin and auger us into a snowbank. We sink into a giant hole that is being created by the spinning tracks.

Then the snowcat begins to list, 20 degrees to the right on an embankment.

Then the snowcat slides back into a giant snag of dead timber. I wonder for a second if a snowcat can roll. Right at the same time, someone speaks aloud, "These things are really hard to roll."

Ragan spends ten minutes expertly jockeying the LMC back and forth, like doing a 50-point turn, until he is able to get the tracks to pack down the snow and gain purchase. He gets the snowcat unstuck, drives out of the hole, and continues across a snowfield that may or may not be the Wagon Road, which may or may not be above the Cloud Cap Road exit.

Ragan is an expert at this—there's no one I'd rather have behind the controls of the LMC.

In clear weather on firm snow, the 9-mile drive down the Wagon Road and out Cloud Cap Road takes forty-five minutes. This descent takes us two hours. We get down Wagon Road, and then exit east on the relatively flat Cloud Cap Road, where we are all relieved a bit. Faster now, perhaps 10 miles an hour, Ragan motors to the trailhead. We lumber into Tilly Jane Trailhead at 4:30 a.m.—the woman still in pain, still curled in a ball, still with no treatment. A sheriff's deputy and Parkdale Fire volunteers wait with an ambulance.

I must admit, at one point in this harrowing descent—probably when the snowcat felt like it was going to tip over and roll down the hill, in the middle of the night, in the middle of a storm, in the middle of the wilderness—I had been a bit concerned. Okay, call it frightened, or scared. We were taking a bit of a risk. But we'd made it down, safely. Our job is mostly complete.

After unloading the patient into the Parkdale ambulance, I sign out the patient to the paramedics and Ragan drives us back up the mountain. With the coming of the glow of dawn and the slight abatement of the storm, it is easier to drive the LMC uphill. Plus the route is now packed down so Ragan can follow our tracks. By 6:00 a.m. we arrive at the cabin at daybreak, pile out of the LMC, and find that Scott and Dale have cooked a full hot breakfast for us. After recounting the rescue and eating, I ski with a few Crag Rats down to my car parked at Tilly Jane Trailhead.

The snow is excellent quality: light, dry, fresh. I am back to my car a little before noon, then drive 30 miles home down the twisty Highway 35.

Once home, I dump my gear in my mud room, scarf some snacks, and jump in the shower. Out of the shower, I feel slightly more awake. I'm ready to get some real food, settle down to relax for the evening, check in with my kids, and go to bed early.

Then, my phone buzzes again just as I'm thinking of lying down for a quick nap.

Kids? Nope.

My new romantic interest, Margaret? Nope.

Parents? Nope.

Another mountain rescue callout? But of course. Blood drains from my head, hands. I get dizzy and shake my head to clear my brain. I have ten seconds of dread, knowing my evening is ruined. And then I decide to respond to the rescue, and adrenaline kicks in again.

Injury. Tilly Jane. Need responders. Snowcat still at trailhead.

This time, a person is injured at the Tilly Jane A-Frame, the building that is 100 yards from the Guard Station. Not only had I just returned home, but the entire crew had just closed up Cloud Cap Inn, just returned to the trailhead, and just loaded the snowcat on the trailer at the Tilly Jane Trailhead. They had planned to leave the snowcat parked on the trailer at Tilly Jane Trailhead and fetch it the next day. All Crag Rats had returned home after spending between one and four nights at Cloud Cap Inn.

I grab my gear, still packed from the night before. I quickly dig out my empty water bottle and wet clothing. I pull on clean, dry ski clothes— long-underwear tops and bottoms, ski pants, fleece sweater, puffy vest, calf-high ski socks. I grab my ski boots, still dank from the weekend: they stink badly. I hunt around for dry gloves and a clean hat. I fill my water bottle and grab a handful of energy bars.

And I head back up the mountain.

I drive back up Highway 35 to Tilly Jane Trailhead and meet the crew: Bernie Wells is here to drive the LMC, equally skilled as Ragan. Bernie is a long-time member and current treasurer, a relatively permanent position. He's the soft-spoken owner of Wells Construction, now mostly taken over by his son Todd. Bernie knows more about the Crag Rats than most, having devoted thousands of hours of his personal time into maintaining Cloud Cap Inn, the Hut (our meeting hall in Hood River), our relationships with the Forest Service, and the lore of our group. Bernie, Ragan, and Bill Pattison make up the core of our elders.

A half-dozen Crag Rats have responded, mostly fresh from not attending the Winter Outing. We clamber in the snowcat and head up the mountain. Back up Cloud Cap Road. Back up Old Wagon Road. Back up to the Guard Station. At least it's still light out and the storm has abated. The sky glows blue and yellow as the sun begins to drift toward setting; we are running low on daylight. It's easier driving now since the track up the Wagon Road is packed down from the multiple snowcat trips that day, from both the rescue and the Winter Outing.

At the Guard Station we park the snowcat, slap climbing skins on our skis (adhesive on one side, the strips of fabric stick to our skis to provide traction for skiing uphill), click into ski bindings, and ski 100 yards to Tilly Jane A-frame. The snowcat can't make it to the front door of the A-Frame because of Tilly Jane Creek. From the Guard Station, we have to ski 20 feet down into Tilly Jane Creek, cross a bridge, which is buried in 4 feet of snow (luckily we know where the bridge crosses the creek), and then ski 20 feet out of Tilly Jane Creek. Past the amphitheater and past the dilapidated cookhouse, we arrive at the A-Frame. Inside, a dozen people are huddling around a young boy. The boy is lying on a picnic table and is attended by two bystanders who happen to be summer river guides.

"Hi, Doc Van Tilburg," I say. "What happened?"

"Sledding, careened out of control, and hit a tree," says one of the river guides. "We've taken pulse and blood pressure every fifteen minutes for two hours: he's stable," says the guide, showing me a first-responder notebook with the log of vital signs. This is ideal data: I instantly know this is not a helicopter evacuation for the same reason as the woman I'd examined earlier that morning. Pulse: stable. Blood pressure: stable. Good color. Talking and breathing normally. Chest and hips have no apparent injury. His abdomen is slightly tender.

"How you feeling?" I ask.

"Okay. My side hurts." The differential diagnosis—the list of possible causes for his pain in the setting of trauma—includes rib fracture, spleen laceration, liver laceration, compression fracture of his lumbar spine, and pelvis fracture.

I have a bag of IV fluids in my jacket that the volunteer firefighter handed me when leaving the snowcat. But considering that the boy has been stable for two hours, he's lying on a dirty picnic table in a dirty, dark cabin, and pediatric IV starts are difficult because kids' veins are small, I defer putting in the IV. Not to mention, I'm not nearly as skilled as a nurse or paramedic at placing tiny catheters into tiny veins.

"Are your parents around?"

"No," says the boy.

"He's here with a Boy Scout troop," says a man. "I'm the leader. He was sledding and hit a tree. I'm so sorry about this."

"Look, don't worry. He's stable. We'll get him down the mountain," I reassure him.

We carry the boy outside, put him in a litter, and ski him over to Tilly Jane Creek. Before crossing the bridge, I ask Walter Burkhardt to set up a safety rope. Even though we only descend 20 feet into the creek, the entrance to the creek is a steep side hill and we have to traverse the off-camber hill 20 yards upstream to get to the snow-covered bridge. So, to keep the litter from sliding down into the creek before we reach the bridge, we want a rope.

We pause for Walter to set up the rope, and then descend into the creek, cross the bridge, and struggle up the opposite bank—pushing, dragging, and shoving the litter uphill through the deep snow—to the waiting snowcat. We pile in and head back down the mountain. Down the Wagon Road. Down Cloud Cap Road. At Tilly Jane Trailhead, for the second time in twelve hours, we transfer a patient from the LCM to an ambulance and Parkdale volunteer firefighters. They are probably just as exhausted as we are. For the second time in a day, I went up and down the mountain. For the second time in a day, I return home from a mountain rescue mission utterly exhausted.

If we get a third callout, I'm not going.

CHAPTER TWO

Blackout

ANOTHER MOUNTAIN RESCUE CALLOUT COMES AT 6:30 P.M., ON A NIGHT smack from the opening scene of an action-adventure movie trailer or one of those paperback thrillers you find at airports: dead dark, wintry chill, bitching blustery wind, and rain pouring in buckets from the dank black sky.

I get nauseated just thinking about another rescue at night.

Night missions are often long and grueling. They are dangerous above and beyond just the normal hazards—rock, ice, snow, mud, rain, wind—because visibility is poor and we are nearly always tired, given our circadian rhythm has normally put us in bed. And we seem to have more night than day rescues nowadays. I get queasy just thinking about the ill feeling of being up all night on the mountain.

I've had my fair share of both night rescues and all-nights work shifts, after working as an emergency physician and a mountain rescue doctor for two decades. At one point I worked one night shift per week for ten years. Night shifts are something I never got used to. After a decade in the adrenaline-infused high-stakes emergency-medicine career, I decided that I needed a change. I needed a new career, a new challenge, and a new schedule. The ER doctor schedule is all over the map, a smattering of days and nights, weekends and weekdays. Any week's schedule is unlikely to be similar to the last. And the nights are horrible. So, midway through my medical career, after a divorce, I put my emergency-medicine career on the back burner. I found a new job.

I joined a struggling three-day-per-week occupational and travel medicine practice at the local hospital, 2 miles from my house. A third of my job was workers' compensation, mired in so much paperwork that no one else in our town seemed to want to tackle it. A third of my job was advising travelers headed on overseas adventures: defense contractors working in austere locations, students studying abroad, relief workers working in underdeveloped countries, and adventure travelers making classic tips to Machu Picchu, Everest Base Camp, or Mount Kilimanjaro. The final third of my job was medical clearance exams for military folks, merchant marine captains, airline pilots, truck drivers, firefighters, and such. No weekends, no nights, and a regular schedule. I maintained part-time shifts in the ER (no nights, no weekends) and continued to work ten shifts a season at the Mountain Clinic, a small emergency facility at the ski resort on Mount Hood.

But I still couldn't rid my life of night-time mountain rescue missions. I don't like night missions. No one does.

Now, here we go: another night mission in another storm.

When I get the callout, I have just returned from the day's work at my new job. The rain noisily spatters the roof and windows of my house, which is tucked in a grove of sky-reaching ponderosa pine in small, rural, generally happy Hood River—the overused but accurate word is *bucolic*. Our county, population 23,000, is a mix of fruit growers, blue- and white-collar working folks, thrill-seeking athletes, and boutique owners. Let me explain.

Hood River County is relatively smallish geographically, 533 square miles, compared to the rest of the state's counties. But topographically, we are extra-large. More than 60 percent of the county is thick, rugged terrain of the Mount Hood National Forest. These are rolling hills, mountains, cliffs, rocky pinnacles and crags, and deep canyons. Much of it is roadless, or crisscrossed by primitive logging roads and trails for motorcycling, hiking, and mountain biking. We've got all or part of three large wilderness areas: Mount Hood, Columbia Gorge, and Badger Creek. Our county includes the north and east half of Mount Hood, which you will come to learn is the predominant figure in our county, in our rescue missions, and in my life.

If the giant, legendary, ominous Mount Hood with the surrounding national forest and wilderness areas is not enough, we have an equally legendary, voluminous river. Our county hosts a 25-mile south bank of the 1,243-mile-long Columbia River, the land adjacent to which is the Columbia Gorge National Scenic Area. This giant waterway separates Oregon from Washington, is bordered by 4,000-foot-high walls of basalt and andesite lava cliffs, and is encased by thick forests, the patriarch of which is the tall, lanky Douglas fir. The forests are also packed with a thousand shades of green: big-leaf maples, western red cedar, mountain hemlock, ferns, poison oak, huckleberries, Oregon grape, and various green ground covers, green shrubbery, and miscellaneous greenery. The canyons are steep and rugged, and many end in cliffs. The streams are clear from glacier meltwater and choked with gurgling rapids, spectacular waterfalls, and giant logs. The waterfalls—in fact, hundreds of waterfalls in the Columbia Gorge—are reason alone for many tourists, hikers, backpackers, and photographers to visit.

The Hood River Valley, which stretches from Mount Hood to the Columbia River, is fertile and the community has always been a hub of orchardists growing cherries, pears, and apples. We have grape vineyards, wineries, and our own Columbia Gorge American Viticulture Area (and a section of Columbia Valley AVA). We've got blueberry fields, apricot orchards, and lavender farms.

Aside from the long-term fruit growers, windsurfers came to the river in the 1980s for the howling, steady, persistent winds on the Columbia River. The marine layer from the Pacific Ocean creeps over Portland, 60 miles to the west. The hot air in the Eastern Oregon and Washington desert bakes. When the cool air is sucked through the gorge, the Venturi effect accelerates the wind to well over 30 miles an hour on a regular basis. And the windsurfers never left. Eventually, the town turned into a world-renowned sports mecca, beyond windsurfing. We've got world-class watersports (kayaking, river rafting, windsurfing, kitesurfing, stand-up paddle boarding, and outrigger canoeing), trail sports (mountain biking, trail running), year-round snow sports (skiing, snowboarding, mountaineering), and air sports (paragliding, speed flying).

Of late, a third industry, smoldering for years, blossomed beyond fruit growing and recreation: tourism. People make the drive from Portland, Seattle, and elsewhere to visit the bourgeoning collection of high-end boutiques, brewpubs (close to a dozen now), wineries, vineyards, fruit stands, and art galleries.

So, it's a busy community packed with athletes and farmers, locals and tourists, exploring the vast Oregon greenery bookended by a gargantuan glacier-clad mountain and a gargantuan blue-green river.

So, as a result, we get mountain rescue calls all months, any time of day or night. Mostly, it seems, at night.

Crag Rat callout. Lost skiers. Cooper Spur. No callout coordinator available.

So after 10 seconds of dread, I decide to respond to the rescue. Instantly, adrenaline electrifies my nerves and shoots to my muscles. My muscles tense and my brain sharpens. I am immediately on duty. My kids are at their mom's house for the week and I sheepishly text to cancel yet another date with Margaret. I have no idea how she will react when I readily and nonchalantly cancel a date for a mountain rescue mission. But I have to.

I quickly shuck my doctor clinic clothes for winter storm attire: insulated, lightweight, waterproof garb of nylon, polyester, down, and wool. I grab my pre-stocked ready pack of avalanche-rescue and winter-survival equipment, toss the pack in my 4x4 Toyota SUV, and head up the mountain, into the night, and into the belly of the wicked winter storm.

Normally, I'd text the Crag Rat coordinator, Penny Hunting, to let her know I am driving to the staging area, Cooper Spur Mountain Resort. But, apparently dispatch couldn't get ahold of Penny and paged the Crag Rats directly. I'd done this drive three score times already this winter: taking my daughters Skylar and Avrie and their buddies skiing, backcountry ski touring with friends, and working at the ski resort clinic.

I call Crag Rat Dennis "Deno" Klein, because I had received another text message that he is responding.

"I'm trying to get out of my house but my phone keeps ringing," Deno grumbles when I call him. A skilled, senior member of our team, Deno is the default incident commander because his day job is mountain manager of the Cooper Spur Mountain Resort, he lives only a few miles from the ski area, and his depth of knowledge about search and rescue—about saving lives in the mountains—runs deep.

"Oh, sorry," I say. "I'm on my way." Three more Crag Rats, Dick Arnold, Joe McCulloch, and Brian Hukari, are not far behind. Dick and Brian are seasoned, skilled members of our team. It is Joe's first rescue—but he's been in the mountains for many years and, of late, has been our chief gourmet cook on training and social outings. Nothing like a monster blizzard for his first mission.

Rain in the lower valley has turned to snow as I gun my truck up Highway 35 toward Mount Hood. In twenty minutes, I turn off Highway 35 onto the twisty Cooper Spur Road, where the snow thickens. The snow is 8 inches deep and the road is unplowed, so driving becomes difficult, even in four-wheel drive. I slide a bit through the corners, so I slow down. Visibility is horrible: my headlights reflect off the falling snow instead of piercing the night and I can barely distinguish the bright white snow-covered road from the bright white snow-covered roadside. The sky pukes fat, colorless flakes at an inch per hour, which sparkle annoyingly in my headlamps. I slow the speed of my truck even more, and quell my nerves.

Just past Tilly Jane Trailhead, where we had responded to two rescues on the Winter Outing weekend in the last chapter, the road ends at the tiny, one-chairlift Cooper Spur Mountain Resort. It is 8:00 p.m. and the large, powerful night-skiing lights illuminate the ski runs in artificial glow. Deno has turned on the resort lights. The closed ski slopes are eerily vacant. A sheriff's truck is parked haphazardly in the parking lot and has its red and blue roof lights rotating, bathing the white snow in Fourth of July colors. I quickly walk to the quaint, wood-paneled one-room ski lodge. In the basement, the ski rental shop, I find the initial stages of a search mission. Deno huddles over a map. He is flanked by another ski resort manager and Chris Guertin, a deputy sheriff search-and-rescue coordinator, who is in charge.

The mission: lost skiers in the side country, the area adjacent to but outside the boundaries of the ski resort. After riding the chairlift earlier that day when the resort was open, a pair of skiers had apparently wanted to try out their new backcountry ski equipment. From the top of the chairlift, the skiers followed one of the two out-of-bounds cross-country ski trails, either Polallie Ridge or Tilly Jane, to the southwest, up the mountain, into the backcountry. This is a big deal nowadays: backcountry skiing is one of the fastest-growing segments in the ski and snowboard industry. The problem is that people buy backcountry ski gear and then head into the backcountry. Some omit purchasing avalanche-safety and mountain-survival gear. Some omit learning how to use the gear. Some omit grabbing a partner, checking the weather, consulting a map, or looking at their watch to see if they have enough daylight.

The twin trails of Polallie Ridge and Tilly Jane are fairly well marked and relatively easy to follow . . . in bluebird daylight . . . if you stay on the trail. Unlike the Wagon Road Trail from the last chapter, which is just around the mountain a bit to the west, the Polallie Ridge and Tilly Jane trails have small blue triangle blazes hammered into the trees every 50 yards or so to mark the trails. But if you go off trail in search of a few tracks of fresh powder snow—late in the day, in a storm, at dusk—the world changes.

In Doe Creek, a thick collection of snags from the 2008 Gnarl Ridge Fire makes the forest disorientating, the same fire that made it difficult for even us experts to find the Wagon Road in the last chapter. Everywhere you look the forest appears the same, with stark white snow and charred deadhead spires littered across the glades like silver spears. At night, without a compass, you wouldn't even be able to tell which way is north. Beyond Doe Creek lies Polallie Canyon, a gargantuan glacially carved fissure in the earth: steep-walled, deep, avalanche prone. In Polallie Canyon, if you don't get caught by an avalanche in the steep couloirs, stymied by the headwall cliff at 6,000 feet, or stuck by a another steep section at 5,000 feet, you simply may not be able to climb back out in deep snow, at night, in a storm.

The skiers had a dead cell phone and no Global Positioning System receiver, map, or compass. With an earlier 911 call, dispatch was able to get a GPS fix on the couple's cell signal before the battery died—more and more common these days with smart phones. With the cell phone GPS coordinates and the description of the couple's route from the one and only 911 conversation with dispatch, Deno had approximated their position in the Doe Creek, a few miles from the mountain resort lodge. Deno knew this area better than anyone on our team.

Deno has the ski resort snowmobile ready to drive us up the mountain to the top of the only chairlift, but I can't head into the field without a partner. First priority is safety of oneself. Team is second. Patient is third on the list. Deno doesn't have his ski gear, so we scour the tiny lodge for snowshoes so that he can come with me. We come up empty. So we wait anxiously: poring over the map, reconfirming the location, and finalizing the plan. When Joe, Dick, and Brian show up, we are ready to pounce on the mountain. Deno fires up the snowmobile to shuttle Joe and me to top of the ski resort. I am juiced to head into the field. This is what I live for, one of my *raisons d'être* or my *plan de vida*: the dark stormy night, the wind blasting through the big conifers, and the powder snow dumping from the sky. Missing skiers—we can save them.

Those who have read my book *Mountain Rescue Doctor: Wilderness Medicine in the Extremes of Nature* will find this mission all too familiar. The zing of adrenaline on a callout, the dangerous foreboding mountain, the skier in peril, and our team of Crag Rats, mountain search-and-rescue experts, heading into the dark, cold, stormy wilderness to save the nearly dead, find the lost, and carry out the deceased. But *Mountain Rescue Doctor* is not just a summation of years of mountain-rescue missions: it is also a tome of how I was able to merge my chosen profession of doctoring with my love of outdoor adventure and the wild high country. It is about balancing my life between work and play. It is about teaching my daughters Skylar and Avrie about volunteerism, mountain culture, and adventure.

After publication of *Mountain Rescue Doctor*, my life was moving forward at rocket speed, all things positive. I was speaking around the country on the topics of outdoor risk and responsibility, mountain safety, and cost of search and rescue. I had the new part-time clinic job, to which I rode my bike. I trimmed my ER shifts to the minimum—for the first time in two decades of doctoring I worked no night or weekend shifts and I had no on-call duties. I had a divorce behind me and I was spending a lot of time with my girls: coaching Avrie's soccer, volunteering in Skylar's school. I was skiing, surfing, biking, and hiking around the world, often with my two daughters in tow. I raced cyclocross competitively with a twenty-member team of all my best friends. I had just signed with a national magazine to write a blog. I was preparing to help teach a wilderness first responder course and provide medical relief in Haiti. To make things so much better, I met Margaret. Perfect, just perfect, I had thought: Margaret was smart, pretty, educated, funny, fun-loving, adventurous, athletic, and—perhaps rather elusive qualities—a family-oriented woman who had a zest for athletic endeavors and a love of mountain adventure. And she had that Midwest wholesomeness, a no-frills, down-to-earth character. Things were about as good as they could get with my daughters, health, family, career, and life.

And, as if nothing could get better, I reveled in the unique opportunity that very few people in the world experience: to ski into mountains, into the night, into the storm, to save a life. I hated the cold, the fatigue, and lack of sleep of a night mission in a storm. But I loved it all the same.

So, no, this is not the opening scene from a mountaineering cinematic epic. Not airport kiosk fiction. Not a pop confabulation for Hollywood.

This is a real winter storm, at night. This is a real search-and-rescue callout. And this is my real life as an emergency mountain rescue physician with my trusted, highly skilled colleagues (many of whom, as you will learn in these stories, are much more skilled than me when it comes to navigation, survival, patient packaging, rope-rescue techniques, and orchestrating meetings with county, state, and federal officials).

I clutch the back of the snowmobile as Dennis guns the heavy machine and races directly up the smooth, groomed, steep snow slope of the ski area. The machine smells of foul exhaust, littering the otherwise clear mountain air with fumes of gasoline and oil. Deno drops me off at the Polallie Ridge trailhead at the top of the chairlift and circles back to fetch Joe—since the slope is too steep for Deno to haul us up the mountain together. While waiting for Joe, I poke a bit into the trail. The lights of the ski resort fade quickly. I pierce the night with my xenon-bulb headlamp and look for tracks. None to be found. I quickly assess that with snow falling about an inch per hour for two hours, I would not necessarily see remnants of the skiers' tracks, if the missing skiers had taken this trail several hours ago. When Joe arrives, we set off on our mission to ski Polallie Ridge Trail, into the backcountry. After I radio SAR Base down at the ski resort lodge to confirm plans, Joe and I enter the thick woods of the Polallie Trail. We see faint tracks: bingo. We're on the way.

Then suddenly: "Hey, help!" We hear a yell. "Hey!"

Out of the blackness, out of the midnight snowstorm, two skiers, a man and a woman, stumble into our view, below us and to our right, through a thick glade of lodgepole pine. We are barely a few minutes into our ski up the trail. The couple is a hundred yards away, but to reach them, we descend through a forested, snow-covered slope, covered with thick trees, boulders, and downed timber. It is painstakingly difficult: we make a few turns, clamber with our skis and packs over big logs, then make a few more turns. Joe catches a ski under a log and tumbles: then he gets up quickly. I nearly fall seconds later, by doing the same thing: catching my ski under log. *Be careful*, I remind myself. *Self first, team second, and patient third. Don't get hurt.*

When we reach the skiers, they are, as is common with rescued victims, relieved, gracious, and thankful. The woman is visibly exhausted and shivering. The man is wincing in pain. A shudder of relief passes over the two, which can sometimes push patients into shock. This happens when the brain is so relieved, it stops conserving blood for the vital organs—heart, lungs, brain—and relaxes. This allows blood flow back to all the non-essential organs like the skin and extremities, which drops blood pressure, and can cause one to faint.

The story was that earlier that day, the two rode the chairlift relatively late in the day and decided to try out their new backcountry ski equipment. They went out of bounds on the Polallie Trail and unknowingly dropped to the north into Doe Creek Canyon, which has gentle low-angle slopes, but is still rugged wilderness. The man had a ski binding malfunction near dusk, in the bottom of the canyon. Walking uphill in deep snow without skis or snowshoes is extremely difficult. He was *post-holing*, sinking up to his knees or hips with each step, carrying his skis strapped haphazardly on a tiny backpack, the kind mountain bikers and trail runners use to carry hydration bladders. If the broken ski binding and clambering in deep snow weren't enough, he twisted his knee. It was just a minor sprain, but enough that trudging painstakingly uphill in deep snow was exhausting. The woman stayed with him.

"We got them," I radio search base. Deno returns with the snowmobile and I mark the point of contact with the sheriff's GPS, standard procedure now for all incidents referred to the Oregon Office of Emergency Management. Just before he whisks the pair away on the loud, smelly machine, Deno yells over the din of the snowmobile.

"You want a ride down?" he asks.

I look at Joe, and shrug. Joe shakes his head.

"No. We'll ski down," I yell back.

Joe and I prefer to peel off our climbing skins and click into our ski bindings. We ski the fresh untracked powder snow down to the lodge, a one-run bonus at the end of a short, successful search and rescue mission.

Back at the lodge, I check my phone, hoping it isn't too late to salvage the date with Margaret. But a voicemail says she's gone to the movies with friends.

As if the night rescues are not bad enough, the ones in midwinter, in storms, are doubly awful.

One rainy night in October, our mountain rescue group was holding our monthly business meeting at our Pine Grove Hut, a meeting hall we built in 1972. We are an all-volunteer, not-for-profit group that responds to rescues under the authority of the Hood River County Sheriff's Office. And we're old: established in 1926, we were the first mountain rescue team in the nation.

Our monthly business meetings are full of colorful discussions on building maintenance, equipment purchases, rescue debriefs, training recaps, and the general business of running our non-profit, all-volunteer club. We have two buildings: the Pine Grove Hut and Cloud Cap Inn, which we lease from the Forest Service but on which we do most, if not all, of the maintenance. We have two vehicles: the LMC snowcat and a small Cushman Trackster, a four-person mini-snowcat. The Sheriff's Office owns the 4x4 pickup we use, but we maintain the $30,000 worth of high-tech rescue gear inside the pickup. We are a 503(c)(3) non-profit club, which requires managing donations, equipment purchases, taxes, and such. We have liaisons with agencies including the Hood

River Ranger District of the Mount Hood National Forest, the Sheriff's Office, the various fire departments, and occasionally other agencies. We belong to the Mountain Rescue Association as a charter member and the regional Oregon Mountain Rescue Council, which manages our certifications. Plus, we send a representative to the Mount Hood Search and Rescue Council, a collection of agencies that meets monthly in Portland to debrief rescues on the mountain. We have trainings to organize, a dozen or more a year, and the latest rescues to dissect and discuss. In other words, we are quite busy.

Our sheriff's office, I should add, has search-and-rescue capabilities that extend well beyond the Crag Rats and the mountain-rescue response. Because of the varied terrain in Hood River County—mountain, forest, and river—the sheriff's office also has a snowcat, plus a pair of snowmobiles, three off-road vehicles, an aviation unit with a Piper Super Cub airplane, and a marine patrol unit with a boat. Our group specializes in mountain rescue—technical rope extrication, avalanche and crevasse rescue, snow searches, and trail searches in rugged terrain.

We get two dozen callouts per year, several of which are multi-day rescues totaling about thirty to fifty mission days per year and about 1,500 hours of volunteer time. We have a core of thirty responders who cover the bulk of the rescues, another twenty or so Crag Rats who respond to a few rescues per year, and a dozen who help with non-rescue tasks for our group. The trainings, agency meetings, and equipment maintenance add up for another 2,000 hours annually at least.

During one such business meeting, we are deep in discussion about training requirements when a rescue page zings to one of seven Crag Rats coordinators, as we are the first to get the page from the Sheriff's Office. Usually, one of the coordinators takes the call and then organizes our responders and passes on information—rescue details, equipment needs, staging area—instead of having a half dozen Crag Rats calling dispatch for the same information. A sheriff's deputy will take command of the rescuer operation at the trailhead.

Two hunters lost on Pinnacle Ridge.

Earlier that day, two men had been hunting on Elk Cove Trail, around 4,000 feet elevation on the north side of Mount Hood, when they decided to cross the steep, thick Pinnacle Creek drainage to the Pinnacle Ridge Trail and return to their car. Seems simple—up Elk Cove Trail, 2 miles across the drainage on contour of the same elevation, and down Pinnacle Ridge Trail. But Pinnacle Creek, which collects water from the Ladd Glacier on the north side of Mount Hood, is steep and covered in thick brush and downed timber. And it was late in the day. And it was raining. The two somehow got separated. One hunter made it across the drainage, found Pinnacle Ridge Trail, hiked down to his vehicle, and drove home. A few hours later, when the second hunter didn't show up at home after dark, the first hunter who made it home called 911.

We send a team out in the pouring rain. I coordinate the rescue initially from the Crag Rat meeting and then from home. Coordinating means I get the rescue details from dispatch, send out a text to the fifty or so Crag Rats on our callout list, and then wait for people to respond. Usually a few Crag Rats call in right away. Sometimes I send out a second and third text every ten minutes to get an initial crew to head up the trail, called the *hasty team*. This night, we get a hasty team of four—two hike up Pinnacle Ridge Trail and another two hike up Elk Cove Trail. Night, rain, and cold add up to relatively risky conditions. The theme is recurring. You get the idea. But that night, no luck: no hunter.

The next morning, the rain abates and I head up to the staging areas with new member Cully Wiseman, a general surgeon, and seasoned veteran and regular responder Brian Hukari, an orchardist. We meet Deputy Sheriff Mike Anderson, who is putting together a plan. We drive our beat-up, secondhand, manual transmission 1993 Chevy 4x4 Crew Cab pickup, which is stocked with rescue gear that costs more than the truck is worth. Deputy Anderson is in the com rig, a jacked-up 4x4 van with an ambulance box that now sports a dozen radios (marine, CB, search and rescue, law enforcement), maps, a computer, and a printer. He hands me a printed sheet of a topographic map with our assignment. Brian, Cully, and I are to go up Elk Cove Trail to the point last seen, traverse the Pinnacle Ridge drainage above a cliff band, and come down the Pinnacle Ridge Trail. Basically, repeat the hunters' planned route before they separated. Up and down the two trails will be straightforward. But crossing the Pinnacle Creek drainage will be full-on bushwhacking.

We drive a mile from Pinnacle Ridge Trailhead to Elk Cove Trailhead. After parking and getting our gear, Cully, Brian, and I set off on the trail. It's lightly raining but warm. So despite wearing rain gear designed to keep me dry, I'm sweating with the gear on and thus getting wet. In no more than five minutes, our cell phones beep in tandem: the stand-down page. The hunter, prepared with rain gear, had built a small fire under a stump, waited out the night, and walked out.

Such is often the case: we search for missing persons and they actually are prepared.

Sometimes, we get a third party SAR mission, in which someone calls in a problem, which turns out to be not a problem. Take the Table Mountain rescue at night one winter. A hiker on Table Mountain thinks he hears a call for help on a drizzly, blustery Pacific Northwest winter day. The trail is steep and rugged and the terrain off trail is laced with rocky canyons and thick forests. A half-dozen of us leave Hood River at dinnertime in our old, beat-up SAR truck, drive an hour to Skamania County in Washington, and arrive at dusk. After some delay, we deploy at 7:15 p.m. after being assigned to hike to the summit of Table Mountain. Rick Ragan, who is waylaid by injury, shuttles us via a 4x4 quad from the staging area near Bonneville Hot Springs Resort to the junction of the famed Pacific Crest Trail. The Pacific Crest Trail is the 2,659-mile-long trail completed in 1993 that begins at the US–Mexico border in Campo, California, and terminates at the US–Canada border in Manning Park, British Columbia. It traverses California, Oregon, and Washington, crossing the Columbia River right here, at Bridge of the Gods between Cascade Locks, Oregon, and Stevenson, Washington.

Again, we deploy at night. Again, in the rain.

Ragan doesn't come up the trail but he ends up working as hard as the rest of us by driving the off-road vehicle up and down the trail for the duration of the night, constantly shuttling rescuers to and from their deployment spots. Our team hikes up the west leg of Heartbreak Ridge Loop on a steep and muddy trail. We get wet from the downpour. And then we get wetter: As we climb higher, the wind accelerates as it comes up and over the ridge, pelting us with spray. Then we hit snow at 2,800 feet.

After several hours and a few thousand feet of climbing, we reach the summit of Table Mountain. From there we are designated to do a grid search in deep snow just south and below the summit. While walking about 20 feet apart, we crisscross a section of forest. We sink up to our knees except where the snow turns to ice, where we slip and slide. We beat our way through thick trees and brush. Once we make a complete pass, covering a quarter-mile-long, 100-yard-wide swath of forest, we mark the search area with GPS and tie surveyor's tape to the trees in a very dark, very windy, and very drizzly night. Then we repeat the grid search just below, to cover a new area. We work our way down the hill, covering the slope, back and forth. We complete the grid search of our assigned sector when the slope terminates in a cliff, which we have to be mindful of in the dark. We have a small group huddle, and decide we are going to ask SAR base not to reassign us to a new search task so we can go home. It's midnight. We are cold, tired, and wet. And it's dark.

In the end, the missing person turned out not to be a missing person. It was an owl perhaps? Or just the wind?

Night rescues suck. Have I mentioned that? And they are risky. We are always tired and visibility is awful. We often don't know exactly where to search or what we are searching for. If the weather is bad: double risk. Often it's hard to get a crew. Most of us have work or family obligations in the morning. If the call is for uninjured hikers with a known location in mild weather, we sometimes toss around the idea of letting the victim spend the night if they can clearly do so safely. It is safer to walk out in the morning. But, if the call goes out, we send a hasty team up the trail. No matter the weather. No matter the time of day or night.

Sheriff Matt English comes to one of our meetings and explains the rationale of night rescues. The sheriff must take every SAR call seriously since his office is charged with SAR in Oregon. In most states, this is the norm: the county sheriff is responsible for search and rescue. A few exceptions exist. In New Hampshire the State Fish and Game is responsible, in Hawaii it's the fire department, and in Alaska it's the state troopers. For every SAR call in Oregon, the deputy in charge processes an SAR Urgency Worksheet taking into account factors including number of subjects, medical and physical condition, known punctuality of the subject, reliability of information, experience, physical condition, clothing, equipment, and terrain and weather hazards. They put that into a rating system and come up with an Urgent, Measured, or Evaluate and Investigate response. Unfortunately, the sheriff often doesn't know at the time of the report what the exact situation is. A call for a possible heart attack once turned out to be a person stuck on a log in a river, uninjured and not in pain. The noise on Table Mountain turned out to be either the wind or an owl. The Pinnacle Ridge hunter was uninjured and not lost—he just got stuck after dark.

Once back home from the Cooper Spur night mission for the out-of-bounds skiers, I type up a short mission summary. And I reflect on how to work this story and others into another book on mountain rescue. Many readers had asked me for more adventure tales, and they didn't want *Mountain Rescue Doctor* to end. However, I am looking for deeper meaning to my life's work and storytelling. I want to pen a volume greater than the summation of harrowing, adrenaline-filled mountain rescue missions. So I filed this rescue away, tucked in a digital folder on my laptop.

Then, nine days later, another accident occurred on the big mountain—Mount Hood, one of the most-climbed peaks in the world. It was a big accident. A life-and-death story. This time, the thrill that would course through my body was not the juice of getting amped for a callout. Rather it was adrenaline—the *fight or flight* hormone that saturates our brain, muscles, and blood in tense situations—which would keep me alive, anchoring me precariously on the edge of a giant, gaping crevasse of death. It was an accident that I became intimately familiar with, one that I would obsess over, dream about, recount a million times, analyze in depth, smile about, cry over, and try to replay over and over and over. It was a big accident, a long, harrowing course of action, and a recovery that would extend for many months. The story had a steamy romance, then a broken heart. It had a heartwarming tale of close family and friends. It featured Skylar and Avrie, for whom I would be thankful until world's end. And it culminated in a scar down my abdomen.

That's because it was my accident. The mountain rescue doctor— nationally known speaker on mountain and outdoor safety, author of a dozen books on the outdoors, and educator on wilderness and travel medicine—instantly, in one second, metamorphosed into a wilderness shock trauma patient high on the snowy peak of Mount Hood, the massive mountain in the forefront of my life, my work, my dreams. The irony of me getting hurt, critically injured, would neither haunt nor plague me, but spur me curiously into a search for the meaning of risk and reward.

Because I almost died.

CHAPTER THREE

Guardians of the Mountain

WE ARE NOT THE GUARDIANS OF THE MOUNTAIN.

We are not guaranteed to respond, guaranteed to reach you, or guaranteed to get you out, should you call for help in the backcountry in Hood River County. Indeed, the Sheriff's Office has a duty to address and respond to every call for help. And Crag Rats will respond to every mission somehow. But we are still volunteers with expert outdoor skills and expert mountain rescue skills, and yet with families, work, vacations, and household duties to attend to. And sometimes we can't initiate a rescue if weather is dangerous, terrain conditions are hazardous, or we simply don't exactly know where you are.

Fortunately, not all rescues are at night. Not all rescues are complex. And many rescues—in fact the majority of rescues it seems, by my unscientific guesstimate—are for people who have been acting responsibly. They just have a mishap: trip and fall, lose their way, get cold. Really, it's not all yahoos who get into trouble. And luckily, with cell phones, our lives as rescuers are much easier. That is, if you have a cell phone, if you're able to get cell reception, and if you don't have a dead battery.

One such call comes via our cell phone text group when I am at work at Mountain Clinic at Mount Hood Meadows mountain resort, one of the busiest resorts in the West because of its close proximity to Portland, Oregon's, population of 1.5 million. Even though I'm busy doctoring, consulting, writing books, teaching, and lecturing—not to mention the international travel that is in my blood—the job at the ski resort, where I have worked ten shifts a season for two decades, pays next to nothing.

But I get great satisfaction working as a ski resort doctor: I show up for work in ski gear, strap a radio to my chest, and ski until I have a patient. I get to hang a bit with ski patrol and make a connection to the ski resort community. Job satisfaction comes from the being able to help people in a remote mountain setting and forming a connection with kindred spirits of the ski resort.

At Mountain Clinic, we are able to render advanced medical care immediately when a mishap occurs in the ski resort. Without our clinic, patients would need to be transported 40 miles away, often on snow-covered mountain roads, to the nearest hospital. On weekends, the clinic can be busy with patients, especially when the sun is out and the resort is at capacity. I tend to work weekdays, when the resort is less busy. When we do have patients, we offer nearly full-service emergency care. We have digital x-ray, an electrocardiogram, splinting material, suture supplies, a full complement of medications, advanced life support equipment, and high-speed Internet to facilitate medical communications. In addition to a doctor, we have a clerk, nurse, and x-ray technician on duty. The typical problems are orthopedic: sprains, strains, fractures of wrists and legs, and dislocated shoulders. Frequently we get a head and or neck injury; often a minor sprain or concussion. Sometimes a serious injury rolls in the door: angulated arm or leg fracture, serious concussion, or dislocated hip or elbow. Sometimes the injuries are so concerning that we send a patient via ambulance to the hospital. Once in a while we call a helicopter. Once every year or two, we have a fatality.

Today is a clear, sunny, warmish day on the mountain, midwinter. My shift is about to finish up at 4:00 p.m. I'm skiing out of bounds in the side country, all the while staying within the required fifteen-minute response time to the clinic. A collection of meadows and tiny bowls just beyond the roped border of the resort provides gentle, low-angle slopes. From the scattered meadows, I can see the ski resort a few hundred feet away. I cruise through the powder snow 300 feet down and hike back up for several laps. The side-country meadows provide excellent powder snow, a great workout, and solace from the busy ski resort of mechanized lifts, groomed runs, and crowds. I love skiing out of bounds, and like skiing uphill almost as much as downhill.

When my shift is nearing its end, I pack up my gear and wait for the evening doctor to arrive. Then a mountain rescue callout page pings my phone.

Hikers stuck in a gully/stream on the Tamanawas Falls Trail. Unknown injury. Possibly in the water. Need rope.

Tamanawas Falls, a Chinook term for *spirit* or *guardian*, is a spectacular 150-foot waterfall on Cold Spring Creek, just off Highway 35, right down the road from the ski resort. Our county is loaded with them—waterfalls, that is, not guardians. Tamanawas Falls lies 4 miles up a trail that doesn't gain much elevation as it ducks into the woods and follows the creek west. Normally, in three seasons, it's a fairly straightforward trail (notice, I'm not calling it "easy"). In winter, however, the trail can be treacherous. This week, a recent weather cycle has made the trail particularly hazardous: snow, rain, cold. The trail received snow, which then got soaked by rain, and then froze hard. This, combined with many people using the trail and compacting the snow, turned it into an ice rink—the same combination of weather that would later provide fodder for my accident.

"The deputy said no one's going up the trail without crampons or snowshoes with spikes," says Meredith Martin, this rescue's Crag Rats callout coordinator. I have all my ski gear, and my response time is immediate: I can leave when the night doc shows up for duty and I'm ten minutes from Tamanawas Trailhead. But I have no technical climbing tools. As adrenaline is ramping up, I can't sit still so I get up and pace around the clinic. The crew coming from Hood River will take forty-five minutes at least. But I would be relegated to sitting in the parking lot if I showed up without snowshoes or crampons. Driving home to get my gear would mean nearly 60 miles round trip.

I have an idea: I'll borrow gear. I run upstairs from the clinic and burst into the ski patrol room.

"Can I borrow some snowshoes or crampons?" I ask Mel Toney, ski patrol director and wife of Crag Rat Tom Scully.

"Sure," she says. "What's going on?"

"Rescue at Tamanawas," I say. I explain that some hikers slipped off the trail about 3 miles up the trail and that I'm just about off duty at the ski resort.

"Oh, I know the spot," says Mel, being a seasoned ski patroller and hiker. "Right past the boulder field, where the trail enters the woods. It's steep there."

"I guess that's the place," I say, unsure since it's been years since I've hiked the trail.

"That's the spot. They in the water?" says Mel.

"Don't know, they called for a rope rescue," I say. "I need to take traction, but my crampons are at home."

"The person might be able to walk down the creek and eventually reach the trail."

"Okay, good to know," I say.

"Or you can go up the creek to fetch them instead of rappelling off the trail," she says.

"Okay, I'll find out when I get there."

"You can take one pair, but we should keep one here in case we have a rescue here." Another patroller holds out a set of crampons for me. "That trail is bad when it's icy," Mel adds. "It's slippery. Be careful."

"Thanks for info and gear. I'll bring them back tomorrow or send them up with someone," I say as I scurry out the door. Just as I walk into the clinic, my replacement doctor arrives, so I jump in my car and drive to Tamanawas.

At the trailhead, I find a patrol deputy, not a search-and-rescue deputy, organizing the rescue. A few Crag Rats have just arrived at the scene. All we really know is that two people have fallen in a creek. John Rust, a lawyer by training but educator by profession, is already up the trail with a Forest Service law-enforcement officer from Gifford Pinchot National Forest in Washington, who happened to be driving by while off duty and heard the call on his government radio.

"The crew took up ropes and ice axes," says the deputy. "No report yet from the scene. Still waiting to hear."

I want to know if the patients are wet and hypothermic, in which case we'd probably need to take a litter up the trail to haul them out and maybe the defibrillator, since hypothermia can cause cardiac arrest. If they are wet but ambulatory, that would mean they can walk out.

"No word from the scene?" I confirm.

"No word yet. The hasty team is still trying to reach the spot where the two fell."

"I'll head up the trail," I say. "We will stage two Crag Rats here until we find out what gear we need."

I get my pack and prepare to head up the trail with new members Cully Wiseman and Hugh Brown. Right as we were leaving, Joe McCulloch and Walter Burkhardt arrive with our SAR truck.

Walter jumps out, ready to sprint up the trail in full outdoor gear with hiking poles Joe walks up to the truck.

"If you two can stage here, and wait to see if we need to haul up a litter," I say. Joe and Walter are ready to do whatever it takes to help the rescue, even if that means waiting at the trailhead. Like most Crag Rats they will drop everything—if they are not at work or with family—and come on a rescue.

The story is that a few hours earlier, a pair of hikers stopped to assist a third hiker—a woman who had fallen on the trail. The woman had fallen in an icy spot where the trail crosses a natural slide path. The slide path is a steep, slippery chute, made more dangerous with the recent rain and freezing temperatures. It's a sheer, slick ice chute about the same pitch as a slide on a playground. When hikers cross the slide path, they normally try to step in footsteps from previous hikers, being careful not to slide down the chute. It is a 10-foot crossing that takes a few seconds. However, due to the ice, one wrong slip, and a hiker would slide down the chute to the creek about 100 feet below. That's exactly what happened: in the process of helping the woman, the couple slipped, fell, and careened down the 100-foot, 40-degree slide path into the creek. They were soaked up to their waists. When attempting to climb back out, the man was able to scramble up the steep embankment by grabbing trees and kicking steps in the ice with his boots. The woman climbed out of the water, slipped again, and landed back in the creek. Unable to climb out up the slope while wearing rubber boots, she stayed put. Luckily, the man was able to call 911.

At the scene, John Rust rappels down the chute, reaches the woman, and ties her into the rope. The Forest Service officer is about to start hauling the two up the rope when Cully, Hugh, and I arrive at dusk, after a brisk thirty-minute hike up the trail.

I quickly put on my borrowed snowshoes to utilize the traction from the spikes on the bottom. Cully straps on traction spikes designed for snow running. Then we help with the rope. Quickly, we haul John and the woman back to the trail and find a spot to give her a seat before we untie her.

Cully and I do a quick assessment. The man is alert, warm, and talkative. The woman is shivering, a good sign since shivering stops when you fall from mild to moderate hypothermia. Hypothermia is a cooling of the body's core temperature. Mild is usually marked by shivering. Moderate occurs as the body cools more and shivering stops; patients become confused and have difficulty walking. Severe is when the body cools to a dangerous, near-death state. Frostbite, unlike hypothermia, occurs when skin freezes, usually on the fingers, toes, nose, and ears. We check her feet and hands quickly, and then help her change into dry gloves someone hands us. This woman is alert, talkative, and speaking clearly: a good sign. I go through a quick review of systems to see if anything is injured: arms, legs, chest, and abdomen reveal no injuries. I do a cursory exam by checking head, neck, arms, chest, ribs, collarbones, abdomen, pelvis, and legs: nothing painful, moves all extremities, neck okay.

The best treatment for moderate hypothermia is threefold. Food: calories are needed to generate heat. Dry clothes: wet clothes hasten heat loss. And start walking: movement generates heat. At a certain point, when hypothermia changes from moderate to severe, shivering stops and patients become confused. Those are ominous signs, in which case we'd have to haul her down the trail. Just in case, I radio SAR base and ask Joe and Walter to bring up the portable litter called a SKED. We normally use a cage stretcher with a wheel attached so we can wheel a patient down a trail. But in this case, with the snow and ice, it would be easier to use our vinyl stretcher that rolls up like a burrito to haul it up the trail, and then it slides on snow on the way down.

I packed extremely light and just have my personal ski pack from being the mountain doctor at the clinic that day, so I don't have much gear. Cully pulls out an extra puffy jacket, some energy bars, and a spare headlamp for the woman. He gives the woman his traction grippers, too, and we strap them on her slick rubber boots. Her friend, the man, I can see has now started shivering.

So the woman warms up a bit with dry clothes and food and the man cools down since he'd been standing around idle for the last thirty minutes. I'm anxious to get these two walking.

"Let's get going," I say. "Can you walk?"

"I think so," she replies.

"You good?" I ask the guy.

"Yup," he replies, teeth chattering.

"Let's get going. Cully will walk in front, I'll walk in back. We'll help you all the way down. We'll go slowly." I speak to the patients, and then turn to John. "Cully and I are going to start down to get them moving."

"Okay, we'll follow after we break down the rope," says John. By now, Walter and Joe have shown up with the litter. They, along with Hugh and the Forest Service officer, start shoveling out the section of trail where the couple slipped to make it flat to decrease the chance of future accidents.

We hike back in the dark with headlamps, down the slippery ice, slowly. We arrive back to the cars by 7:00 p.m. to complete a short, successful rescue.

Risk comes in all forms for the Crag Rats. Not all of our rescues are life and death. Not all our rescues are highly technical. But all have some level of risk.

Risk is a thorny problem because until something bad happens, risk is a potential loss, not an actual loss. Once something happens—an accident or illness—loss is no longer a risk but a reality. Risk is simply the *potential* of losing something of value. It the case of outdoor athletes and recreational enthusiasts, the risk is usually physical well-being, an injury like a sprained knee, or illness like hypothermia or frostbite. But, the catch is, we can take risk repeatedly without any bad outcome. Then, one day, like my accident, a risk becomes loss.

In the wilderness, we generally speak of two distinct types of risks: objective and subjective. Objective risks are constants. They are avoidable, but not totally escapable. In the mountains, objective risks include high altitude, difficult terrain, foul weather, sun exposure, rock fall, difficult trail conditions, and avalanches. The objective risks of the Tamanawas Trail are always present: tree fall, creek crossings, weather (storm and sun alike), and difficult trail conditions like slippery ice, deep snow, loose dirt, and thick mud. These omnipresent hazards can be mitigated essentially by avoidance, or, because nobody wants to totally avoid the outdoors, by minimizing exposure. To totally avoid, one would have to not go into the outdoors at all, which has its own set of risks.

The second type of hazards, subjective risks, are within our control. These are factors we can directly prevent by staying hydrated, nourished, and well rested; taking good equipment; avoiding losing one's way; and staying within our skill level of the particular activity. These risks are best mitigated by preparation and planning, obtaining skills and experience, taking good equipment, and, occasionally, either hiring guides or going with friends who have advanced skills.

Just how do we orchestrate risk prevention? Preventing such accidents is not difficult, if one is aware of the danger to begin with. Therein lies the first problem. We have to understand, or at least be aware, of the risks and how to minimize them.

Primary prevention is to avoid exposure altogether—none of us are going to want to stop going into the backcountry or stop enjoying life to its full potential. But sometimes it is important to exercise that option. We've all turned around on an adventure or outing at some point when conditions were dangerous and the fun factor was dwindling due to said conditions. Turn around, make a different plan. Stay home and watch *Keeping Up with the Kardashians* with your teenage daughter if the mountain is unsafe.

But what interests me more is secondary prevention: accept risk, but limit probability of a bad outcome and curtail the consequences if one does occur. This involves preparation in the before-you-go stage by using proper tools and equipment, training, education, and experience, and staying mentally and physically healthy.

Tertiary prevention is escaping, or reversing, a situation once an accident occurs. We'll get to that later.

In the case of the Tamanawas Falls rescue, the risk could have been mitigated with the proper footwear by wearing traction spikes or by choosing a different trail that was not so icy. But that presumes one is aware of the risks in the first place. The hikers may not have known the conditions were dangerous.

The more I investigate the concept of risk in outdoor recreation and adventure travel, the more I realize how vital understanding risk is to success. But to understand risk and reward, the more complex components of risk need to be dissected—the twin, intertwined components of risk: probability and consequence.

The *probability* of an accident is the likelihood that it will occur. This is what normally comes to mind when we think of risk. What is the chance of slipping off the steep section of Tamanawas Trail in the ice without proper footwear? Unfortunately, so many factors impact the probability that it is difficult to accurately predict: We cannot just add up objective and subjective factors on any given outing.

Probability of an accident is influenced by three components: the frequency of exposure, duration of exposure, and the quality of exposure. We all know that frequent exposure, long duration, and severe terrain and weather conditions increase the probability of an accident. I have a friend who quit his job to spend the summer rock climbing the big walls of Yosemite National Park. He has a higher probability of an accident compared to another friend who goes rock climbing a few times over the summer, climbing single pitches with a top rope on a local crag in good weather. So to maximize safety, we aim for activities that have a trifecta of safety margins: limit exposure duration, limit exposure frequency, and limit exposure in difficult terrain and foul weather. Simple. Obvious.

But how do we know which activities are the riskiest? Unfortunately, I don't find statistics helpful. Ask yourself what is riskier: dying from a Mount Everest summit bid, a shark bite, a malaria-laden mosquito bite, or rabies-carrying dog bite? Which is more dangerous: dog, shark, mosquito, or the world's tallest mountain?

The odds of someone dying from rabies after being infected by an animal bite and going untreated are 1/1. In other words, rabies is universally fatal without treatment, and 60,000 people die every year worldwide from rabies, mostly because those people are bitten in a developing country by an unimmunized, infected dog and then don't seek treatment.

The odds of dying from trekking to Mount Everest Base Camp are 1.3/1,000. Trying to reach the summit is much riskier: 42/1,000 western climbers trying to reach the summit die, and this excludes the recent tragedies. The 2014 Western Cwm avalanche killed sixteen Sherpa ice fall doctors and the 2015 Nepal earthquake triggered an avalanche that killed eighteen western climbers and Nepali Sherpas. Those were just the fatalities at Everest Base Camp. The earthquake killed 7,250 overall, and injured 14,122.

Are mosquitos and sharks worrisome? The odds of dying from malaria globally are 0.1/1,000. Sharks are safer: The odds of dying from a shark bite are 0.001/1,000. In comparison, the national statistic for dying in a car accident in the US is 24/1,000—riskier than both mosquitos and sharks. And, in fact, almost as risky as a Mount Everest summit attempt.

It turns out, however, that statistics are a guide, but not a great guide. Statistics like those above are based on all comers, with separate sets of skills, experience, equipment, cognitive function, and awareness. Rabies risk can be reduced from 100 percent to nearly zero by a) avoiding getting bitten by a dog, monkey, bat, skunk, raccoon, or any other furry creature, b) immunizing dogs, and c) immunizing humans with either pre- or post-exposure vaccine—a classic example of how vaccines save lives.

Malaria death similarly can be reduced to nearly zero by a) avoiding bites by using protective clothing and insect repellents, b) avoiding malaria if bitten by a malaria-carrying mosquito with medication prophylaxis that kills the microbe in the bloodstream and liver before it causes damage, and c) early treatment with medications if one does get malaria. Still, there are 500 million cases of malaria per year in the world and one million deaths worldwide, most in underdeveloped or developing countries that have neither insect repellent nor medications.

Risk expert Dr. F. Session Cole, chief medical officer at St. Louis Children's Hospital, explains how risk assessment can be overestimated with statistics. "The problem is that the public assumes that any risk to an individual is 100 percent risk to them." In other words, just because someone becomes ill or injured, that doesn't mean that you have the same risk. In fact, the probability of a freak or once-in-a-lifetime accident recurring maybe *de minimus*, or so minimal that it is equivalent to no risk.

So, I'd like to forget about statistics. Often, in mountain rescue, people are not taking huge risks. In fact, sometimes they are doing *mostly* everything to be safe, yet the small percentage of risk still nails them. Bad things do occasionally happen to good people who are doing nearly everything right. Like this Tamanawas Falls couple who slipped on an icy trail trying to help another hiker, slid down a gully, and got stuck in a creek bed. Several small things contributed to the accident: icy trail, improper traction, and helping an elderly woman who had fallen. Fortunately, the couple fell on a known trail, with lots of bystanders and good cell reception, in the middle of a sunny day, and on a weekend, when several Crag Rats were readily available to help them.

Therefore, probability notwithstanding, an equally, if not sometimes more important, aspect of ascertaining risk is *consequences*. Probability is the chance of something occurring, but consequence is the effect of that event once it occurs. Consequence is highly variable in the wilderness, largely dependent on access to help. This is something we don't think of as often.

Consequence of an event depends usually on the environment, or the distance to help. For example, if a surfer gets bitten by a shark on a beach in Florida, he or she most likely can readily get help. Other surfers, bystanders with cell phones, and EMS personnel are likely available. Compare this to the exact same injury to the exact same surfer who is riding waves at a remote surf camp at Garangan, Indonesia, where access to care is difficult. Assuming the probability of injury for the sake of discussion is equal, these two locations have much different consequences. If my accident had happened, all things being equal, on a day that the mountain was closed and I was backcountry skiing solo, the outcome likely would have been different.

So, risk is a combination of both probability of an accident (exposure duration plus exposure frequency plus severity of conditions) and consequence if an accident occurs. It makes more sense to look at the two together on a continuum, using a green, amber, and red model, like a traffic light.

Risks that have low probability and low consequences are green; we're not going to worry too much about them. If you are hiking on a flat trail, only a few miles from your car, in sunny weather, with a backpack of food, water, and survival gear, then the probability *and* consequence of an accident are low. You have a low probability of spraining or fracturing your ankle. But if you do, you are close to your car on a straightforward trail with access to help.

Risks that are low probability but have high consequences occur frequently in mountain rescue. These are amber: caution. For example, we set up a rope-raising system to pull the injured hikers out of the Tamanawas ice slide. If we've done everything correctly, the probability of a rope breaking is very low. Our ropes are rated to a strength of 6,000 to 8,000 pounds for a workload of 600 to 800 pounds (tenfold margin of safety). Often we use two ropes: a main haul line and a backup belay. The latter is solely in case the first rope fails (double the tenfold safety margin). Our carabiners and webbing and other hardware are similarly rated to thousands of pounds. But, *if* the rope system were to fail for any reason, the consequences would be catastrophic—a rescuer and patient could plunge into the creek. Thus, low probability but high consequence is amber: *use caution.* This might be similar to investing your entire life savings in a Vanguard Index Mutual fund: the probability of the fund catastrophically tanking is low, but if you lose your life savings, the consequence is huge.

High probability but low consequence events also occur in mountain rescue, but they are bit less concerning. I remind my team members all the time that if they respond to a trail rescue in summer wearing shorts, they have a high probability of getting a poison oak dermatitis, a nasty rash that is so itchy it becomes debilitating. That's a low consequence for the rescue, but two days later when the rash develops, it becomes a problem. Low consequence is less worrisome, but still amber: *caution.*

High probability and high consequence are red: *extreme risk.* When these risks are present, we have to pay special attention to these rescues. When we get called for a rescue in the middle of the night, in the middle of a storm, high on Mount Hood, the probability of hypothermia and frostbite is high and the chance of avalanches is high. Thus the consequence of a mishap to rescuers high on the mountain in extreme conditions is ginormous. These situations are dangerous, so dangerous that we've been known to delay rescues until conditions—probability and consequence of an injury to rescuers—have improved. We are not guaranteed to come immediately, or at all, in these situations. In other words, we are not the failsafe automatic responders, or guardians of the mountain.

What I'd like readers to think about is this: Risk is not just the probability of getting into an accident, but also the consequences of an accident if it occurs. I see this regularly windsurfing and kitesurfing in the Columbia River, when in midsummer people decide not to wear a wetsuit. Sure, the air temperature is 80 degrees and the water temperature is 65 degrees. The probability of getting stuck in the river with equipment malfunction is perhaps quite low. But, if an accident occurs for any reason, the consequences of being in the water without a wetsuit can be life-threatening. A kayaker on the Columbia River died one year after being caught in turbulent wind and waves, losing his boat, and spending an hour in the water—on a sunny day, in midsummer, with mild water temperatures. He made it to shore and had hypothermic shock the minute he was pulled from the water. He did not make it. So: dress for the swim, even if the likelihood is low.

We go after all sorts of calls up on Mount Hood. Many are very straightforward. Again, still risky and challenging, but straightforward like the Tamanawas Falls slide-for-life couple. Many are low risk, and low to moderate consequence. But even the easiest rescue is still challenging, physically taxing, and somewhat risky. The drive up the mountain sometimes is the most dangerous aspect of the rescue.

One spring day we receive a 5:30 a.m. call for a missing hiker at Wolverine Lake. A man had been camping with friends. Sometime the night before, with a fair bit of alcohol, they'd wandered off on a night hike in the Mount Hood Wilderness. The group seemed to remember that the missing man "decided to rest on a log" sometime after dark. After the night hike, half of the group drove an hour to Hood River, booked a hotel room, reported the guy missing, and went to bed. The other half of the group crawled into a tent at Wolverine Lake and slept.

That morning, then-Sheriff Joe Wampler fires up the Piper Cub and spots the man 3 miles from and hiking back to the primitive campground at Wolverine Lake. Bruce Hukari, Micah McNulty, and I load up in our old 4x4 crew-cab long-bed pickup, drive a half hour up Highway 35 just past Tamanawas Falls, and then continue another half hour on rough gravel roads to Wolverine Lake. At the lake, we interview a few other campers, and then locate the tent from which we wake one of the missing man's companions. They are of little help. So we set off on the trail, and within one minute, we find the man straggling back to camp. He is barefoot, dehydrated, hungry, and hungover. He's got scrapes on his legs. We give him some food and water and turn him over to the friend, who has arisen from the tent.

Then we make the two-hour drive back to Hood River.

On another mission, we are called for a rescue in August at Cooper Spur Ski Resort. The lift maintenance crew is working but the place otherwise looks vacant. A maintenance worker called 911 when a man came wandering into the parking lot looking for a stretcher and asked the employer if a gate could be opened so the man could drive up the chairlift access road. His girlfriend had been injured on the mountain. When scrambling up a scree field, a boulder was knocked loose, tumbled down, and struck the woman in the head and chest. Lose consciousness? Maybe so, maybe for a few seconds. A group of friends is slowly bringing her down by using an old ski resort sign and some bamboo poles to fashion a stretcher.

No, they don't want help. The girlfriend is being carried down the mountain. They are self-sufficient. Nonetheless, we go after them. Joe Wampler finds the injured woman with the Piper Super Cub below Cooper Spur, which still has patches of snow in late August.

We muster a crew, drive up to the ski resort, and check in with the deputy running the rescue. A ski resort employee drives us up to the top of the chairlift. From there, we set off to find the woman.

When we meet her coming down the mountain, the woman is alert and orientated, has stable vital signs, has short-term memory loss of the incident, and sports an abrasion across her upper chest wall. The wound is dirty from the pumice and sand on the ridge. Tentative diagnoses: closed head injury with loss of consciousness and chest wall abrasion. Might have a broken rib or broken collarbone, but not likely. Might have a collapsed lung, but not likely. Probably has a concussion. Doubt a neck fracture, but certainly possible.

With the loss of consciousness, we are obliged to immobilize her spine in case she has a neck fracture. Although more recently, I try to "clear the cervical spine" in the field, meaning I try to determine if the patient has a low probability of a neck bone fracture based on clinical assessment. If one can clear a cervical spine in the field, it may mean avoiding a dangerous evacuation by a stretcher. If one can't clear the spine, then we put the patient in full spinal immobilization and carry him or her out in a litter. We have a few different criteria to use: the North American X-ray Utilization Study, or NEXUS, recommends five criteria to clear the neck: no midline neck tenderness, no neurologic abnormality, normal alertness, no distracting injury, and no intoxication. In this situation, the woman can't be cleared: chest wall injury and loss of consciousness with some residual memory loss make her higher risk for a cervical spine fracture.

We rig up the backboard and the SKED stretcher, a vinyl stretcher that rolls up like a burrito so it's easy to carry uphill. Once packaged, we carry the woman down some rocks, across a snow patch, and down more rocks. A light wind has picked up and is blowing sand and dirt across our group. It's getting in our eyes. Once we reach another patch of snow, the blowing sand stops. At the snow patch, we rig up a rope and belay her down the snow, on which the SKED easily slides. Eventually, we enter the woods and carry her out to the ski resort.

She refuses ambulance transport to the hospital.

"I'll be fine," she says after I warn her of the possibilities of a concussion, collapsed lung, and scarring from all the dirt and sand in the chest wound, which needs to be scrubbed clean lest it permanently tattoo the skin. I give a stern warning. So does the deputy. She signs out, against medical advice. It's dusk, so we head home.

In another rescue, we respond to a boy with hypothermia near the top of Gnarl Ridge, at the 6,000-foot level on the north side of Mount Hood. In addition to nearly an hour's drive to the Elk Meadows Trailhead, we hike two hours up the trail carrying a litter searching for a hypothermic boy. The story was that two days prior, a family of five left Timberline Lodge on a backpacking trip. On the first day, they crossed White River and got wet. The next morning, they got further soaked by rain. By that afternoon, day three, the young boy was shivering and dad called 911.

We run up Elk Meadows Trail with a lightweight litter and find the family by 6:00 p.m. They are huddled around a fire, with the young boy in a tent wrapped in a sleeping bag. He is warm, dry, uninjured. He is not hypothermic. He's looking pretty happy. Lisa Rust, a lawyer turned teacher and veteran climbing guide (as in Everest) pulls out a spare down jacket. We wrap the boy, sleeping bag, and tarp, plop him in the stretcher, and hike back out Elk Meadows Trail, across the rocky Newton Creek, to Mount Hood Meadows. We make it back right at dark, 8:30 p.m.

In all these straightforward—I won't say simple or easy—rescues, the biggest risk for us is probably driving to and from the mountain and stumbling on the rough terrain. Sometimes people are foolish; other times they are doing everything right. Fortunately for us, not every rescue is a harrowing life-and-death situation. But nonetheless, they're still risky to some degree.

We debrief at our next meeting. Mostly, we discuss recurring themes. Sometimes we worry about the lack of response from volunteers: some rescues only require a small hasty team but others require a large number of responders, especially when carrying a heavy person, over rough terrain, or for a long distance. Sometimes we question why some callouts seem to be for people who should be self-sufficient—such as with the hung-over man, the non-hypothermic boy, and the woman who didn't want our help. Why are people not more prepared? Why do we always get called at night?

The sparse turnout of responders, particularly at night, is a bit worrisome. I think volunteer participation ebbs and flows, depending on how busy one is and what crisis or time-sensitive issues are occurring in people's lives. People get busy with work, family, and social lives. We have more burdensome training requirements now with the post-911 Incident Command System mandated by the Federal Emergency Management Agency and more rigorous training from the Oregon State Sheriffs' Association guidelines. The minimum requirements for Oregon SAR personnel are a CPR and first-aid class every two years and thirty hours of training and missions annually. For a group of volunteers, some of whom come out to only a few rescues per years, this can be somewhat laborious. These are inherent problems of volunteering: finding time to go on rescues, meeting training requirements, and completing all the ancillary jobs like maintaining our buildings, vehicles, and equipment.

But, as Sheriff English explains at one of our meetings: none of these problems trumps the legal obligation of the sheriff's office to respond. The sheriff must respond, and by default, he must send the Crag Rats or a group from a neighboring county. And so although we respond, we are not, by any means, guaranteed to respond, guaranteed to respond immediately, or even guaranteed to find you if you're lost. We take an urgent or measured response, but still can't afford to risk an injury to a Crag Rat. We will brave the terrain and weather to make a good faith attempt, but it's not guaranteed.

I hope people understand that self-reliance is vital to minimizing risk and minimizing consequence—because the Crag Rats are not the guardians of the mountain.

Chapter Four

Wy'East and Pahto Fistfight in Heaven

Many more powerful forces exist here than Tamanawas, guardian of the mountain. These geographic features do far more than define
the landscape: It is this great river and these great mountains that are
intrinsically part of how I connect with this land that I call home.

The tribes that lived here years ago spoke of a giant rock bridge
that spanned the raw, wild Columbia River, once called Nch'i-Wana, a
Sahaptin moniker meaning "Great River," the stream that connected the
great forests of the north and south. People lived and prospered: Hunting
and fishing provided bountiful harvests, the forest provided shelter, and
the streams gave pure mountain water. The land was at peace for many
years, presided over by Great Spirit who lived in the sun.

Great Spirit had two sons, Wy'East and Pahto, who were rabble-
rousers and quarreled regularly. One day, Great Spirit gathered his sons
and had them each shoot an arrow in opposite directions and gave them
each land to preside over. Pahto picked the forests to the north and
Wy'East took the forests to the south, leaving Great River to divide their
territories. Great Spirit built a giant bridge crafted from andesite and
basalt to provide passageway for people and animals.

But the brothers continued to fight. Great Spirit became angry,
and stopped the sun from shining on the lands. The people got cold. It
rained. It snowed. The wind blew. And darkness fell. Great Spirit, try as
he might, could not reverse his punishment and could not cause the sun
to shine again.

Then one day a wandering old woman named Loowit came bearing a special gift: fire. Great Chief, dismayed at having taken away the sun, asked Loowit to create fire so that all the people could warm themselves.

"Build us a fire and I will grant you any wish you desire. We will die without it."

"I want to be young and beautiful," she said. So Loowit created fire, sparking warmth in both lands. The next morning, the fire rose and warmed the hearths of both villages, and the sun shone again. And next to Bridge of the Gods, alongside the banks for Great River, sat a beautiful young maiden.

Peace reigned over the land for some time, until the brothers began favoring Loowit, and they became jealous of each other, like brothers do. Then, they fought once again, like brothers do, but with raging fire, cascading mudflows, billowing winds, torrents of rain, and flying boulders. Great Spirit was so angry that he struck down the Bridge of the Gods and turned the brothers to stone, ice, snow, and dirt. Wy'East became Mount Hood and Pahto became Mount Adams. Some say they continued to spit rock and fire at each other as present-day volcanoes.

The legend is a bit foggy as to what happened to Loowit. Some versions say she became Mount St. Helens. Others say she escaped the fiery land. And yet others say she dispersed her soul into every maiden in the land.

These great mountains and forests and rivers are a deep part of the landscape and the lore. They are majestic and revered. We don't always need to climb to the tops of these snow-clad peaks. I have circumnavigated Mount Hood on skis at the 9,000-foot level during a one-day ski tour around the mountain. I have ridden around the base on my road bike: 100 miles of pavement, save the 5 miles of gravel on Lolo Pass Road. But I have not yet completed the rite of passage of many Oregon hikers, backpackers, and ultramarathon runners: the Timberline Trail.

Mount Hood's Timberline Trail is fairly unique as far as loop hikes go: It's a 43-mile circumnavigation of a volcano at the 6,000-foot level on a rugged trail built in the 1930s by the Civilian Conservation Corps. Most people start at Timberline Lodge and hike either clockwise or counterclockwise in two to five days, although trail runners do the loop in a day. The trail undulates up and down for a total of 8,000 vertical feet uphill. Along the way, hikers ford log bridges across bubbling streams of Newton, Sandy, and White Rivers, and tramp through thick Douglas fir old-growth cathedrals that lead to mesmerizing cascades like Ramona Falls. The wildflower kaleidoscope at Elk Cove is among the best in the West, chock full of Western pasque flower, bear grass, witch's hair lichen, western trillium, purple lupine, bright red Indian paintbrush, and ever-green huckleberry, the fruit of which is delicious in late summer.

Mount St. Helens has the Loowit Trail, which is a 30-mile loop, and Mount Adams can be circumnavigated via a more primitive back-country trail. The Pacific Northwest, in fact, has other volcano loop hikes. The 46-mile Three Sisters Loop circles North Sister, Middle Sister, and South Sister volcanoes near Bend, Oregon. And probably one of the most famous hiking trails in the world is Mount Rainier's 93-mile Wonderland Trail.

So one midsummer week, four hikers set off from Cloud Cap Inn to hike the Timberline Trail. They started walking clockwise over the course of four nights and five days: across the pumice and sand of treeless Cooper Spur, over craggy Gnarl Ridge, down into the wildflowers of Elk Meadows, underneath the chairlifts of Mount Hood Meadows, down, across, and up the great glacial chasm of White River, into Timberline Lodge for a burger and a pint at Blue Ox Bar, down Zigzag Canyon, across the Sandy River, up to Ramona Falls, around Yocum Ridge, around Bald Mountain Ridge, through Cairn Basin with more wildflowers, around Barrett Spur, and past the pristine, tiny, glacier-fed pond of Dollar Lake. Now, day five, they had one long traverse back to Cloud Cap Inn: across the raging Eliot Creek and the thick steep Eliot Glacier moraines, the twin mounds of sand, silt, rocks, and scree that border each side of the creek and the tongue of the glacier.

And it is here that they have a problem. Five days deep and five days tired, their dusty red Nissan Sentra is an hour away at Cloud Cap Saddle. They have the same problem everyone has when trying to complete the Timberline Trail: the bridge over the Eliot Creek is gone. A flood took out the bridge in November 2006 and the Forest Service has not replaced it. In fact, it's more than just the bridge that washed out: The section of

Timberline Trail that descends the West Moraine down into the Eliot Creek and Eliot Glacier has been obliterated. Officially, this segment of trail is closed.

Even if you can get safely down West Moraine scree slope—a sandy, rocky 300-foot descent on a 50-degree slope that terminates right in the creek—the stream is too wide, just barely, to jump across and too deep, by a long shot, to wade across. Midday, midsummer, the stream is raging at full tilt because the sun is melting the Eliot Glacier, a half-mile upstream, by 2 feet per day, and pumping meltwater into the creek.

So, three options exist for crossing Eliot Creek. The safest first: Hike down to Lawrence Lake and take a car shuttle around to Cloud Cap Inn.

The most enjoyable second: You don't go down into the Eliot Creek Basin but rather cross higher on the Eliot Glacier. This means you hike a mile and 1,000 vertical feet up the West Moraine and cross on the snow-covered glacier at 7,000 feet—there's a flat bench on the Eliot Glacier that is free of crevasses and seracs. After crossing here, you hike back down the east moraine to reconnect with the Timberline Trail. This takes about two to three hours of extra time, when you consider the average person going at a good clip hikes uphill 1,000 vertical feet in an hour.

Alternatively, the least safe but quickest way: down the moraine. At the point where the Timberline Trail ends at the West Moraine, you can descend a rope that someone has tied to a rock. The rope—battered by wind, sand, sun, and rocks—provides a hand line to scramble down the moraine (read: dangerous). Then once down the 300-foot scree slope, you hike twenty minutes upstream to the headwaters of Eliot Creek, where the water seeps from the tongue of the glacier. At 6,500 feet elevation, the headwater of Eliot Creek begins as several small streams that emerge from the melting ice. Although there are several braided channels to cross, they are much smaller compared to where the bridge was washed out. Once across the braided channels of the creek, you hike back downstream. Then, you need to climb out of the canyon back up to the East Moraine to rejoin the trail: another rope and another 300-foot slope of scree and sand, boulders and pumice.

This group decided to take the most difficult way. The first man descended the West Moraine scree slope and made it down to the edge of the creek. Then his girlfriend made it down. Then, the next woman started making her way down, lost her footing somewhere near the top of the rope, fell backwards with her heavy pack, hit the scree slope on her back, bounced, cartwheeled, and landed smack on a boulder, about 2 feet from falling into the raging, 10-foot-deep Eliot Creek. Luckily, she did not injure her head or back. However, she smacked her shoulder and dislocated it as she struck the boulder. The man came down. As he descended the steep scree slope, he knocked down a pile of sand and scree that barely missed the woman.

The men tried to yank the shoulder of the woman for a bit to try to put it back into its socket, but it hurt too much. And they were more bookish than outdoorsy. So, they called 911. Luckily, on a clear day above tree line, cell phone reception is excellent on Mount Hood.

So off we are again, on a gorgeous midsummer afternoon, heading up the mountain. Todd Hanna, Ron Martin, Meredith Martin, and I meet at the county yard, pile into our truck, drive to Tilly Jane Trailhead, and then continue on the gravel-dirt, pot-holed, rough Cloud Cap Road 9 miles to Cloud Cap Saddle Campground, just a few hundred feet below Cloud Cap Inn. The drive takes an hour.

At the campground we meet two other hikers who give us good information.

"You see an injured hiker?"

"Yes, across the Eliot Creek. Lying on a boulder. Right at the bottom of the West Moraine rope." We know the exact location. The approach hike will take twenty minutes. The woman has a dislocated shoulder, so we go light: no litter.

We set off on a brisk trot up the mountain and through the woods, where we emerge on the East Moraine, the vast rocky ridge with an expansive panorama of the mountain, the giant Eliot Glacier, and the Eliot Creek headwaters. From the East Moraine we can't see the bottom of the creek because the slope is too steep.

We scramble down the scree slope of the East Moraine. Partway down, we see the creek bottom and the tiny figures of the foursome on the opposite bank. About halfway down, the slope steepens and we find the rope someone tied to a rock, the hand line to help hikers up or down the slope. The rope is frayed and faded: not too safe, by my judgment. We continue hiking down the slope without touching the rope, going slowly so as not to slip. Our boots slide a few feet downhill with every step in the scree.

At the creek bottom, we are walking on boulders that range in size from bowling balls to small cars. When we are not scrambling over boulders, we walk on sand and rocks. We make our way to the creek directly across from the hikers. But the creek is too loud for us to yell. So we signal to the three hikers that we are coming. Todd, Meredith, Ron, and I search for a crossing, but we can't find a safe one immediately in the vicinity: too wide to jump, too deep to wade. We start hiking upstream.

In fifteen minutes, we reach a small cascade, the headwaters of the Eliot Creek. After scrambling up the rocks around the 10-foot waterfall, we find the spot where the creek emerges from the glacier in three or four spots. Each is a separate channel, which is much smaller than the raging Eliot Creek just below us.

Ron and I decide to cross, so we hop across boulders, stream by stream, and make it to the other bank with dry feet. Ron has hiking poles, which helps give him balance.

Todd and Meredith decide to stay on the east side of the creek to find a better crossing spot. Ron and I make our way down the west side of the creek, which turns out to be difficult because the West Moraine butts right up to the creek. We clamber across the side hill of sand, scree, and boulders. The sand finds a way into our boots and grinds at our ankles and feet like sandpaper. In a few spots, we hop boulders inches from the Eliot Creek.

Bernie Wells shows up and radios us from the top of the West Moraine rope.

"I'm at the top of the West Moraine rope," he says. "I'll stay here." He's not coming down.

"Can you watch for rock fall?" I ask Bernie on the radio.

"Sure, no problem. I'll hang out here in the sun," he replies. I'm concerned that a loose rock might peel off the sandy slope of the moraine and come careening our way. The creek, which was probably raging at 2:00 p.m. when the woman fell, has abated a bit as the afternoon sun begins to dip lower in the sky. I can see the high-water line, a wet, dark spot on the boulders, about 6 inches above the current stream level.

After fifteen minutes, a quarter mile of descending the west bank, we reach the foursome.

"Hi, we are search and rescue. I'm Christopher, a doctor, and this is Ron. What happened?"

"My shoulder. I dislocated it," says the woman, who is not wincing until she moves. She is absolutely stoic.

"I tried to put it back in, but it was too painful," says the oldest of the men.

"That's okay. I'll take a look," I say. As I examine the patient, I run through a brief *review of systems*, a verbal survey from head to toe that doctors do to make sure there are no other issues. No head injury. No headache or blurred vision. Neck fine. Chest, no. Abdomen, no. Legs, okay.

The patient is lying on her stomach on a large boulder with her left arm hanging down off the rock, the position of comfort . . . or rather, the least pain. I palpate her shoulder through her shirt and feel the head of the humerus out of socket and a depression where the joint is. I check the ribs and clavicle: no obvious pain. I check her wrist pulse, finger color, and hand sensation to make sure blood flow and nerves are not being impeded by the dislocation. She is breathing normally: I don't have a stethoscope but can tell that generally she is in no acute distress—until she moves a bit, and then she winces in pain.

After confirming the patient has a dislocated shoulder, I am ready to *reduce* it, put it back into socket. I have what we doctors call a PARQ conference: procedure, alternatives, risks, and questions answered. Procedure: put shoulder back into socket. Alternatives: hike out with it dislocated, or worse, we fetch a litter and carry her out. Risks: could be fractured, could cause pain to reduce it, and could cause nerve damage or a fracture by trying to pop it back into place. Questions: none.

"Let's do it," she says. She is one tough hiker.

"We'll help," says one of the hikers.

"I think Ron and I can get this, but stand over here," I point to an area that is out of the way as far from the creek as possible.

With Ron helping me, we gently help the woman sit upright on the giant boulder, which is right below the scree slope and right next to the raging waters of the Eliot Creek. From a sitting position on a rock I give her a small square foam camping pad; she sits on it for comfort.

Many ways exist to reduce a dislocated shoulder. I use the "Snowbird" method, the moniker given because the doctors who described the procedure in the medical literature worked at the Snowbird Winter Resort in Salt Lake City. First, I have the patient sit. I tie a cravat in a loop, place the loop around the patient's arm at the crook of her elbow, put my foot in the cravat loop, and gently push down on the woman's arm by using my foot in the loop. This allows me to use my foot as traction to pull the humerus bone out of the dislocated area, while keeping my hands free to guide the humerus head back into socket. I instruct Ron to keep the woman from falling off the rock with a gentle bear hug. I have both hands free, since I'm using my foot to pull the arm back into socket, so I support the woman's arm and shoulder. It may sound painful, but after three seconds of traction, the humerus bone pops back into place with an audible and palpable "clunk."

"Wow, I felt that," exclaims Ron.

"Oh gosh, that is so much better," says the woman, who has instant pain relief. She sits up straight and moves her arm a bit. The older of the hikers heaves a sigh of relief.

"Don't move it too much," I explain. "We don't want it popping back out while the muscles and joint are loose."

I complete a quick post-reduction assessment. The pain is nearly resolved and the woman can move her shoulder about 50 percent of normal range of motion. She has a strong wrist pulse, normal finger color, and normal sensation: no nerve or blood-vessel damage. I construct a makeshift sling and swath by pulling up her T-shirt tail, cradling her arm in the T-shirt, and using safety pins to affix the shirttail to the shirt body. I take 2-inch-wide medical tape and put wraps around her torso, effectively taping her arm to her chest. Ron gives her a hiking pole for her free hand. I call Meredith and Todd on the radio.

"We're ready to move," I say. I don't want to spend any extra time here because of the danger of rock fall. Plus, we have a walk out that will be doubly dangerous if we hike out at dusk, which is an hour away. "Where should we cross?"

"Nowhere safe down below," says Todd. "You'll have to go back upstream."

"Okay, we're headed that way." I can see Meredith and Todd across the creek, but the noise of the Eliot makes shouting futile. "Bernie, can you see us?" I ask on the radio.

"Yup, I got you. All good from here," the radio crackles.

"Okay, we are moving upstream," I say.

Ron asks one of the men to grab the woman's pack.

"Be careful hiking out," says Ron. Ron and I spot the injured woman from front and back. With her left arm immobilized, even a small stumble would make it difficult for her to catch herself.

We start the walk out, up the west bank a quarter mile, across the creek where Meredith and Todd are there to help us wade through the water, and then back down the east bank, now with all four rescuers and all four hikers collected.

To back get up the East Moraine scree field, where Bernie is perched on the rock in the fading sun, Todd and Meredith set up rope to use as a safety line. We tie a smaller-diameter 10-foot-long cord to the rope using a prussic knot. A prussic is designed to slide up the rope, but with sudden downward pressure, the knot cinches and stops sliding. So, the patient has a sliding cord tied to the rope that gives her a hand hold all the way up the slope. Todd and I walk alongside to spot the woman should she fall. Meredith and Ron escort the other two hikers up the slope. Atop the East Moraine, we pack up the rope, and make the straightforward hike back through the woods to Cloud Cap Saddle campground.

Reducing a dislocated shoulder is something I do regularly in my job at Mountain Clinic. At the mountain, reducing a dislocated shoulder is often fairly straightforward, because patients come right from the ski hill via ski patrol, barely ten minutes from dislocation. From the Eliot Glacier mission, the reduction of a dislocation may seem easy. But I do this procedure on a regular basis. And it's not without risk. One big controversy in the outdoor recreation industry is how much medicine should be taught to non-medical personnel. Should guides and mountain rescuers be taught to give allergy medicine like epinephrine, to administer antibiotics for infections, and to reduce dislocated shoulders? It is difficult to learn a shoulder-reduction procedure without physically doing it under supervision, such as in medical school.

On one hand, if a river guide is stuck with a client with a dislocated shoulder on day three of a seven-day river trip, reducing the dislocation could mean continuing the trip with ease, and would also speed healing. A dislocated shoulder left unreduced could mean a lengthy and dangerous evacuation. Imagine popping a shoulder back into joint quickly, when the alternative is immobilizing an arm for a raft trip down dangerous rapids, where if one falls out of the boat, he or she would have difficulty swimming.

On the other hand, does this procedure have any risk? Sure. You can create a fracture by reducing a shoulder dislocation. You can turn a stable fracture into an unstable fracture (one that doesn't heal properly) or cause damage to blood vessels or nerves. And you can cause a fair bit of intense pain and muscle damage if you pull too hard and too long.

Much of risk mitigation is balancing benefits against risks and consequence. But as you will see, striking an equilibrium is a thorny, elusive, but obtainable quandary.

In this accident, primary prevention would have been to avoid descending the scree slope and to take the long way around Eliot Creek. Secondary prevention would have been to use a new rope to descend the slope slowly, possibly lowering backpacks down one at a time. And tertiary prevention would be to call for help, as the foursome did. But how does this look to the Crag Rats? Sometimes we can't avoid going into the wilderness to help someone, so we need to rely on a more complex system of secondary prevention to avoid accidents.

We mitigate risk through five components: experience, training, practice, equipment, and well-being. The Crag Rats don't necessarily do these formally, but the steps are vital to risk management, even at the informal level. Sooner or later, to be a professional you have to gain experience, participate in training, practice, use good equipment, and stay fit . . . both mentally and physically. Let's look at each separately.

First, Crag Rats are perhaps a bit unique and certainly a bit insistent when it comes to *experience*. Our group is composed partly of docs, nurses, paramedics, firefighters, forest service rangers, climbing rangers, and ski patrollers with some level of medical, crisis management, and technical experience. We also have professional rope riggers (firefighters and movie set). But we also have hard-working, trail-tested team members who work as lawyers, judges, farmers, orchardists, carpenters, builders, and engineers. The unified skill we bring to the group is acquired *before* we join: we are ski mountaineers. The bare minimum to join our group is that you have to have summited Mount Hood (11,249 feet) and Mount Adams (12,281 feet). Along with Hood and Adams, "Life Membership" in the Crag Rats entails summiting Mount Jefferson, North Sister, Middle Sister, and South Sister in Oregon, and Mount Rainier, the big one at 14,411 feet high.

In addition to coming to the group with a skill set, experience comes from simply attending rescues: simple or complex, large or small. In other words, potential new members with no outdoor skills can't just sign up with Crag Rats and then expect to be formally taught mountain-rescue skills. We don't teach people to become mountaineers, skiers, or mountain rescuers. Many SAR groups in larger communities have an academy or training year, during which the groups formally accept applications and then train accepted applicants over the course of a probation year. But the Crag Rats bring in members with mountaineering experience and have them gain rescue experience by attending trainings and missions. The reasons: first, we simply don't have time to train people with all the other tasks at hand: rescues, trainings, building maintenance, equipment maintenance, non-profit functions, and liaisons with all the agencies we work with. Second, it's a tradition that dates back to the earliest Crag Rat days: We accept mountaineers as members, we don't make mountaineers. At first I questioned the requirement of having climbed Hood and Adams, because several potential members who had not bagged Hood and Adams still had well-honed expert skills in rock climbing, skiing, and hiking. But then I realized that we need this gauge, this basic requirement to assemble a team of kindred spirits.

Second to experience, we try to train regularly. But considering we have about fifty members to respond to thirty callouts a year—while maintaining jobs, families, and household duties—it can be a burden. Twice a month we have meetings. The first meeting of the month is a business meeting, and a few years ago Ron Martin started a pre-meeting mini-training, a thirty-minute brush-up on a skill like patient packaging, splinting, or hypothermia treatment. This is usually something quick to teach, or a refresher of skills we already trained on. The second meeting of the month is a two-hour training on a variety of topics: GPS, avalanche rescue, rope rescue, patient packaging, cell phone and radio communications, and the like. We also have trainings a few times a year on Mount Hood, especially for avalanche rescue. Beyond Crag Rat trainings, some members seek outside training through search-and-rescue, rope-rescue, or wilderness-medicine courses.

Two issues are important with regard to training and risk. The first is training quantity: How much training is enough? I already mentioned that reducing a dislocated shoulder can be a critical procedure, but is also risky without proper training. Doctors run into training issues regularly and sometimes select ourselves out of procedures if we don't practice or perform them often enough. Similarly, with mountain rescue, if you set up a complex rope-rescue system once a year in training, is that enough to be proficient? Probably not. The best training is one for skills you can use regularly, and thus can constantly reinforce. This is why the best rescuers are the ones who are recreating in their daily lives—hiking, rock climbing, trail running, backcountry skiing, mountaineering—because we are constantly using the rescue skills in daily recreation.

Which leads me to the second issue: training quality, or the complexity of training. At one time, the Crag Rats tended to train at the extreme end of our skill set. In other words, we trained on rope rescue and avalanche rescue. We love to set up complicated rope-raising systems using high-tech hardware on the training tower we built with telephone poles in the gravel parking lot of our hut. But when I looked at a decade of rescues, about twenty to thirty calls per year, a third are medical, most are trail rescues or searches in the woods for lost people, and a third are on one specific single trail, the most popular hiking trail in the Columbia

Gorge. About five missions per year are rope rescues, and all but one or two per year are complicated rope rescues. Setting up highly technical, complicated rope systems is a skill we don't use much in the field. So, training on the basics is as important as training on the extreme end of a skill set for the most complex rope rescues. When in doubt, one can always rely on the basics.

The third component is practice, which I consider separate from training. Training is formal or informal instruction on a certain technique or skill. Practice is repeatedly employing that skill so it becomes routine. A classic example is attaching our wheel to the bottom of our stretcher. It seems like a simple procedure: the attachment system is a frame with webbing that wraps around the 1-inch-diameter tubular rails of the litter and then tightens with a simple ratchet. But it can easily, and often does, bind if you don't first pull the excess slack. We still tend to put it on wrong sometimes during rescues so that the wheel is not firmly attached and then rattles all the way down the trail. This happened once on the Eagle Creek trail and we had to come down with a wheel shimmed with sticks because the webbing was jammed in the ratchet. So, someone can demonstrate how to put our wheel on our litter, and you can do it once under supervision, but if you don't practice it regularly, you may end up doing it wrong.

We've all been there: you learned to do something on a computer but forgot the procedure without practicing it. I love practicing because it helps me master skills. I have practiced writing for the last three decades. I need two hands to count how many books I've written that have not been published and more than two hands to count how many fifty-page book proposals I've written. But, it's practice. Malcolm Gladwell wrote in *Outliers* that it takes ten thousand hours of practice to become an expert at an activity.

Beyond experience, training, and practice, equipment becomes the next vital piece. And herein lies the sexy part: gear. We love good equipment. All the Crag Rats carry personal safety and rescue gear for multiple capacities.

In winter, I carry a full avalanche-rescue and winter pack replete with winter clothing, helmet, alpine touring skis, climbing skins, ski crampons, and avalanche safety gear, which includes an airbag backpack, beacon, shovel, and probe.

For summer trail rescues, I carry a lightweight pack. Everyone has a slightly different version of their ready pack. I carry a long-sleeve polyester shirt, medium-weight jacket, work gloves, medical gloves, radio, two headlamps, extra batteries, Mount Hood and Columbia Gorge maps, a roll of tape, GPS, and a small survival kit. I carry personal rope-rescue gear, which includes a helmet, goggles, 20 meters × 7 mm rope, three locking carabiners, three prussic cords (to ascend a rope), a belay device (to descend a rope), a 10-meter length of webbing (to make an emergency harness on a patient or wrap a loop around a tree to rappel), and a personal harness. I also have a bottle of water and a few energy bars always stocked in my pack. It's a *ready* pack: I can grab it at short notice, knowing it's got the basics for a rescue.

I have extra gear in two bins. In my summer trail-rescue gear bin, I have a wetsuit and life vest, extra clothing, and extra climbing gear. In my winter mountain bin I have boot crampons, ski crampons, an ice axe, and extra mountaineering gear. I have an advanced-life-support medical kit handy. The biggest problem nowadays, given the spectacular performance of rechargeable lithium ion batteries, is keeping everything charged: radio, headlamp, cell phone.

We have group gear in our truck. We had been driving around a 1994 Chevy crew cab long bed pickup. It was fairly hammered. Once driving to an Eagle Creek rescue, I was behind the wheel driving 70 miles per hour and we heard a subtle "pop," hard to hear over the road noise with the windows down. I looked at Joe.

"What was that?"

"Dunno."

"Maybe we have a flat." Pause. "I think we have a flat."

We pulled over and changed the flat tire on the shoulder of Interstate 84. The fire department completed the rescue. After that Sheriff Matt English bought us a new truck: a 2016 Ford F350 Crew Cab long-bed pickup.

The team gear in the truck is costly and highly specialized. We have two frame litters (aka stretchers) with backboards and attachable wheels.

One wheel is wide, like an ATV or golf cart, and the other is narrow like a mountain bike. We have a lightweight Skedko SKED vinyl litter that rolls up and is designed to be easily carried in rough terrain or to slide on snow. We have a vacuum mattress, which is a large air bladder filled with Styrofoam pellets. It inflates so we can put an injured patient on it, and then deflate it, compress the pellets, and form a firm, hard litter to protect a patient's spine. We have Styrofoam floats for the stretchers to use for water rescues, and a spine immobilization vest for crevasse and canyon rescues. We have a slew of ropes, a slew of climbing hardware, and some basic medical gear including a weatherproof automatic external defibrillator. And we have more basic safety gear like life vests, helmets, harness, headlamps, and radios.

We have two caches of extra gear: some extra gear is stored at the Hut in the basement, like spare ropes, extra webbing, extra litters, and outdated equipment. We have a basic supply of gear at Cloud Cap Inn: a litter with a wheel, a litter with handles that allow us to ski with it, an extra Sked vinyl litter, a defibrillator, a few extra ropes, and spare medical supplies. In addition, we have a collection of antique rescue gear, not field deployable, that has been collecting at Cloud Cap Inn over the past six decades: old ice axes, old steel crampons, old ice screws, and a wood leg splint dating from the 1950s.

I tend to look at getting a new piece of equipment based on balancing benefit versus risk. Is new gear lighter, stronger, smaller? Can it do the job of multiple pieces of equipment? Some innovations change the world forever, like the invention of the ice axe. Before the ice axe, mountaineers used long wooden poles called *alpenstocks*, which provided stability when climbing and could arrest a slide if one should fall. In 1796, when Jacques Balmat and Michel-Gabriel Paccard made the first ascent of France's Mont Blanc, they carried both alpenstocks and small axes to cut steps in the steep sections of the glacier. Eventually, the ax and alpenstock began to merge into one tool when climbers began shortening alpenstocks and putting a pick on both ends. Yvon Chouinard helped further design in 1966 when he built ice axes with a curved pick, which aligned with the natural curve of a swing and stayed embedded in the ice better when a climber put his or her weight on the axe. This invention revolutionized climbing performance—allowing climbers to ascend ice much steeper than before—and dramatically improved safety.

Similarly, battery technology has dramatically improved rescues. I now bring my 1,000-lumen headlamp, designed for mountain biking at night. It's ten times brighter than the average, small 100-lumen headlamp. And the great brightness of modern headlamps is possible because of the compact lithium ion battery—the same technology that powers computer tablets, smart phones, and electric cars.

In my day job as a doctor, electronic medical records are changing the way we do medicine. If I have a difficult case in the emergency room, such as an infected knee, I can take an image of the knee with my phone, upload it to the patient's chart, and call a consultant 60 miles away in Portland. He or she can view the image to give me advice. With telemedicine, we can have real-time audio and video conferences in Mountain Clinic with a neurologist or neurosurgeon in the city if we are concerned about a head injury or possible stroke.

Once in a while, equipment is not too practical for mountain rescue. Take the femur traction splint. If someone fractures their leg near the hip, it can cause life-threatening bleeding and severe pain. Sometimes, putting on a special splint that puts traction on the femur to straighten it can alleviate pain and lessen bleeding. But, for use in mountain rescue, one medical study looked at the application and found that we rarely needed it because we are responding to patients who are stable because it takes so long to get to them, lay rescuers rarely remember how to use the splint, and the splint can make transportation in a litter difficult because it sticks out beyond the stretcher. And another problem with this specialized splint, specific to mountain rescue, is that it is yet another device to take up space and weight in our pack, where space and weight are at a premium as we haul gear up the mountain.

I tend to be a minimalist. I favor lighter, more compact gear. I like multiuse tools, as long as performance is not compromised too much. We must have light packs, as we are going into rugged terrain in austere conditions and need to take both personal safety and survival gear, plus equipment to address the patient's injury and predicament. Of late, I'm using a GPS app and the camera on my iPhone instead of carrying a separate GPS and camera.

So, the last component to mitigating risk—beyond training, practice, experience, and equipment—is the thorny issue of rescuer well-being, aka fitness. Physical fitness is important, which is why Crag Rats tend to gravitate toward members who are naturally in the outdoors every week, skiing, hiking, backpacking, climbing. But fitness goes beyond just being physically fit. Mental fitness, proper sleep, good nutrition, and adequate hydration are all vital aspects of safety.

But I'll have to cover that later. As I sit at my desk working on this book, another page zings to my phone. *Need hasty team. Male adult lost and dehydrated on Wygant Ridge. No other injuries. Have GPS coordinates.*

It's 7:50 p.m. on a Sunday. I'm hoping it's not going to be an all-nighter, as I have to see patients in my office in the morning. I'm exhausted from a three-hour mountain bike ride earlier that day and trying to focus on this manuscript. Walter rock-climbed all day with his kids, Brian was in harvest on his orchard, and Cully biked that day, too. We are about to show up at 9:00 p.m., pre-fatigued. We will have to hike an hour up the most difficult trail in our county, with a tall, healthy bumper crop of poison oak plants lining the trail. We will quickly find the man by using GPS coordinates from his phone. He will be dehydrated, with heat cramps, which we will correct with fluids and food. Turns out he will likely have rhabdomyolysis, a condition that causes muscle cells to break down and rupture: a combination of excess hiking while being out of shape, lack of fluids causing dehydration, and heat causing hyperthermia (aka heat exhaustion). The condition, more simply, is overuse of muscles in extreme conditions, which causes them to fail. After hydrating and feeding the man, we will slowly make our way back to the trailhead, sometimes with him scooting on his butt down the steep sections. We will make it back home just after midnight.

So, I'll finish this chapter—interrupted in life again with a mountain rescue—as I grab my pack and head to the trailhead with my colleagues, friends, and fellow mountain rescuers.

Chapter Five

Life, Interrupted

Once in a while, we go after dogs. Here we go again, at night. Again, on the mountain. And yes, again, in a storm.

One wintry night we are called to White River, the gargantuan basin that drains the White River Glacier on the south side of Mount Hood, equally as large and dangerous as the Eliot Glacier on the north side. The staging area tonight is a parking lot on Highway 35, at 4,400 feet elevation, where the river crossed the road under a large conduit. This is a popular destination for cross-country skiing and sledding.

Earlier that day a pair of cross-country skiers noticed a dog acting strangely, barking and running in circles, 2 miles up the canyon. It seemed to be focused on some trees near the creek. The skier tried to approach the dog, but it barked and ran away. The dog didn't follow the skiers when they called to it.

The big questions: Why is the dog circling the trees? Is the owner down in the snow? The sheriff gets the call and needs to investigate.

My quiet evening at home interrupted, I grab my gear and drive to the mountain. The drive up is light snow and fog, but when I reach White River parking area, right as I turn from the east to the south side of the mountain, the storm abates, the clouds clear, and the sky turns black and starry.

Some teams are already on the mountain. Although the call came in at 3:30 p.m., Teams 1 and 2 couldn't deploy immediately. They were on-duty Mount Hood Meadows ski patrollers who could not get permission to go out of bounds until they were off duty. So at 5:00 p.m., two teams of two patrollers each start making their way from the ski resort at 5,500 feet, out of bounds, through thick trees, down Iron Creek and Green Apple Creek drainages into the giant chasm of White River. A Team 3 composed of two Crag Rats along with a prospective Crag Rats member leaves White River parking area and skis up Iron Creek, the thickly forested drainage just east of White River. Team 4 is Crag Rat Tom Rousseau and me, our first callout together. We are assigned to ski up White River basin proper, the wide open, treeless, snow-covered canyon that has the White River carving troughs through the sand, scree, and pumice boulders. Tom and I are directed to "a clump of trees" where a dog was running circles. We set off on a beautiful starry night up the canyon. The snow is 3 feet deep and fresh, so even with skis and climbing skins, we sink a foot. It's less like skiing and more like walking or snow-shoeing: we pick up a ski, slide it forward, step down in the soft snow, and sink a foot deep. We're not gliding at all. Tom uses skinny cross-country skis, so I break trail with my wider alpine touring planks.

Tom has a GPS unit and I have two radios strapped to my chest: my Crag Rats VHF radio, which has Oregon State SAR frequency, and a sheriff's department UHF radio, which has the ski patrol frequency so I can communicate with Teams 1 and 2.

After twenty minutes of skiing up flat terrain through 3 feet of fresh snow, Tom and I run into the first of many obstacles that will plague us all night. First, we hit logs and boulders that we attempt to scramble over without taking off our skis. Then, we hit the braided channel of the creek: White River headwaters come from multiple spots in the glacier, just a mile up the quarter-mile-wide, treeless, rocky canyon. The canyon has been scrubbed of vegetation by past floods and the glacier. The creek here is a series of braided channels, mostly 3 to 6 feet wide. They make it impossible to ski in a straight line up the canyon. Just as we cross a creek and ski a few minutes uninterrupted, we hit another creek crossing blocking our path. Some of the channels run south straight out of the canyon, and others meander east and west like a snake. It's like we are inside a giant pretzel: We are trying to find our way out but keep crossing the same creek.

On some of the narrow trickles we can ski right over the water; the streams are a foot wide and our skis span the snowbanks on either side. The wider streams we toss our skis across, then either jump or gingerly step on rocks or logs. A few of the shallow ones we step in with our ski boots.

Protect your feet. Do not get them wet, I think to myself, knowing wet feet would be a disaster. Despite the heavy foam liners and plastic shells of ski boots, I'm still careful not to let any water in. Our progress is laboriously slow. On one crossing, Tom cracks his ski binding on a rock. We stop as he straps it together with a stretchy polyurethane strap. It holds. We are able to continue.

After an hour of laboriously trekking up the White River Basin, I hear on the radio that the non-Crag Rat volunteer on Team 3 wants to head back. Not sure why: uncomfortable with the night, deep snow, or creek crossings? Tired? Afraid? Team 3 is only a half-hour from the parking lot.

"We're sending Charley back. He wants to return," says Crag Rat and ski patroller Paul Klein on the radio.

"Negative," says the seasoned deputy Mike Anderson sitting in his warm Sheriff's Office pickup truck in the White River parking lot. "You have to stay together. If one comes out, everyone comes out."

"Can we send him over to Team 4?" asks Paul. Tom and I are Team 4: we are in the canyon. Team 3 is out of sight on bench about 30 feet above the creek in the woods, about 100 yards away from us. If it were not for the creek crossings and the deep snow, it might take ten minutes for Charley to ski to us. But it was likely more like thirty, if even possible with the creek crossings, deep snow, and cornice that has built up on the edge of the creek. And it would be dangerous to do so alone.

"We've got lots of creek crossings and deep snow here," I say into the radio. "There's a cornice leading into the creek also."

"Negative, Team 2," says the deputy. "Team 2 needs to stay together. If one comes out, the entire team comes out." I know Paul, a seasoned mountaineer and ski patroller, is bummed to leave. We have an unwritten mantra in mountain rescue: protect self first, team second, and the patient third. We have to be wholly well and present on mountain rescue missions.

Being well means staying physically fit, which is really the only reason we can walk all night, climb all night, ski all night—as I was explaining in the last chapter before being interrupted by the Wygant Ridge rescue.

We live in a fairly robust outdoor community. Mount Hood was first climbed in 1857 by Portlanders W. S. Buckley, W. L. Chittenden, James Deardorff, H. L. Pittock, and L. J. Powell. The Mazamas mountaineering club was formed on the summit in 1894. The Mount Hood Ski Patrol began here in 1937, and the Mountain Rescue Association was formed in 1959 at Timberline Lodge. Some ten thousand climb the mountain yearly and we have year-round skiing and snowboarding because of the glaciers.

So, to keep up with mountain rescue and the general robust recreation we do, mountain rescuers, as a demographic, tend to stay fit and stay well.

Adequate nutrition and hydration is vital. I'm a big proponent of the Michael Pollan mantra he wrote about in *In Defense of Food*: eat real food, not too much, mostly plants. Dan Buettner in *The Blue Zones* has the same idea: mostly plants, limited portions, don't snack too much. Moderation.

I'm also a ginormous fan of sleep. Although some people might argue that humans sleep away a third of their lives, if you respond to rescues in the middle of the night, in the middle of storms, in the middle of mountains, you have to be rested or you just can't function. In other words, without adequate sleep and rest, you may indeed have more waking time, but you won't be very functional.

In addition, staying mentally fit is vital too. Stress at work or at home can clog up one's brain. I think perhaps we all have stress to some extent, but from what I can tell, when a mountain rescue call goes out and we respond, the Crag Rats seem to leave extraneous external stressors at home. We seem, as a group, to roll up our sleeves and focus on the job at hand.

Unfortunately, we don't plan mountain rescues. They come at all times of the day and night, mostly night. Sometimes rescues catch us off guard, interrupting life when we are tired, hungry, or distracted by stress of home or work.

Chatter continues on the radio, with Deputy Anderson checking for team status updates. Since skiing down is faster than skiing up, one Mount Hood Meadows ski patrol team reaches the dog sometime around midnight. They search the area, and find the dog but no human.

Tom and I hear the stand down and start the ski out under a starry ski with the moon shining bright, reflecting off the snow. We don't need headlamps. Tom's broken binding holds together as long as I lead and mash down the snow. On a few creek crossings, the water nears the tops of my ski boots, but my feet stay dry. Nonetheless, they are still cold.

Team 1 brings the dog out behind us, following our tracks back to the parking lot.

This is not the first dog rescue for the Crag Rats, and not the last, I'm sure. People get into trouble because of their dogs. Once, in Eagle Creek, a dog was zipping down the trail, apparently not being fully cognizant of trail hazards. Like a cliff. It ran, then jumped or fell off the trail into a steep gully, one that was a few degrees shy of being a cliff. Mica McNulty and I ran up the trail with rope-rescue gear and slung a rope around a tree. We met the Oregon Humane Society Technical Animal Rescue team—I never knew there was such a team. I lowered Mica into the gully, and then hauled him back out. We came up empty. No dog. Disappeared.

Another time we raced up Ruckle Creek Trail to rescue a woman stuck in a creek because she went after his dog. Off leash, the dog fell into a steep creek canyon, got stuck, and disappeared. A team ran up the trail, found the woman in the creek canyon, dropped in a rope, and hauled her out. But no dog. Cully Wiseman went up two days later, searched the creek for the dog, found the dog, and brought it out.

And it's not always dogs and humans we search for, rescue, and recover. We have been called on to set up forensic reenactments of rescues that involved criminal charges. We've rappelled off cliffs to search for evidence. We once searched a local Washington landfill when body parts of a missing woman from a county 300 miles away turned up in garbage.

Once on Mount Hood we went up to retrieve bones and a backpack on the Coe Glacier that were discovered by Timberline Mountain Guides. We sent a team up and retrieved the backpack and the bones. The bones turned out to be coyote. The backpack turned out to have been lost on a rescue in in the 1980s that the Crag Rats responded to and Brian Hukari remembered. The owner of the backpack, who was tracked down in Seattle, came to Hood River to retrieve the backpack, four decades after losing it.

In all our rescues, unusual or routine, in addition to taking care of ourselves we take care of our group, with teamwork. This is sometimes a challenge when the Crag Rats don't have a clear leader in the field. The Crag Rats are known for showing up and getting the job done, the way we've done it for nine decades, with fewer formalities than other groups. We know by default who should be medical, who should be rope supervisor, and who should help the sheriff's deputy plan the mission. We fall into roles without necessarily having formal designations like other mountain rescue teams.

Group dynamics can be difficult, especially with regard to communications. Sometimes groups can overestimate power and mortality, rationalize warnings, and disagree on decision-making authority. They can ignore or miss important warning signs and get wrapped up in the excitement of a rescue or activity. Individuals in groups may not speak up because of pressure to conform so they are not seen as weak or unadventurous. The 2012 Tunnel Creek avalanche in Stevens Pass, Washington, the subject of a *New York Times* article, *Snow Fall: The Avalanche at Tunnel Creek* by John Branch, and a book, *Deep: The Story of Skiing and the Future of Snow* by Porter Fox highlight this perfectly. A dozen skiers, all industry professionals and highly skilled, plan a last-minute backcountry ski tour. Despite dangerous conditions, no one bails, no one speaks up, no one says they shouldn't go. On the ski down Tunnel Creek, an avalanche kills three.

In search and rescue, post 9/11, we have some checks and balances. We now use the National Incident Management System, which minimizes some of the dangerous group dynamics. The NIMS is a system for responding to incidents, regardless of cause, size, location, or complexity. It gives organizational and operational procedures by dividing up tasks using a hierarchy for command. It gives us common language for communication and a common national radio frequency for search and rescue. We work with the Forest Service rangers, the private ambulance paramedics, firefighters, ski patrollers, and other technical rescue groups. NIMS gives us clear supervision by Sheriff Matt English and the sheriff's deputy on site, as well as division of workload when appropriate, a common language, dispute resolution, and feedback.

Normally, our missions are small. A sheriff's deputy SAR coordinator is in charge as incident commander and we're divided up into teams, sometimes with a leader in each team. When missions are more complex rope rescues, we occasionally have a safety officer who is in charge of checking the rope system and making sure the situation is safe. Usually we designate, often by default to the person with the most experience, a rescuer to be in charge of the rope system, and another to be medical responder. Fortunately, working with other teams, often volunteers, we never seem to have too many problems. Perhaps that is because, paid or volunteer, we are all professionals. When someone feels unsafe, people pay attention. When there's a medical decision or rope-rescue situation, we defer to one who has the most experience. When we work with other groups, we quickly cite our credentials. I may be experienced from a medical standpoint, but others are infinitely wiser than me when it comes to navigating, route finding, rope-rescue systems, and search planning.

The Crag Rats have been doing it this way since 1926—sometimes traditions and habits are ingrained over decades and generations. Sometimes, or rather many times, change is hard for a ninety-year-old group.

A perfect example of how the Crag Rats operate is a cliff rescue in the City of Hood River. It is a snowy day and we are paged to Indian Creek Trail. A woman was hiking with her dog, slipped on the ice and fell down an embankment. It's a mile from my house, so when I get the page, I grab my gear, jump in my Toyota, and drive to the staging area.

Once there, I find Mark Wiltz, the only other Crag Rat on scene, assessing the situation along with a half-dozen law-enforcement officers. The woman is perched on a ledge, 50 feet below us and 100 feet above Indian Creek.

"You go over the edge," says Mark. "I'll set up a rope."

"Okay, I'll go down. I've got a rope," I say, pulling out the 20-meter line I carry in my pack.

We quickly set up a rappel, while other Crag Rats start showing up with more gear. We have a good turnout of rescuers because the rescue is within city limits, but no one thinks to grab our SAR truck. Crag Rats start pulling out their personal gear. I put on mountaineering boots and ski pants. I don a harness, helmet, and work gloves. I tie into the rope that Mark has secured to an 8-inch-wide white oak trunk and I'm about to step off the edge.

"Be careful," says Sheriff English. "We are not sure how this woman will react. She might be pretty scared."

"Okay," I say. "I'll be careful." From one professional to another, Sheriff English warns me—otherwise, it would not have occurred to me that she may be panicky. I make a mental note to keep myself on a separate rope, and stay uphill at all times. I'm not necessarily scared, but cautious. I've interacted with difficult patients enough in the ER to know the warning signs of fear, anxiety, panic, and desperation—which usually come in that order.

"I'm staying on my rope," I say to Mark. "When more gear arrives and you get a second rope, I'll clip her into that separately."

"Okay, we're rigging another rope now," he says. I see Jim Wells, Jay Sherrerd, and Walter Burkhardt have arrived and are setting up a raising system using a collection of personal equipment.

I go over the edge and rappel through the snow-covered brush.

"You okay?" I say as I reach the woman. "I'm going to wrap this harness around you and tie you into a rope," I say using a stern, friendly doctor voice. "We're going to get you up the cliff." I stay uphill and an arm's reach away. I look down, and see the creek below us.

"Think I would have made it if I'd fallen all the way?" she asks.

"Dunno," I say, as I'm trying to focus on putting the harness on her, tying her into the haul line, and keeping a fair distance uphill from her on a ledge that is loose mud and snow.

The crew above then begins to pull the woman uphill. I crawl up the embankment on my own, sliding a prussic knot up my rope to hold me in case I slip. Up top, a cadre of Crag Rats pulls the woman to safety, helps me onto the trail, and quickly breaks down the rope system. We're done in an hour, and head home—our truck never having made it to the scene.

As part of both group safety and learning from the rescue, we usually try to debrief as a group. Our debriefings come in several flavors. The best are the quick debriefs at the end of the mission: we are all anxious to go home. Often it is a quick check: everyone got down okay, no equipment broken, patient handed off to EMS.

We review rescues quickly in our monthly business meeting. We chat about radio communications, rope systems, and equipment that needs to be repaired, replaced, and cleaned. Should we have waited for our SAR truck instead of using our personal gear for the woman on the cliff? Why don't we get called sooner, when dispatch hears about the call an hour or two before we get paged? Why do we have to go out at night? Can we wait until morning? How do we get more Crag Rats to show up for rescues? What the heck was the subject doing up the trail at dark without a headlamp? (You can insert anything here: up a trail without a map, or up the canyon without enough food, water, and clothing.) We don't necessarily judge or criticize, but sometimes we have to laugh. If we don't laugh, we would not be able to do this job. It's a good-natured, private laugh.

We return to the problem of not enough responders, since we are a volunteer unit. Volunteer groups are often plagued with participation problems. If we have too many rescuers and too few rescues, people tend to get bored and lose interest. If we have too few rescuers doing all the work on lots of missions, people get burned out. Fortunately, we have a continued core of responders of thirty or so Crag Rats who respond to many rescues, with another twenty or so who help out occasionally. Those who can't necessarily respond to rescues due to work, family, health, or other issues often take on ancillary duties: maintaining our Hut, maintaining the Cloud Cap Inn, keeping the snowcat and Trackster running, meeting with the Sheriff's Office and Forest Service, serving as callout coordinators, attending Oregon Mountain Rescue Council and Mount Hood Search and Rescue Council meetings, and helping to run our nonprofit club by paying bills, doing the taxes, getting insurance quotes, or rounding up firewood. It's a fair bit of work.

Only rarely do we have a full sit-down debrief, only on big rescues, usually those that occur on the mountain, usually with deceased victims involved. After rescues and recoveries, all we want to do is get home, quickly repack gear for the next day (whether it's skiing with kids, working at the resort, or waiting for the next callout), get some food, and go to bed (or work if that's the case). Dog or deceased person. Lost or stranded or injured. Get it done, get home, and go to bed.

CHAPTER SIX

Ten Fatal Seconds

ONCE IN A WHILE, ON AVERAGE ONCE YEARLY FOR THE CRAG RATS, A victim pays the highest price for risk. The Crag Rats get called out for something no one likes doing, but we pitch in and get the job done.

A body recovery.

On a warm summer evening, the sun graces our small town. Barbecues heat up for free-range Eastern Oregon beef burgers and Columbia River salmon, windsurfers and kitesurfers eke out the dregs of the day's wind, mountain bikers spin off the trails, kayakers and stand-up paddlers load up their boats and boards from a day on the water, and our cell phones vibrate and ring with another mountain rescue callout.

The rescues on Mount Hood have long since wrapped up for the season. Long days and warm temps of summer usually bring us to hiking trail rescues, where most people are enjoying trails and creeks of the beautiful Columbia Gorge. On the mountain, the ski mountaineering and mountaineering season has mostly wrapped up due to dangerous conditions: warm temperatures and blazing sun melt the snow and ice, causing the crevasses to open and rocks and ice to fall from the high cliffs into the climbing routes. We're already a few months into trail-rescue season and most of us Crag Rats have stowed our mountaineering gear in exchange for our summer trail gear.

When the callout comes with a glacier rescue so late in the climbing season, every Crag Rat pays attention.

The summer scene on the south side of Mount Hood is relatively unique; it's one of a few places in the world that has year-round skiing and snowboarding. Timberline Lodge was built on the south flanks of Mount Hood from 1936 to 1938 as part of Franklin Roosevelt's Works Progress Administration. The lodge perched at 6,000 feet is iconic of the "Cascadian" architecture typical of many Pacific Northwest buildings of the era: a timber-frame style with locally sourced hand-hewn beams, board-and-bat Douglas fir siding, steep snow-shedding cedar-shake roof, and indoor and outdoor stonework from volcanic basalt rocks.

From Timberline Lodge, two chairlifts, the Magic Mile and Palmer, run all summer. The reason is that Palmer Glacier is crevasse-free and rises 2,000 vertical feet from Timberline Lodge. Thus, Timberline Lodge ski area can keep the slopes open all summer so ski racers can train in the off season. Professional skiers and national ski teams come from around the world and youth ski racers come to attend ski camps. Snowboarders and freestyle skiers come to ride the terrain park jumps, rails, and half-pipes. The scene in the small village of Government Camp, or *Govy* (one street, population 193, named after a US Calvary encampment from 1849), 6 miles down the mountain, is thriving. Teens and professional racers alike pack the tiny town. Skiing starts early with 7:00 a.m. chairlift rides, and closes at 2:00 p.m. when the snow turns to thick slush.

In addition to the race camps, the South Climb of Mount Hood is one of the busiest mountaineering routes in the world. The US Forest Service estimates that more than ten thousand people attempt to climb Mount Hood annually, but the agency does not officially keep stats. For Crag Rats, some of us zip to the summit several times during the spring to ski from the top. From the parking lot, the summit is a three- to five-hour climb. But Timberline also allows a "climber's ticket," a one-ride trip up the two chairlifts to the top of Palmer Glacier; this saves two hours of hiking.

Normally accidents on the south side, which is mostly in Clackamas County, are diverted to our colleagues with Portland Mountain Rescue. However, the county line is right on the eastern edge of the Timberline Lodge ski area permit area, on the West Moraine of White River Glacier. The moraine in summer is a sandy scree ridge that divides White River and Palmer Glaciers. Thus anyone going out of bounds into White River Glacier, to the east, drops from Clackamas County into Hood River County.

And that's exactly what happened.

Earlier that day, a twenty-five-year-old snowboard camp coach had completed work duties at 2:00 p.m. He decided to take a group of young campers out of bounds to look for a good spot to take a video. They hiked fifteen minutes out of bounds, leaving the Timberline Lodge permit area on Palmer Glacier, and dropped into White River Glacier. Unfortunately, what is quite safe inbounds on the Palmer Glacier, which is manicured by snow-grooming machines, governed by ski patrol, and accessed by chairlift, is a different world than the rest of the mountain wilderness. The White River Glacier is chock-full of towering seracs, deep crevasses, giant basalt cliffs, boulders that tumble from the Steel Cliffs 2,000 feet above, and, down at the bottom of the expansive canyon, a raging braided river running full tilt on a seventy-degree summer afternoon.

White River Glacier is raw backcountry: wild and dangerous.

The problem was knowledge, or rather lack thereof. The man was likely unaware of the extremes of a glacier, in the midsummer sun, with temperatures well over seventy degrees. The heat and solar radiation melt the glaciers so that everything becomes unstable. Boulders frozen into the ice let loose, towering seracs crumble and fall, snow bridges over crevasses collapse, and the slopes that are firm and icy in the morning turn to a gooey, thick mush. Of course, the possibility exists that the man did indeed understand the dangers of being on a massive glacier in the middle of a hot afternoon in the middle of the summer and he just decided to take the risk. But if so, it was a gigantic risk.

When the off-duty coach and four campers dropped into the glacier by easily hiking 300 feet out of bounds and looked for a suitable spot to take images, they unknowingly put themselves in the wrong place at the wrong time. They put themselves into a high-probability, high-consequence situation. As they explored an ice cavern, the ceiling—a block of snow the size of a school bus—collapsed.

The man was instantly crushed dead by the 4,000-pound slab of snow and ice. Buried deep.

When the call comes in that evening, we send a hasty team to the scene. By the time a crew drives an hour to Timberline Lodge, assembles in the parking lot, catches a twenty-minute snowcat ride up the glacier, and hikes from Palmer Glacier, over the scree ridge, into White River Glacier, and into the crevasse, it is well after dark. The snow has refrozen rock hard. The crew chips away briefly at the burial site with small avalanche shovels and probes. But it's not much use in the rock-hard ice. Based on the reports from the four uninjured campers who witnessed the accident, it is clear that this was not survivable.

Sheriff Matt English wisely decides to pull the team that night and assemble an extrication crew at first light. He calls on both the Crag Rats and our colleagues from Portland Mountain Rescue. We send out muster texts to our teams.

"You'll need shovels, picks, and axes," reports Jay Sherrerd as a member of the hasty team. "It's rock hard. We tried to dig into the ice, but couldn't even get a probe in the snow," he says, referring to the 3-meter-long, 1-centimeter-thick pointed aluminum avalanche probe designed to poke through snow to locate a buried person. Once the sun went down, the ice froze solid.

"You'll need long-handled shovels and picks," adds Jay. We need farm implements, not sports equipment like the tiny compact portable avalanche-rescue shovels we carry in our packs. "Avalanche shovels were useless."

Then someone with a brilliant idea sent out a text: *Bring chainsaws.*

"I've got one," texts Brian Hukari.

"Me too," responds Paul Klein.

At 4:00 a.m. I meet Brian Hukari, Paul Klein, and a crew at the county yard to load up our truck and drive an hour to Timberline. Brian loads his oily chainsaw and gasoline, which looks odd juxtaposed against the high-tech ski mountaineering gear we pile in the truck. We make the one-hour drive up the mountain at daybreak. The sky is cloudless and the air is already warm, upwards of forty-five degrees. The ice will begin softening likely at midmorning and be melting dangerously at midday.

We check in at SAR base, stationed at the Timberline Lodge backcountry climber's parking lot, at 5:00 a.m. Fifteen rescuers show up from Crag Rats and Portland Mountain Rescue. We're toting high-tech carbon-fiber and fiberglass mountaineering skis in one hand and dirty, well-worn farm tools—chainsaws, long-handled shovels, grain scoops, and picks—in the other. At the parking lot briefing, Sheriff's Deputy Mike Anderson discusses safety in a stern, direct tone.

"We are taking no chances up there. This is a confirmed fatality. We are not risking rescuers," he says to the group. We all nod. "At 11:00 a.m. I want you guys out of there, if you've recovered the body or not. We'll come back tomorrow if we need to."

He asks for two volunteers to be safety officers. I and Rocky Henderson from Portland Mountain Rescue step up. We are not the team leaders; that's a separate function.

"Your job is safety of rescuers," he says. "I don't want you to help with extrication. I want you watching everyone and everything—watch for rock fall, ice fall, crevasses."

We pile into a snowcat provided by Timberline Lodge and ride up to 7,500 feet on Palmer Glacier, on the east edge of the ski-resort permit area. From there, we carry the chainsaws, shovels, and a litter across the West Moraine scree field, which turns out to be a huge mound of rocks and sand. From crevasse-free, manicured ski runs of Palmer Glacier, we cross a knoll of basalt pumice and sand and descend into the massive White River Glacier—which is otherworldly in comparison. The massive glacier has enormous towering ice seracs, giant gaping crevasses, and huge boulders of andesite and basalt that likely peeled off the Steel Cliffs 2,000 feet above sometime earlier that month. The boulders leave huge divots in the snow where they land and then, from repeated melting around the boulders, they sink into the snowpack. This is the quintessential wild, rugged backcountry of a glaciated peak. Mount Hood has twelve glaciers, mostly above 6,000 feet and covering a good portion of the entire mountain, save for pockets of rocks, cliffs, and headwalls. From Timberline Lodge clockwise, they are: Palmer, Zigzag, Reid, Coalman, Sandy, Glisan, Ladd, Coe, Langille, Eliot, Newton Clark, and White River.

Experienced mountaineers know being in a crevassed glacier at 2:00 p.m. on a seventy-degree summer day is dangerous—the melting ice is extremely unstable. So, when we drop in and start chain-sawing and shoveling, we are cautious. And with an 11:00 a.m. evacuation time, we have three hours to extricate the body before the glacier becomes too unsafe.

This is back-wrenching work; all fifteen of us pitch in. Brian and Paul run the chainsaws to start cutting blocks of ice from the bus-size piece that fell. They begin by reaching overhead to cut away three-foot-wide blocks of ice. When the blocks tumble to the ground, another five or six rescuers line up to clear the blocks from the chainsaw zone. In another section, a few other rescuers dig by hand with shovels and picks—one person picks to loosen the ice and a second clears away the loose fragments, and two or three more scoop the ice out of the way. Extra hands are simply moving snow out of the crevasse and shoveling it down the mountain into a pile. It's tedious, constant, manual labor like digging a ditch. We never really take any breaks, but try to rotate positions—except the chainsaws. Paul and Brian keep running the power tools, removing ice, block by block.

The Crag Rats unfortunately go on one or two body recoveries a year. Often people die in high-risk, high-consequence situations. It's not fun. But it is part of being a Crag Rat. We just get the job done.

A fifty-seven-year-old priest visiting from New Jersey climbed Mount Hood via the south side on a sunny day in late July one year. He reached the summit with his climbing partners in the early morning. Once atop the peak in the warm summer day, he walked to the edge of a cornice, which had built up over the north-facing rock cliff from the prevailing west winds and had begun to soften. As he got too close to the edge, he fell right through the cornice, hit the rocky ledge 700 feet below, and died.

The rescue was on hold for a few days, once a helicopter confirmed fatality. Then, when the weather and climbing conditions looked safe, we sent Brian Hukari and three other Crag Rats up to the summit from the south side and then down the northwest side to the Coalman Glacier and a flat spot in the snow and rock called Queen's Chair. They recovered the body and lowered it down the north side of the mountain to a second team stationed at Snowdome, a crevasse-free snowfield. Then the body was loaded into a helicopter at 9,000 feet.

A few years before that, a Polish military officer was in the Columbia Gorge training with a company that builds unmanned aerial vehicles. On his day off, the man climbed one of the most difficult routes on the mountain, the Eliot Glacier headwall, a steep mixed route (*mixed* means rock, ice, and snow) that ascends about 2,500 feet, at 50 to 70 degrees steep, from the top of the Eliot Glacier to the summit. He fell from very near the summit and landed at 9,100 feet. Although the sheriff continued for several years to get repeated requests from the Polish government to recover the body, it was determined to be too dangerous for us to go after the body—it's still there as of the last sighting a few years ago.

One winter, we were called to help Portland Mountain Rescue search for three climbers, all in their mid-twenties, on another difficult yet famous climbing route called the Luthold Couloir. Three climbers set out and somehow either fell, or got caught in a storm, or both. I was the only member from Crag Rats to respond that day, so I was paired with two from Portland Mountain Rescue. On the day I went up in a storm, we were assigned to climb to Mount Hood's summit. We set off about 9:00 a.m., first taking a snowcat to 8,000 feet where it was misting rain with a 30- to 40-mile-per-hour wind. As we ascended the mountain, the air became colder and the fine mist froze on our jackets and pants into small, beautiful, dendritic crystals called rime. Our rime-encrusted clothing initially was damp, but once we climbed to 9,000 feet, the air temperature cooled and our clothing instantly became stiff. Now it was cold enough to snow, and all the while the wind kept howling. We continued to ascend, in gray overcast, inside "the ping pong ball": the clouds and the snow were the same color so we couldn't see a horizon.

At 10,000 feet, the bottom of Hogback Ridge, I voiced some concern. First, the snowpack was fresh, the wind was blowing, the temperature continued to plummet dramatically the higher we climbed, and the visibility was nil. Second, with the new snow and the wind depositing it around the mountain, avalanche danger was high. Third, I was cold. My toes were freezing. *Turn around*, said my gut, *it's not safe*. The visibility on the summit would be nil anyway. One rescuer from PMR wanted to continue, and the second didn't care. I insisted we turn back: It wasn't safe, it wasn't worth the risk, and the stakes were too high for the benefit. In other words, high probability and high consequence would net very little reward. The scale was tipped, not in our favor. So we turned back.

Our summit team was reassigned to a lower elevation, Illumination Saddle, where another team had just found a body of one of the climbers and needed help with extrication. That alone was difficult in the storm, but we managed to ski to Illumination Saddle and help. The climber was recovered that day near the bottom of the Luthold Couloir at the 9,000-foot level. We used a rope to bring him up the gully to Illumination Saddle. Then we had to ski him out in a travois over to Timberline Lodge navigating by GPS. Luckily we had a big team with plenty of help. A second body was found on the Reed Glacier at the bottom of the Luthold Couloir six months later, once the snow and ice on the mountain melted. The third, like many climbers who have become lost or died on this giant peak, is still missing.

There are 122 known fatalities, or missing and presumed dead, on Mount Hood since 1883, when a soldier named Bernard from the Vancouver Washington Army Barracks was lost when camping at Timberline. Some are never found; they're lost in the caverns, ice caves, crevasses, and creeks. A few, like the Polish military officer, are found but in too precarious a spot for us to safely reach. Many fatalities are on the South Climb or Cooper Spur Routes, the latter being the most common spot for fatalities.

Not all of our body recoveries are on the mountain. Once a hiker on Eagle Creek jumped, for fun, off a 70-foot cliff, fell into a plunge pool, got sucked under by the hydraulic pressure of the waterfall, and drowned. The sheriff called in a dive team to rescue the body. Our job: help the dive-rescue team get their gear up the trail and bring the body down the trail once it is pulled from the water. We rolled up our sleeves to get the job done, so we could be home for work or dinner or bed.

Another time a group of canyoneers descended Dry Creek Falls. After the five-pitch rappel, they were completely done with their descent. They were a half-mile from their car down a road. When they went to pull their rope from the final rappel down 70-foot Dry Creek Falls, the rope got stuck. They had three options: leave the rope, repeat the entire canyoneering descent with a new rope, or free climb up the 70-foot waterfall. They took the latter option. One climber scaled the cliff, nearly reached the top, and then fell and died before he could get to the rope.

Some fatalities occur from simple, yet tragic, errors in judgment, rather than from foolhardy attempts at pushing to the extremes. Once, a group of friends was camping in the Mount Hood National Forest, just off remote Road 4410. They had a few beers around the campfire. When they decided to head to bed, they all retired to their tents. In the morning, the group woke to find one of their buddies missing. After a search of the area, they found him at the bottom of a 30-foot rocky outcropping—upside down, in a tree, dead. Apparently, he left the campfire to head to bed, but first walked up to the rocky outcropping to urinate. In the dark, perhaps with a few beers onboard, he walked right off the cliff.

Sheesh, I thought, as I was packing up the body in a body bag with a Forest Service law enforcement officer. *This could happen to anyone camping with friends and having a few beers around the campfire.* Above, the rest of the Crag Rats used a rope-raising system to haul the body in a SKED litter up the cliff. Todd Wells had brought the small Trackster snowcat to the scene, so we loaded the body onto the Trackster and Todd drove the body out to the road.

Some fatalities are seemingly so easy to prevent. A man was flying a drone in Eagle Creek, crossed a fence, hiked past a cliff warning sign, and walked to the edge of a cliff above Punchbowl Falls. Somehow he lost his footing, fell 150 feet, and died. When Portland firefighter and prospective Crag Rat Gary Salzay and I arrive at the scene, we first have to don life jackets and swim across the freezing-cold creek to confirm the fatality. Once that is done, we wait in wet clothes for Joe McCulloch to swim out with our litter, floating with the help of Styrofoam tubes strapped to the rails. Gary and I then place the body into a body bag, lift it onto the litter, and slide the litter into the water. The team on shore pulls the litter 150 feet across the plunge pool, lifts the heavy package to attach our wheel, and then wheels the litter down the trail.

After transferring the body to the mortuary van, we rinse out the litter in the creek. Crowley takes one rope home to dry it. The second rope, my personal line, I wash in the washing machine, leave to dry on my back deck, and then notice a frayed end that travels up the rope several feet. I decide to decommission the rope and replace it. Gary offers to get some decontamination supplies for the truck. And that's a wrap: we're all business. Go home, wait for the next callout.

Some fatalities are not so easy to prevent. In 2014, I led a wilderness medicine field seminar to Everest Base Camp (EBC) with a group of doctors, nurses, and their family members. Our small group trekked over eighteen days to EBC, eating and hiking together, bunking in tea houses, sharing laughs and beers. On this sort of trip, people tend to become close-knit quickly. One of the trekkers was Eve Girawong, a physician assistant who was just beginning a career in wilderness medicine. She was there to experience the EBC trek and gain education in wilderness medicine. She was quite literally one of the happiest persons I've met: always smiling, always cheerful. The trip was marked by a catastrophic accident. We had landed in Kathmandu the day sixteen Sherpa "icefall doctors" died while putting up the climbing route. So when we arrived at our ultimate destination, Everest Base Camp, ten days later, the place was eerily somber. Without the icefall doctors to set up the ropes and ladders through the Khumbu Icefall, all climbing expeditions were canceled that year. The entire place was eerily vacant, with the few remaining expeditions packing up. If that's not sad enough, the next year was the great Nepal earthquake that injured 14,122 people and killed 7,200, including 22 people who perished in an avalanche that hit EBC. Eve had gone back to Nepal that year to serve an expedition as a team physician assistant, and unfortunately, she was one of the 22 who died in the avalanche at EBC.

And then there are the seemingly untouchable extreme athletes who pull off amazing feats of human endurance, skill, and achievement, and who push the limits too far. Too many times they put themselves in harm's way and are plastered all over the news, sometimes coming across as being heroic. Pioneer extreme skier and ski mountaineer Doug Coombs died at age forty-eight from falling off a cliff at Couloir de

Polichinelle in La Grave, France, while trying to rescue his colleague Chad Vanderham. Big-wave surfer Mark Foo drowned while surfing a big wave at Half Moon Bay, California, while chasing big surf around the world. Legendary rock climber Dean Potter, known as one of the world's best at free-solo climbing (climbing without a rope), highlining (walking across a slackline set up between cliffs or rocky pinnacles), and BASE jumping (jumping off buildings, antennae, spans, and earth) died along with Graham Hunt in a wingsuit accident in Yosemite National Park. Extreme skier and ski BASE jumper Shane McConkey: a ski BASE jump in the Dolomites, Italy. Skiers J. P. Auclair and Andreas Fransson: an avalanche at Monte San Lorenzo, Aysén, Chile. Matilda Rapaport: an avalanche in Farellones, Chile, while filming a video game. The list goes on.

When you combine high risk and high consequence, people die. It's often due to ignorance or lapse of judgment—they get too close to the cornice rim, go out of bounds, drink too much alcohol, push through a storm, or tackle a route beyond their skill level. Sometimes a fatality is not due to ignorance but simply to pushing the limits in search of the adrenaline buzz, or a bigger sponsorship, or a personal challenge to go deeper, farther, faster, higher.

I don't particularly like writing about fatalities. Nor do I want to foster any disrespect for families and friends who lose loved ones. But, unfortunately, this is part of what we do. I have to include these stories in this book, to give a full account of mountain rescue and risk. They are tragic and sad, but a necessary component.

When I crashed on Mount Hood and was rushed into emergency surgery, it was a few days before I could reflect on what happened in my near-death accident. Going a bit too fast? Maybe. Mind preoccupied with Margaret? Probably. Not paying attention to the snow conditions? For sure. Should I have stayed home? Absolutely not.

Sometimes I replay the accident in my head. It comes to mind when I get distracted, such as when riding my mountain bike or skiing. I have a momentary pause when I realize: I'm jacked on adrenaline, my mind is preoccupied with positive thoughts—work, romance, kids—and I'm going fast. I get an eerie feeling that brings me back to the seconds before

I crashed on Mount Hood. I was relatively high on life that day: romance with Margaret, good book sales, great powder, upcoming trip to Haiti. I have, occasionally, a repeat of that momentary fleeting glimpse of adrenaline, distraction, and speed. I recognize it, and then I slow down, focus on the task at hand, and pay attention.

One thing was clear when I crashed: I had to trust the people taking care of me. I had to trust my friends, my family, my doctors, and my nurses. They were the experts, and had to put me back together. And then, I had to trust my instinct not to stop adventuring or rescuing people after the accident that nearly killed me. In fact, I couldn't really stop adventuring. By now, dear reader, you can see mountain adventuring and mountain rescue are deeply ingrained in my personality and passion. I did not really change my approach, because I rarely put myself in high-risk, high-consequence situations to begin with. But I have to say, I now am a bit more cautious.

Before my accident, in *Mountain Rescue Doctor*, I talked much about balancing life. I balance work and play quite well. I balance family time and personal time. I balance hitting the trails and mountains with my friends with going out on rescues with my colleagues. I even try to balance my writing: I have written blogs, medical journal articles, novels (unpublished), young adult books (unpublished), teleplays (not yet picked up by Hollywood), book reviews, and newsletter bits for professional societies. But the one thing I did change—perhaps as the result of a combination of getting divorced finally, getting my kids prepped for college both mentally and financially, paying off my house, and getting critically injured—is that I now say yes to more varied adventures. I didn't want to stop adventuring, and in fact, I wanted more and different adventures, to make sure I wasn't missing out on a component of life.

So as a result, I became more adventurous, but with a different focus.

I began working as faculty for medical seminars with an adventure travel company, for which I traveled to the mountains and rivers of five continents. I did a stint as a cruise ship physician. And I jumped at the chance to lead a relief trip to Haiti. In other words: I kept on adventuring, albeit a bit more cautiously.

I learned to recognize the dangerous combination of speed, distraction, and dangerous terrain, and to dial things back a bit.

In White River, we found the snowboarder's body after an hour and a half of removing blocks of snow and ice with chainsaws, shovels, and axes. We were well before our absolute turn-around time on the mountain. I confirmed death, texted some images to Deputy Anderson, and packaged the corpse in a body bag. We wrapped the body bag in a SKED litter, and, using a rope belay, hauled it 300 feet out of White River Glacier onto Palmer Glacier. After loading the body into the snowcat, Brian and I skied down midmorning, carrying the chainsaws.

It will not be our last body recovery, but fortunately, over the course of the past decade, the Crag Rats have only had about one per year. We will talk about the recovery at our next Crag Rat meeting by discussing only the technicalities, to avoid becoming emotionally involved. In fact, we may even chuckle at the meetings, a coping mechanism.

The only lesson I can bring to the table with these essential stories is that the ultimate consequence is one to fend off with a vengeance. That takes a bit of knowledge and judgment. It takes a bit of balance. And unfortunately, when bad accidents happen and we are on duty as professionals, it takes a bit of detachment.

One of the most vivid memories I have of this body recovery is very self-centered, probably a coping mechanism. I remember skiing down Palmer snowfield, among the ski racers and freestyler skiers and snowboarders, with a full mountaineering pack and a chainsaw. I remember thinking to myself, *Well this is a first: skiing down Mount Hood carrying a chainsaw.*

CHAPTER SEVEN

Lost, Lived, Found

ONCE IN A WHILE, RESCUES ARE COMPLEX. WHICH MEANS RISK IS magnified.

On a classic midwinter day, we are having our annual banquet, the eighty-ninth anniversary of the Crag Rats. When I say classic, I mean Pineapple Express classic. The same weather system that caused my accident.

We live in a maritime snowpack, meaning much of our weather comes from the gigantic Pacific Ocean. When the storms roll in from the north, as in Canada, they can be bitterly cold and drop little precipitation. This doesn't happen too often. When the storms roll in from the west or northwest, usually from the Gulf of Alaska, we get snow in the mountains. Often the snow is light, but not super-light like in Colorado or Utah. With maritime weather, we have mild temperatures and warmer weather systems compared to the Rocky Mountains. The snow usually has 10 percent water content, meaning it is a bit "heavy" or "thick." If you catch it right, less than a foot of snow can be bottomless with skis or a snowboard. If you catch it wrong, it is affectionately known by a variety of distasteful monikers like *Pacific Northwest cement*, *Cascade concrete*, or *mashed potatoes*. If the storms come from the southwest, generated around Hawaii, they are warm, often too warm to drop snow, and rain comes to the mountains, often up to 8,000 feet, above all the ski resorts in Mount Hood. Thus these storms are unaffectionately called the *Pineapple Express*.

So it wasn't just raining in Hood River Valley, it was pouring buckets.

At the banquet, we have heaps of traditions, the first of which is showing up in cultish black-and-white checked buffalo-plaid shirts, the uniform of the early days when our group was established in 1926. We open the banquet at our meeting hall, the Hut, with a traditional reading of our first rescue in 1926 and the formation of the Crag Rats. We eventually move into awards such as Hat of the Year, the one who has done a good deed, and Rat of the Year, the one who has done the silliest deed. Nominations shoot out from the crowd of one hundred or so Crag Rats and guests, and are voted on based on subjective loudness of applause.

I happen to be working the front door as the year's Pip Squeak, or secretary, a job I'd shunned for a solid two decades before I ran out of excuses. In our club, once you are voted in as Pip, you enroll in a six-year leadership commitment. After Pip, you become Little Squeak (vice president), Big Squeak (president), and then trustee for three years. Each officer has specific duties beyond rescues. The officers are in charge of training, keeping the two buildings stocked and running, and our main social functions. In addition to the Winter Outing, we have the *Ice Follies* in fall, during which we sometimes work on high-angle and crevasse rescue training and ice climbing, sometimes with the four other Oregon mountain rescue groups from Bend, Corvallis, Eugene, and Portland. In November we host the *Steak Fry*, a social we have at the Hut to which everyone brings a steak to throw on the fireplace grill. And the last year as an officer, you are in charge of the Annual Banquet.

So, just as happy hour starts, the bulk of the one hundred or so attendees filters in the door, pays their annual dues, and buys some Crag Rat swag like a shirt, hat, or jacket with our insignia, which hasn't changed in ninety years.

"I heard we got a callout," says John Rust as his big frame suddenly fills the doorway.

"What? I didn't receive a text," I say incredulously.

Just then, Sheriff Matt English and Deputy Mike Anderson walk in. I accost them.

"Do we have a callout?"

"Yes, but I was trying to find another group. It's your banquet night," says Anderson. "In fact, I think it may be a Crag Rat who's missing." It turns out that one of the missing men was planning to attend the banquet as a prospective member, but is not a Crag Rat.

Immediately I get amped into high gear and start spreading the word of a callout. I let incoming Big Squeak Tom Rousseau know, and we both discuss heading home to get our gear. I walk downstairs and try to speak over the din of conversations from fifty people chatting and eating appetizers. The general consensus by some of the Crag Rats, those who regularly respond to rescue, is that this is our side of the mountain, so we should go on the rescue. But another faction of Crag Rats has the general feeling that this is their night off.

"It's the only night I have a babysitter this week! I'm not going on a rescue."

"Let someone else take it."

"I just had a beer."

It's another night rescue, and by now readers will understand that night rescues are horrible (even those not in stormy weather), but the norm.

Both Tom, incoming president, and me, incoming secretary, want to go. But Stefan, as current president, thinks we're too germane to the banquet to leave the hundred people assembling. It's an important gathering for the Crag Rats, partly because we have invited colleagues from Portland Mountain Rescue, the Sheriff's Office, and the Forest Service. I'm giving the annual slide show that recaps our rescues.

When Brian Hukari walks in the door, I grab him.

"We've got a callout," I say. "Two skiers on the north side, up Tilly Jane."

"I'll go," he says instantly in his soft and humble voice. He writes a check for his annual dues and immediately turns around and leaves to get his gear without saying anything more. He's been on more rescues than almost anyone in the past decade. Lisa Rust, John's wife, had heard about the missing skiers earlier that day when she and John were skiing with their kids and word circulated around the ski lodge. She had brought her gear to the banquet. She walks in wearing a dress, and when she confirms we are getting deployed, she goes to her car, returns with a duffel bag, and changes into backcountry ski gear. Meredith and Ron Martin also want to go. They had caught a ride to the banquet with another person so Sheriff English calls a patrol deputy to come to the Crag Rat Hut to give Ron and Meredith a ride home to collect their gear.

So, step one complete: We've got a crew. Now, we have to get the teams up the mountain to start the search.

Meanwhile, high on the mountain, two backcountry skiers are lost. The two local men had taken their kids to Cooper Spur Mountain Resort—a small, one-chairlift, 800-vertical-foot, family-friendly ski hill on the north side of Mount Hood—so their kids could go to ski camp. After getting their kids settled at camp in the morning, the two men set off on what was to be a short, half-day backcountry ski tour up the Tilly Jane Trail. They planned to return to the one-room lodge just after lunch, when ski camp finished.

The cross country ski trail ascends 2,000 feet over 2 miles, up the mountain and through the woods, part of which are burned snags from the Gnarl Ridge fire of August 2008. In 2 miles, you reach the Tilly Jane/Cloud Cap Historic District, the collection of buildings that includes the A-Frame and Guard Station, which I described in the first chapters in this book. From here, many skiers continue due south, up the mountain, past tree line.

Above tree line, one can ski the Tilly Jane Creek headwaters, a heavily wooded, low-angle, avalanche-safe drainage that eventually pops out above timberline into a little gully on the East Moraine of the Eliot Glacier—the gully separates Cooper Spur Ridge and the massive Eliot Glacier. Some skiers continue up the mountain and climb up Cooper Spur (the actual ridge, which spans 6,000 to 9,000 feet elevation, is not to be confused with the resort, which is down at 4,000 feet). An old stone shelter at 7,169 feet built by the Civilian Conservation Corps as part of the Timberline Trail is still barely functional in summer; in winter, it's usually plugged with snow. Climbers sometimes make it up to 8,729 feet to a large boulder called Tie In Rock. At Tie In Rock, skiers turn around to descend and summit climbers rope up to ascend the final 2,500-foot pitch to the top.

One issue with skiing the Cooper Spur is that the ridge itself termi-nates at 6,400 feet at the headwaters of Polallie Creek, which happens to be a cliff. So if you ski down Cooper Spur, you have to traverse northwest at 6,500 feet elevation about a quarter-mile to get back to the Tilly Jane Creek headwaters, the gentle slope you had skied up.

Another issue is that since a volcano is a cone, from any point high on the mountain you can't just descend via the *fall line*, the route a rock would follow if it rolled down the mountain. If you descend from high on the peak and you are off by only a few degrees, you could end up in the wrong drainage, and then get exponentially farther from your desired destination. On Cooper Spur, if one is looking downhill and due north, the Tilly Jane is to the left and Polallie Canyon is down the fall line. To the right, northwest and west, there are a half-dozen more drainages: twin branches of Sand Canyon, Fall Creek, North Fork Cold Spring Creek, South Fork Cold Spring Creek, and several unnamed headwaters that collect glacial runoff and spring water, turn into creeks, and lead down through thick forest into the East Fork Hood River. If you pick the wrong drainage, then the more you go down, the farther you get from your desired destination, and the deeper you get into the woods. This is why maps, compasses, and GPS receivers are so essential. As is clear weather.

A similar phenomenon occurs on the South Climb route on Mount Hood, which leads from Timberline Lodge to the summit: the so-called *Mount Hood Triangle*. The south side begins at Timberline Lodge at 6,000 feet and you can see the summit from the lodge as you climb up Palmer Glacier. It seems that you are climbing straight up the mountain. But you climb up with a very slight traverse to the left. So, if you get high on the mountain and then the clouds roll in and eliminate visibility, you can't just descend the fall line when you are on the South Climb. The fall line sends you down Zigzag Glacier, and over the Mississippi Head cliffs, quite far from Timberline Lodge. To get back to Timberline, you have to descend the fall line with a slight left traverse to avoid the Zigzag Glacier, but not too far to the left or you will fall into White River Glacier. Here's a tip: from 9,000 feet just below Crater Rock, you follow due south on a magnetic compass to get down Palmer Glacier to the Timberline ski lifts and eventually to Timberline Lodge.

In good weather this may not be a problem if you have landmarks and you can see. Although it wasn't especially cold on this particular day, at midday clouds rolled in, which means fog and poor visibility or *white out*. The two skiers lost their landmarks and got confused. They were likely in "the ping pong ball," in which the sky and snow all appear the same: white. When the skiers failed to show up at Cooper Spur to pick their kids, they were reported missing by their wives.

The two skiers were lost.

Tonight, we muster a team of five who head up the mountain. Fortunately, a call went out to other SAR teams, and two members from Portland Mountain Rescue responded because they happened to be camping at the Snowshoe Club Cabin in the Cloud Cap–Tilly Jane Historic District.

One Crag Rat team skis up the Tilly Jane Trail, then back down to the Cloud Cap Road to clear the most common means of descent: no skiers. The crew from Portland Mountain Rescue skis a mile over from the Snowshoe Club Cabin to the Tilly Jane area to clear the Guard Station and A-Frame: no skiers. Tom Scully and Brian Hukari ski high on the mountain: up Tilly Jane Trail, up the Tilly Jane Creek gully, and up to Cooper Spur. At night. In the snow. In the dark. It takes them a few hours just to get to their search destination. Tom Scully later said they found tracks high up on Cooper Spur, and the tracks were crazy.

"The tracks went uphill, then downhill, then back uphill. They went south, then north, then south again. The tracks looked like they were created by someone who was lost." They searched all night, and came back down the mountain by dawn.

The sheriff's office pings the missing party's cell phones. With modern technology, dispatch can send a request to a phone number to get the most recent cell tower connection and GPS information location of the phone. The latter function works if the phone is turned on, and its accuracy varies depending on the cell phone carrier system.

No luck that night. No cell phone ping. No missing skiers.

The next morning, we wake to crystal-clear skies and mild temperatures: a beautiful day on the mountain gives ideal conditions for searching. We have a full complement of rescuers to assault the mountain. I coordinate the Crag Rats response and the sheriff's deputies run the rescue at incident command, also called SAR base. Bob Stewart and Mike Ander-

Crag Rats haul the Sked up a cliff of basalt in Mount Hood National Forest.

Ron Martin, Meredith Martin, and Lisa Rust circumvent the washed-out bridge on the way up the trail, Columbia National Scenic Area.

Well after midnight, Meredith Martin and Walter Burkhardt hike down from Table Mountain.

It's never easy navigating the rain, mud, and rocks down the rugged trails of the side canyons of the Columbia Gorge.

Even the most straightforward trail rescues can be dangerous—navigating a trail hewn into the columnar basalt cliffs.

Just one more mile to go, Mark Flaming leads the charge across the log jam.

On the way up the trail, Crag Rats respond in the beautiful greenery of the Columbia Gorge side canyons.

Racing against daylight, Walter Burkhardt and Lisa Rust haul the litter through the burn.

SAR Deputy Mike Anderson gives the morning briefing on day two of a three-day search.

Using a tag line, Crag Rats and Cascade Locks Fire Department bring a patient down another steep, rugged trail.

Cascade Locks Fire Department and Crag Rats struggle over a log in a field of ferns.

Crag Rats belay the Sked litter down a late August snowpatch on Mount Hood.

On the way home, the old truck stops for a picturesque view of the east flank of Mount Hood, just outside Badger Creek Wilderness.

Unloading skis and farm implements, Crag Rats and Portland Mountain Rescue organize for a recovery effort at Palmer Glacier.

Midway through a recovery effort, Crag Rats move snow in the crevasse on White River Glacier.

Brian Hukari (top) and Paul Klein use chainsaws to cut through the ice at White River Glacier.

In the "ping pong ball," Crag Rats and Portland Mountain Rescue traverse Zigzag Glacier in a whiteout.

A crew from Portland Mountain Rescue and American Medical Response regroups at Illumination Saddle.

Ascending Triangle Moraine in a whiteout, with rain turning to freezing rain.

Snowstorms make good powder days: Jay Sherrerd organizing the team for another lap up the mountain, from Tilly Jane Trailhead.

At 4:30 a.m., at Tilly Jane Trailhead, Crag Rats pass off a patient from the LMC snowcat to a Parkdale Fire Department ambulance.

Crag Rats on another training day in deep powder, lead the charge up Ghost Ridge.

Homeward bound, Crag Rats ski down Tilly Jane Trail after a weekend of training at Cloud Cap Inn.

Heading home from a day at Cloud Cap Inn, Penny Hunting (left) and Jennifer Donnelly start the ski down.

Alpenglow graces the north face of Mount Hood, as seen from the deck of Cloud Cap Inn.

son are both seasoned SAR deputies—they run the rescue from the Cooper Spur ski area from the Com Rig, the jacked-up 4x4 ambulance converted to a communications hub. This is a large production. The sheriff's office manages multiple teams on the mountain. Two snowcats—we have the LMC and the sheriff's office has a snowcat also—go up with teams of Crag Rats to stand by for evacuation. Former sheriff and current deputy Joe Wampler flies the Super Cub and searches overhead. Two teams of skiers from Portland Mountain Rescue make their way up to Cooper Spur. A pair of Crag Rats led by Todd Wells heads up on snowmobiles. More Crag Rats show up to help and get dispatched into the field. The communications search-and-rescue team, Mountain Wave, sets up their communication truck to perform radio relay.

I'm coordinating the Crag Rat callout before heading to Mount Hood Meadows ski resort with my daughter and her friends for a high-school freestyle ski competition. My job is to send a text to muster a crew of Crag Rats, and then give out the information on the staging area. The deputies have the much more complicated task of running the rescue.

While I'm on my way up the mountain, Wes Baumann, a Crag Rat, climbing ranger, and ski patroller, calls me with an excellent idea. He wants to drive around to Mount Hood Meadows on the east side of the mountain, 10 miles by road from search base. From there, he wants to take two chairlifts to the top of the ski resort, climb an additional 1,000 feet above the ski resort out of bounds to 8,000 feet elevation, and traverse back to the north side of the mountain. This would put him directly on top of Cooper Spur.

"It's the quickest way to get up the mountain," he explains. "I've already cleared it with Mel," he says, referring to ski patrol director Mel Toney, wife of Crag Rat Tom Scully, who just got home from searching all night. "Asa will go with me." Asa Mueller, a Crag Rat, ski patroller, and firefighter, is highly skilled in the high alpine like Wes.

I call Deputy Bob Stewart to tell him about Wes's idea.

"Let me get right back to you," Bob says.

When I get to Mount Hood Meadows to drop off my daughter and her friends, I hear from the radio chatter that Joe Wampler has spotted the two men from the airplane; they are in the upper drainage of North

Fork Cold Springs Creek. I walk over to the ski patrol room, where Wes and Asa are assembling their gear for the mission, assuming they have permission from Bob at SAR base.

"They just found them," I say.

"Where?" asks Wes.

"Between Cooper Spur and Gnarl Ridge." We pull up a map on the ski patrol office computer.

"We can get there quickly," says Wes referring to riding the chairlift up the mountain and traversing to the north.

"I have to clear this with SAR base," I say. "Get ready; I'm sure it's a go." I call Bob again from the ski patrol land line.

"Oh, I forgot to call you back. What's the plan again?"

I explain it to him again.

"Let me run it by Mike," he says, referring to Deputy Anderson. "And it's all cleared with the ski resort?"

"Yup."

"If it was anyone but those two guys, I'd say no," he says, knowing Asa and Wes are not only ski patrollers and skilled mountaineers, but also have intimate knowledge of this part of the mountain.

Nothing for fifteen minutes. I call back.

"Oh, yeah, it's a go," says Bob. "Sorry I forgot to call you." It's quite difficult running the rescue. Seasoned SAR deputies, Anderson and Stewart, manage multiple teams from different agencies with multiple modes of transportation. The radio, I can hear by listening in, is clogged with chatter. The two missing skiers have just been spotted by airplane; they are hiking uphill. Soon thereafter the skiers are able to make a call to 911. Mike and Bob have to switch from a search plan to an evacuation plan, but also have the difficult task of keeping track of rescuers. I didn't realize it until later, when seasoned Crag Rat Rick Ragan mentioned it, but having multiple rescuers spread out on the mountain with multiple modes of transportation is a difficult situation to manage.

I spend the morning at the high-school freestyle ski competition while fielding calls from Crag Rats wanting to help, and monitoring the chatter on the radio. I send updates via text, and remind all responding Crag Rats that we'll need more help if the men are not ambulatory. If they can ski out, it will hopefully be straightforward. If they are injured, it's going to be a major ordeal extricating them from the backcountry. Joe refuels the plane, then spots the men again from the air: the skiers are slowly climbing out of the gully where they spent the night.

Wes and Asa, true to their plan, ride the chairlifts, climb 1,000 feet above the resort, ski quickly to the north side, spot the lost skiers from above, and ski down to them. Wes and Asa make contact in under two hours, despite other teams climbing up from SAR base for at least five.

Fortunately, the missing skiers had realized they were lost the night before. They hunkered down under a tree in an animal den. They were not hurt, just tired, hungry, and thirsty. They were too deep in the wooded canyon to get cell reception. They decided the next morning to climb back up the mountain to find their way home. Wes and Asa start escorting the two skiers homeward and meet up with the teams from Portland Mountain Rescue. Everyone makes it back by 4:00 p.m. Once everyone is clear from the mountain, I send a stand-down text.

These guys made it, as many do, and sent us thank-you notes and donations. They used good judgment, hunkered in, and stayed the night. In the morning when the weather cleared, they went about finding their way home. Good judgment—mental fitness—is vital for safety. Understanding the levels of prevention—primary (prevention of an accident), secondary (escaping a potentially bad situation), and tertiary (fixing a problem once you're injured, ill, or lost)—is vital for safety.

Now, it's time for all of us to go home to eat, hydrate, and sleep. We'll do it all again soon. It's not always on the snow-clad peak of Mount Hood, though. We have a separate set of gear and skill we use for the other half of our county rescues: the trails, canyons, waterfalls, and cliffs of the Columbia Gorge.

PART TWO

DOUBLE DOWN IN THE COLUMBIA RIVER GORGE

Chapter Eight

A Most Dangerous Walk

I AM ABOUT TO EMBARK ON ONE OF THE MOST DANGEROUS RESCUES IN two decades of mountain rescue. It won't be technically difficult, but rather physically and mentally exhausting, so much so that one little mistake on a straightforward trail evacuation becomes potentially perilous.

The rescue text comes at 7:30 p.m. on a warm, clear summer evening. Therein was the first reason it was dangerous: I assumed it was a routine rescue on a routine trail. Sunrise Falls and the Sunrise Falls Trail network is less than an hour's drive from the 1.5-million-person metropolis of Portland. And it is spectacular.

The trail is a narrow track that meanders along Sunrise Creek among tall Douglas fir and western hemlock, with the occasional silver fir, lodgepole pine, and western red cedar. Although the trees are so gigantic they reach several hundred feet to the sky, they still do not reach the top of the steep, narrow canyon. The creek is a picturesque, bubbly mountain stream replete with tiny rapids, waterfalls that sprout from springs in the basalt and andesite cliff walls adjacent to the creek, and shore-side groves of sword ferns, Oregon grape, old man's beard lichen, and the occasional patch of *Toxicodendron diversilobum*, the dreaded poison oak. The wildflowers are a spectacular rainbow of yellow (clasping arnica, gumweed, jewel weed, St. John's wort, monkey flower), white (Douglas' aster, American waterlily, pearly everlasting), purples (serrulate penstemon, meadow knapweed, hardhack, bull thistle, foxglove), and reds (crimson columbine, Columbian lily, Indian paintbrush).

This is indeed why these trails are part of the Columbia Gorge National Scenic Area: They are unbelievably spectacular. The main Sunrise Falls trail climbs right from the parking lot and never stops ascending; in 10 miles the windy dirt track on the west bank of a north-flowing creek tops out at an elevation of 4,000 feet. In 3 miles, you can take a spur trail down to a spectacular swimming hole. In 4 miles, you cross a bridge over a deep slot canyon. Higher up, part of the trail is hewn into a cliff so sheer that the 100-foot drop to the creek is right below you.

Despite being well maintained and well traveled, the trail is not smooth but rather hard-packed earth embedded with sharp rocks, slippery roots, loose powdery dirt, and puddles from the springs that trickle even in midsummer, when, despite a dry spell, the trail can be still be slippery in some sections.

Earlier that day, an inexperienced hiker was taking his first backpack outing with a new friend he'd met on a social media site that connects hiking partners. Social networking provided an online connection, but the two hikers had never met until that day at the trailhead. They were destined for a single night backpacking trip somewhere near East Lake.

A few things added up to slow progress: a late start, heavy packs, the first backpacking trip of the season for both, and the new friendship. At the Sunset Camp, 8 miles deep, the trail crosses the creek via a series of boulders because a bridge washed out a few years back. When crossing the creek, one of the men slipped on the wet rock and twisted his knee. He was not only in excruciating pain, but the knee had swollen to the size of a softball and he couldn't move. Fractured? Probably so.

Without cell phone reception, the uninjured man walked two hours down the trail to a spot at mile 5 where cell reception is spotty. A few minutes later, once the dispatch confirmed the story and a sheriff's deputy gathered information, a callout went out.

Hiker at Sunset Camp on Sunrise Falls trail, knee injury, reads the text.

Here we go, I'm thinking, *the start of the trail season in the Columbia Gorge. Sounds pretty straightforward: run up the trail with a stretcher and haul him out.*

I was quite wrong.

The Columbia River is 1,243 miles long, starting from Columbia Lake in Canal Flats, British Columbia, and terminating in the Pacific Ocean. The fourth-largest river in the US has one of the steepest drops. The 90-mile section that flows through the Columbia Gorge is marked by 4,000-foot-high basalt and andesite walls with rocky cliffs and promontories, waterfalls, and thick forests. The Columbia River is no longer exactly wild, since fourteen major dams and another two hundred or so dams on tributaries control the water. The forests in the gorge are a wonderland, especially the waterfalls, the largest of which is Multnomah Falls, at 620 feet high. About half of all our calls are to the trails of the Columbia Gorge—not, as one would think, on Mount Hood.

Rescue Coordinator Deputy Bob Stewart, who had come in on his night off to staff SAR base with the Com Rig, tells Crag Rat Coordinator Stefan Gumperline that he needs us at the trailhead for a haulout from Sunrise Falls. We'll need to lug our heavy stretcher 8 miles uphill to Sunset Camp to bring out the patient with a knee injury. But Stefan has a better idea once he looks at the map. With Stefan on speaker-phone, Brian Hukari, Rick Ragan, and I spread the map on the hood of our SAR truck at the Hood River County Public Works Yard at dusk. We decided to drive an hour to West Lake, at 4,320-foot elevation and the terminus of the 16-mile Sunrise Falls Trail. The man is injured exactly in the mid-point of the deep, heavily treed canyon, at the 2,320-foot level. Although the route in from the lake is slightly longer—an hour's drive instead of thirty minutes and one extra mile on the trail—we'll have one key advantage: downhill. The plan is to find the subject, plop him in a stretcher, and then continue to hike downhill to the main trailhead, another 2,000-foot drop. A one-way, 16-mile, 4,000-foot descent, at night, on a difficult trail. But since we so regularly respond to simple rescues on this trail, I mistakenly idealize we'll make it home by 2:00 a.m.

On the way out of town at dusk, we pick up Lisa Rust and Tom Rousseau. Ragan drives us into the pitch-black night up a dusty, rugged, potholed road to the top of the trail. It is so difficult to see driving up the rarely-used, ill-maintained Forest Service road that I press a button on the console that says "take down." A high-powered white light blasts through the forest darkness. At several spots, Rick brings the truck to nearly a full stop to crawl over logs and across deep potholes.

At 9:50 p.m. we set off down Sunrise Trail, bouncing the stretcher down a series of steps carved into the hillside. We tote the stretcher like a cart since it's attached to a single wheel. One person in the front faces forward, reaches behind to grab the stretcher, and pulls. A second person in back steers the litter and keeps it upright. Either position, even with an empty stretcher, is backbreaking, shoulder-wrenching, and neck-twisting work on this uneven trail.

On the map, the trail appears to alternate between following the natural contour of the hillside, meaning flat, and following the stream downhill. In actuality, the specific trail details don't show up well on the topographic maps. The trail is littered with rocks, roots, and loose sand. Several sections have stream crossings and short but brutal uphill sections. At one point, getting anxious to get to the patient, I am in front trotting along faster and faster until I speed up to a slow jog. Suddenly, I hear skidding on dirt a second before the stretcher yanks against my arms, nearly pulling my shoulders out of joint. The stretcher slams into the hillside and Brian slides to the ground. I'd forgotten that Brian's cast was just removed from his recent wrist fracture. He was okay, but he could have broken his wrist again.

At another point, we zip briskly around a corner at a trot only to run smack into a tent that two hikers have set up, right in the middle of this remote, little-used section of trail. I nearly step right inside the tent as I skid to a halt while Brian recoils to a stop behind me by ramming into the stretcher with his stomach. My headlamp blasts the two campers through the mesh screen of the tent. They are startled awake, wide-eyed and scared.

"Search and rescue," I say unapologetically to the campers. I tell myself to slow down. I am all revved up on adrenaline and feeling pressured to get this rescue completed. I have to be to work in less than ten hours.

This is a difficult situation, which adds to the typical dangers already present in the backcountry: middle of the night, fatigued, jacked on adrenaline, pressured to find the man quickly, limited by time, and our guard down because of routineness. Complex, difficult tasks cause stress. Stress causes our brain not to function properly. Cognitive impairment, in varying degrees, occurs in mountain rescue, but also in many aspects of life: a tough project at work on a deadline, a tense family crisis, a frustrating e-mail, a difficult phone call from your boss. One thing's certain: Stress, to some extent, causes our brains to focus intensely on one subject, while blocking out others. If you are highly trained in dealing with stress—law enforcement officer, firefighter, emergency doctor—you may be able to function with minimal mental impairment in your specific field. But even those trained to handle stress in one situation, like people with careers in public safety or medicine, may not be able to handle it in another aspect, like home life. And one day with stress out of normal context can throw even the most experienced professionals off kilter.

In mountain rescue, like many situations, we have a three-fold hit to the brain: "the fight-or-flight" reaction, fatigue, and distraction from multiple sensory inputs. We must intentionally guard ourselves against these three issues, lest the mission turn even more perilous.

Let's look at the fight-or-flight reaction first, aka the "adrenaline rush." In Cro-Magnon days, this reaction was necessary either to stand up and protect oneself against a big furry creature, or to run very fast and very far away from said big furry creature. This stress response occurs not only with fear, but also with excitement, anxiety, surprise, anger, pressure like a time deadline, or any sort of urgency. It is modulated by a series of neurotransmitters and hormones, of which adrenaline, or epinephrine, is the most well-known, but cortisol and serotonin also play key roles.

Epinephrine is secreted by twin adrenal glands, which are perched on top of the kidneys. Epinephrine functions in stress similarly to the shock I experienced in my near-death accident. Only unlike the physical stress of internal bleeding, the stress reaction is triggered by a *perceived* threat from sensory input to the brain. The brain then tells the adrenals to open the floodgates and dump epinephrine into the bloodstream. Epinephrine increases heart rate and respiratory rate to increase metabolism. It limits blood flow to organs not used for fighting or fleeing, such as the kidney and intestinal tract. For those organs vital to fight or flight—heart, lungs, and muscles—the blood vessels dilate and flow increases. The heart increases its rate and pressure to circulate blood as quickly as possible to deliver life-sustaining oxygen and glucose to muscles and pick up toxic carbon dioxide and lactic acid. The lungs change out the carbon dioxide for oxygen as quickly as you can breathe, faster and faster.

Meanwhile, cortisol, a powerful steroid, is also released by the adrenal gland. It triggers maximum quick-fuel dumping into the blood stream—glucose is released from the liver glycogen stores and fatty acids are released from fat—to supply skeletal muscles with quick energy. Cortisol also helps deliver a massive amount of glucose to the brain, to sharpen eyesight, smell, and hearing. It allows the frontal lobe of your brain to focus acutely on an intense task at the expense of blocking out other peripheral tasks. This is one reason that, in the midst of a stress reaction, we can focus intently on the task at hand but may totally miss activity in the periphery.

Serotonin, the third key hormone, is responsible for mood, which is usually anxiety in the heat of the fight or flight reaction. But it is also responsible for the immense good feeling after the stress has been resolved, the so called "runner's high."

Adrenaline, cortisol, and serotonin jack up your system for maximum physical performance, a powerful feeling that is quite useful when climbing a mountain, mountain biking a technical trail, snow skiing in steep terrain, in mountain rescue, or any other difficult task. Sometimes this stress reaction can be incredibly useful, even lifesaving. If you are skiing a steep gully, get caught in an avalanche, and need to instantly maneuver to escape the snow slide before being buried alive, this reaction can save your life. Sometimes, however, it is not helpful. It's not necessarily important to be supercharged on adrenaline when you get behind the wheel of a county-owned one-ton crew-cab long-bed four-wheel-drive pickup loaded with $30,000 of SAR equipment. Nor is it ideal to be revved up when you need to set up a complicated rope-rescue system. Or when you are trotting down a trail to rescue a non-critical patient. Key words here: non-critical.

And the adrenaline reaction occurs more frequently, albeit on a smaller scale, in daily life. A loaded e-mail from your boss or an argument with your teenager can cause anxiety and thus trigger a stress response. We've all been there.

In mountain rescue, we have a second complicating factor that couples with the stress reaction: fatigue. Brian, a farmer, worked all day and went stand-up paddling that afternoon, a celebratory workout after getting his cast off. Lisa, a seventh-grade teacher, had gone for an after-school run. Tom, a retired communications engineer who keeps our radios operable, had gone for a long hike that day. I had gone on a mountain bike ride after work. So, after a full day at work and recreation, we were tired before we even set out on the trail.

And of course, it is night, so that adds to whatever fatigue we have from our physical activities earlier that day. Our natural circadian rhythm insists that we should be at home in bed at this moment.

In addition to fighting adrenaline high and fatigue low, we've got a third complication: distraction, or rather, difficulty in trying to focus with multiple sensory inputs. Often in mountain rescue, like any tense situation, focus requires intense concentration and we are required to process multiple sensory inputs at once, complete multiple tasks simultaneously, and make critical decisions at the same time. We are running down the trail with the litter, watching for rocks, roots, and stumps, occasionally talking on the radio to Rick, trying to regulate our body temperature because we are sweating but a cool night wind has picked up, and following a map and trail signs. And this is the simplest part of the rescue: hiking down the trail to find the patient at a known location with a known non-critical injury.

Much has been studied with regard to multitasking, managing multiple sensory inputs and cognitive outputs. We do it all the time in today's world. We talk on the phone and drive. We type an e-mail regarding one issue while we're on the phone with our boss discussing another. We help our kids with homework while we make dinner. With social networking, we simulcast, with sensory input coming from multiple streams at once, all day long: We quickly toggle between Instagram, Facebook, Snapchat, e-mail, and other apps more quickly than we can fully read or process data. In my office I get communication via my desk phone, cell phone, e-mail (several accounts), instant messaging, and the electronic medical records program "in basket." In the emergency department, I may be dictating a chart on one patient and on hold to talk to a specialist about a second, when the nurse walks in to talk to me about a third.

Studies show that multitasking has two key problems. First, it wastes time due to repeated context switching, or toggling between two tasks, each time leaving one on hold to be later resumed, while quickly starting a second. The brain must restart and refocus when returning to a task, not always returning to the exact bookmark. Second, multitasking causes errors due to insufficient attention—something we can't afford in mountain rescue. If we are setting up a complicated rope-rescue system and then pause to answer a radio call, we could miss a critical step in the rope system by having our attention diverted for even a few seconds.

Driving and talking on the phone at the same time is a classic example. One study showed that drivers talking on phones were more accident prone and had slower reaction time than those intoxicated over the legal limit of blood alcohol, 0.80 percent. But then, any distraction while driving is dangerous: adjusting the radio, looking for sunglasses, eating.

Edward M. Hallowell, psychiatrist and author of *Crazy Busy: Overstretch, Overbooked and about to Snap, Strategies for Handling Your Fast-Paced Life*, said multitasking is a "mythical activity in which people believe they can perform two or more tasks simultaneously as effectively as one." Some functions, routine motor and perception tasks, are somewhat easier to multitask, compared to learning new skills or tasks that require problem solving, in which it's nearly impossible to process two streams at once. In mountain rescue, we have to be very careful, but sometimes we don't have any choice but to multitask.

An adrenaline buzz, fatigue, and distraction add up to a risky rescue, and the most dangerous part is still to come. We mistakenly thought this would be a quick forty-five-minute descent to get to the injured man. That would have been the case hiking by day without carting along the stretcher and our rescue packs, but it takes us two hours to reach the patient—darkness, rough trail, and the heavy litter make for slow going.

We find the patient at 11:50 p.m. just north and uphill from Sunset Camp. He is hunkered in a tent pitched on the side of the trail. His knee is bad: swollen, slightly deformed, and bruised. Tibia plateau fracture? Probably so. A stream from a spring trickles on the rock and soaks the bottom of the tent. The man is muscular: 6 feet tall and weighs at least 250 pounds. And he clearly can't walk.

I know in an instant this is going to be a difficult extrication, and we'll be lucky to finish by dawn. We are tired, it is midnight, and we only have a crew of four. The trail down is steep, rocky, wet, and narrow. We have at least two sections of cliff that are 18 inches wide, one washed out bridge, a half-dozen stream crossings, and one suspension bridge.

It's going to be an all-nighter. Once again. But I have no idea just how difficult this is about to become. Adrenaline and fatigue are wrestling in me, creating a strange sensation. Adrenaline jacks up my brain, ready to solve this problem, but fatigue sets into my arm and leg muscles.

"We are going to need more help," says Lisa.

"We are out of radio range," says Tom.

"Let's get this done," says Brian.

Not only do I know our team is in for a difficult task, but I am dead tired and feeling pressured to get this rescue completed so I can get some sleep before work.

So, how do we address the intense stress of mountain rescue and, in fact, any difficult situation? The trifecta of stress, fatigue, and focus difficulty can compound a difficult situation unless it's recognized and mitigated.

Luckily, a pathway for success and safety can help us mitigate risk in mountain rescues, and this pathway works for almost any stressful situation. The pathway is:

- Recognize the situation
- Take a "time-out"
- Prioritize
- Use a checklist
- Divide up the tasks

Neither step will take too long: we don't have the luxury of time in many mountain rescue situations. And we don't necessarily do any of these steps formally—they're part of the nature of the Crag Rats and the nature of mountain rescue.

First we have to recognize the issue and identify the problem. We need to recognize when we are dead tired or we're running too fast or handling too many tasks at once. We've all been in the situation when we don't realize until it's too late: We've already sent a charged e-mail back to our boss or said something we regret in the heat of an argument with our teenager. Stop, slow down, and think through your situation. Don't react immediately or impulsively!

Second, take a "time-out," a momentary pause to review effectiveness and safety. In mountain rescue, we do this frequently, often without really noticing this informal pause. Before we leave the truck, one of us usually runs a quick check with the group. Everyone have a headlamp, map, food, water? Communication with SAR base? Who is tracking the mission with GPS? During the descent tonight, we stopped at every trail confluence to check the map and the trail signs, even though we know this trail. But this simple procedure is important to eliminate mistakes.

In the hospital where I work, we take a formal time-out before every procedure. It takes only a few seconds but it has been shown to be instrumental in minimizing errors. From a simple laceration repair to a complex surgery, we typically ready equipment and have a PARQ conference to discuss procedure, alternatives, risks, and questions with the patient. Then we have the patient sign an informed consent. Finally, only when we are all ready to go, we take a "time-out" by asking a series of questions that take about twenty seconds. It's a simple procedure that is a redundant but necessary step to help minimize errors. The questions for my hospital, from removing a mole to replacing a total knee, are:

- Identify the patient with two identifiers, usually name and date of birth
- Confirm the procedure
- Confirm the site
- Mark the site

- Confirm laterality
- Confirm the consent is signed properly
- Review safety practices, which often means a quick check to identify the location of the biohazard container for prompt disposal of contaminated bandages and sharp needles.

And in my hospital the steps must be *read aloud for all team members.*

In my day-to-day office, we have a less formal time-out every Monday morning via a "huddle board." The huddle board is an invention by my medical assistant who felt that using up a lunch hour for a long, mundane staff meeting wasn't too productive. We dreaded those meetings! But we needed to check in as a team every week. We have a dry-erase white board in a central location in our back office. During the week anyone can add a topic to the huddle board. Our rule is that if it takes longer than two to three minutes to discuss, it is not appropriate for the huddle board and another form of communication should be used. Once a week, with no scheduled time, we get the staff together and zip through a list that varies from five to ten items long. The list includes quick reminders about billing or office procedures, a recap of a difficult patient, scheduling for the week, and such. The weekly huddle takes ten minutes, tops, so everyone has time to attend.

In fact, I use time-outs in every facet of my life. When I grew up we had a family dinner every Sunday night that my dad called "a meeting of the family corporation," to recap the week and plan the next. I still carry on this tradition by having a Sunday night dinner with my daughters and keeping a notebook of "minutes" each week. Mostly we talk about difficult situations at school, the next week's schedule, and upcoming travel adventures, which is my favorite part.

The United States Coast Guard uses a more formal time-out called, for simplicity, "GAR," which stands for Green-Amber-Red, the three colors of a traffic signal. GAR is slightly more elaborate than our mountain rescue time-out and my office huddles, but GAR still only takes minutes, which is a fundamental factor to having a successful time-out.

It works like this. When faced with a difficult mission, every member of a response team assigned to a mission rates risk in six categories on a scale of 0 to 10: 0 being no risk, and 10 being extreme risk. The rating is done in confidence, because the supervisor is often responsible for the first three categories and subordinates can often be reluctant to criticize their superior. The subjects are:

Supervision: Is the supervisor qualified, focused, engaged, and impartial?

Planning: Are the preparation and plan adequate?

Team Selection: Are members skilled for the job?

Team Fitness: Are members physically and mentally ready?

Environment: Are the weather, terrain, and sea conditions safe or manageable?

Event/Evolution Complexity: Is the allotted time and complexity of the task reasonable?

Once each member has rated the six categories, he or she adds ups the numbers, the sum of which will range from 0 to 60, and plots the score based on three colors. A score of less than 24 is Green, low risk. A score of 24 to 44 is Amber, moderate risk. A score of 44 or more is Red, or High Risk. The supervisor asks each team member's color rating, nothing more. If everyone is Green, mission is a go. With a predominance of Ambers, the supervisor should consider mission modifications in certain areas to lessen risk. With one or more Reds, the time-out mandates risk reduction measures.

So depending on your work or home situation, you can take a variety of time-outs, either formal or informal.

The third key, once you've recognized the problem and taken a time-out, is to prioritize tasks. In mountain rescue, our priority is fairly straightforward and is based on three components: immediate action, prompt action, and delayed action. But, these three factors can really guide making priorities in every aspect of our life.

First decision: Is this situation life- or limb-threatening? If the patient had a displaced knee fracture cutting off blood flow to his foot, immediate action would be required to straighten the leg to restore blood flow. Sometimes immediate action is to move the patient to a safe place, tie him or her to a safety rope, or start resuscitation.

Second decision: What needs to occur rather promptly? In mountain rescue this is usually package the patient and evacuate. Get down the trail. But not always. Sometimes the weather, terrain, and darkness are too dangerous to allow travel, so our priority is to wait until morning. Sometimes extrication is simple: hike a patient down a trail. Other times, it's complicated: rig a rope-raising system to haul a patient out of a canyon or crevasse. Once, we had to feed and hydrate a patient for twenty minutes before we could walk down the trail.

Third, what can be put off until later? This includes actions that we can deal with well after the rescue: repair equipment, replace batteries, talk to Sheriff English about better radio communication, get a better headlamp, practice putting the wheel on the litter, and such.

How does this look in other aspects of life? My daughter got in a fender-bender car accident and called me while I was working a busy emergency room shift. She was upset so I couldn't initially understand her on the phone. First priority, immediate action, is this life threatening? I need to make sure my daughter is not physically injured or threatened—if she is, the task is find her location right away and call 911.

She calmed down quickly and luckily neither she nor the other driver was injured. Whew! So, the second priority is: What needs to be done promptly? Trade insurance info with the other driver, call a tow truck if needed (it wasn't needed, whew!), and call the police to report the accident. The third priority then becomes listing items that need to be accomplished, but can be done later. Write down a narrative of the accident, call the insurance company, and call the repair company. And, she needed to confirm to Dad that she wasn't driving and texting—an important discussion to have later!

Similarly, if you have a stressful situation at work with a coworker or received an emotionally charged e-mail, then that can trigger a stress reaction. You don't want to fire off a loaded e-mail in the heat of emotions like anxiety, frustration, fear, and anger. The immediate response might simply be to acknowledge receipt of the e-mail and say you'll look into it. Prioritize whether the situation requires an immediate, prompt, or delayed action.

How do you keep the priorities straight? For complex tasks, checklists become the go-to tool to get this done safely. When you're clouded with adrenaline, fatigue, and/or multitasking, a checklist can be vital to success.

Checklists became widely used by the Federal Aviation Administration to eliminate pilot error, which turned out to be wildly successful for minimizing aviation accidents. In medicine, especially with surgery, use of checklists has helped eliminate errors, as neurosurgeon Atul Gawande described in *The Checklist Manifesto*. Checklists work because they are created in times of calm, rational thought. Then, when stress is causing impaired brain function in a busy, complex, emotionally charged situation, you can revert to your checklist.

I love checklists. Before I left on a month-long trip to Patagonia in Chile and Argentina, on a trip that involved hiking, trail-running, mountain-biking, and river-rafting gear, all jammed into carry-on luggage, I was a bit stressed with the complex task of packing. I also had a million things to do at work and home before I left. Fortunately, I didn't have to think too hard about packing: I had made a checklist the month before! Similarly, if my daughter gets in another car crash, she can now open the glove box and look at the checklist. First priority: check for injuries, move to a safe spot on the road, and call 911. Second priority: trade insurance information and call a tow truck if needed. Third: be prepared to give Dad a full explanation if you were driving and texting or talking on the phone! I love checklists so much, in fact, that I wrote two books based on my checklists: *Backcountry Ski and Snowboard Routes Oregon* and *Adrenaline Junkie's Bucket List: 100 Extreme Outdoor Adventures to do Before You Die.*

We have an excellent mountain-rescue checklist in the form of a flip chart for trail rescues called *Riggers Guide. Riggers Guide* is a compact spiral-bound booklet on 3 × 5 plastic-coated paper that gives diagrams and checklists for rope-rescue systems, patient packaging, helicopter operations, and such. We all carry it in our packs. In fact, it is so useful that we also have a second avalanche-rescue guide.

The fourth and final piece, after recognizing the problem, taking a time-out, and prioritizing with your checklist, is to take action, usually via division of duties. Division of duties is important for minimizing errors. Take a job, do it well, and trust your partners to complete theirs.

We have defined tasks tonight just by default; we don't really need to talk about it. This is the way the Crag Rats operate mostly—we naturally take the tasks we are most skilled at. I'm medical, Lisa's helping me, Brian is setting up the litter, and Tom is on the radio trying to reach SAR base or Ragan, who might still be in the truck at the North Trailhead, or might have driven home. In the increasingly cold night, we package the patient. First I put on gloves—as I've said before, protecting the rescuer is first priority.

"You okay?" I ask.

"It hurts really bad. I think it's broken," he replies.

"I'm going to take a quick look, splint it, and then we're going to get you out of here," I explain. "Okay?"

"Okay."

With Lisa's help, I unwrap the patient's leg and look at the knee. It is swollen, bruised, and slightly angulated. He winces with every movement and every touch. I straighten his broken knee just a bit and splint it with a malleable aluminum splint, an elastic compression bandage, and several wraps of 2-inch-wide medical tape. The splint is fairly snug: I want to make sure it is immobile but not tight enough to cut off circulation to his foot. I quickly check his foot pulse, color, and temperature: good neurologic and vascular function beyond the obviously fractured knee.

We arc in a very cramped space in a tent perched on a rock covered with trickling water from a spring uphill. Brian has taken the wheel off the stretcher, and he slides the stretcher onto the rock. Lisa and I drag the patient out of the tent by sliding him out on the inflatable camp sleep pad he's lying on. We move the patient from the rock ledge to the stretcher, not gently but roughly, by lifting, sliding, pushing the man and camping pad into the litter. Brian and Tom pick up the man's shoulders and I stabilize his injured leg. Then, as he is a few inches off the ground for a few seconds, Lisa slides, or rather shoves, the litter underneath him and we plop him down roughly on the cold, hard fiberglass.

He yelps in pain. It is a rough transfer. But keep in mind this is the middle of the night, in the middle of the wilderness. We are doing the best we can.

Then we need to reattach the wheel to the litter, which is no easy task. Brian, Tom, and I lift the litter with its 250-pound cargo, and Lisa then slides the wheel under the litter. We are holding it waist-high while she clicks the wheel into place. We then rest the stretcher on the wheel, which only requires two of us to balance it to keep it from falling over. Finally, Brian takes a time-out to check the wheel, to make sure Lisa has fastened it correctly.

Tom takes the patient's backpack, along with his own, and escorts the patient's friend down the trail. Brian, Lisa, and I start wheeling the patient down the trail.

The first obstacles come all at once: wheel the patient off the mud and rocks, push the litter over a few roots, and then haul it up a 10-foot hill strewn with rocks, dirt, and roots. It is as steep and long as a half-flight of stairs. With four of us pushing and pulling, the litter stalls and teeters when the wheel jams suddenly against a root. I try to dig in with my feet to prevent the stretcher from falling over, but I can't get purchase on the soft soil. The stretcher, patient included, tilts at 45 degrees to one side before Brian grabs it, digging his feet into the slippery, powdery dirt. With a sudden jarring back-breaking maneuver, we keep the patient from crashing over into the brush and barely get him up the hill. It takes ten minutes to move 10 feet down the trail. And we almost drop the patient.

I look at Brian, our thoughts exactly the same. *That was close! This is dangerous. We need more people. This is going to take all night.*

The guy cries out: "Please don't drop me."

"We need more people," says Lisa.

"We're going to have to take it slow," I say.

Just then, five volunteer firefighters show up. In the deep canyon, we have no radio communication with SAR base. We knew help was coming, but had little idea when and where they would show up.

"Thank God," I say.

"We need help," says Lisa again.

So over the course of the next six hours, we travel 1 mile per hour. The going is painstakingly slow and dangerous. We tip the man over twice: the litter luckily hits the sidewall of the hill, listing at 45 degrees. The litter does not hit the ground and the patient doesn't fall out, but it is close a few times. We stop frequently to swap out litter attendants. Even though we have nine rescuers and only two guide the stretcher at once for fifteen minutes at a time, it's incredibly fatiguing. Even thirty minutes of walking without hauling the litter is still not enough rest. This is back-breaking, arm-fatiguing, shoulder-jarring work. Every thirty minutes or so, we come to a steep section, a boulder, or a log, where it takes all nine of us to detach the wheel, pass the litter over a log or up a hill, and reattach the wheel. During the cliff sections, Brian takes the rear steering position, since he's the most experienced and the strongest.

At mile 4, Tom gets the first radio communication with SAR base in 3 hours and calls in a status report. It's around 2:00 a.m. and I ask Tom to inquire how we might get home, since we are going to finish the mission 16 miles from where we started.

"Ragan is here waiting for you," crackles the radio from SAR base. Ragan has been sitting in the truck at SAR base all night without any communication from us.

At mile 3, nearing home, just when we think things can't get worse, they do. First, we are so tired that, even with nine rescuers, we still have to take a total break about every fifteen minutes. Two people hold the litter while standing, and the crew rests.

Then, when we drop into a small stream crossing, we smack the litter wheel into a rock and hear a loud "crack." We lift the litter over the rock and try to continue down the trail but the wheel wobbles dangerously. Tom looks at the wheel.

"The flange and axle are broken," he says.

"We have no choice. We have to carry him out."

If readers think wheeling someone out is dangerous and pushing us to the limits of our strength and endurance, you should know that *carrying* a 6-foot, 250-pound man out, without the help of the wheel, is nearly impossible.

We finally reach Sunrise Falls South Trailhead at 6:00 a.m. and transfer the patient to an ambulance. We are exhausted. We still have a half-hour drive home: Lisa, Brian, and I all have to be to work in two hours. Lisa later commented that if dispatch had inquired about the height and weight of the patient, she might have sent her 6-foot-tall husband on the rescue instead; he was home with their young children.

This rescue was so difficult that I get nauseated thinking about it.

A year later at the same camp, we are called to fetch an injured hiker who had fallen off a cliff, scrambled back to camp, and needed to be evacuated. Cascade Locks Fire Department was unavailable, so a call went out to the American Medical Response Reach and Treat team, a backcountry rescue crew employed by a private ambulance company from neighboring Multnomah County.

A hasty team departs about 5:30 p.m. and one of the firefighters has an excellent idea.

"Can I put on my running shoes and run up the trail?"

The runner reaches the patient in two hours. Lisa Rust, Meredith Martin, Ron Martin, and I haul up the litter, with Todd Hanna and Tom Rousseau coming an hour later. The runner reports no rope rescue required and noncritical injuries. The AMR paramedics reach the woman at 7:30 p.m. and report she's banged up and dehydrated, but noncritical.

"Can she walk out?" I ask on the radio, as our team is still trudging up the trail with the litter. And I get nauseated right then. All I can think about is the man we hauled out the year before and how dangerous it was. To evacuate the woman in the dark would be dangerous.

I reach the woman at 8:00 p.m. with about an hour left until dusk. The paramedics did a good job at hydrating her and giving pain medicine. We have a huddle.

"You guys have been with her for an hour. Think she's okay to walk?" I ask.

"Well, we can try it. If it's a problem, we can put her in the litter," says the paramedic. We put a harness on the woman so we have hand holds and so we can clip her to a belay when crossing the cliffs and streams. So we begin the long walk out. No litter, thankfully. I look at Lisa.

"A litter evac will be dangerous. It's really difficult."

"Don't we know."

At the height of the stress in the middle of the night evacuating the man from Sunset Camp, somewhere past 2:00 a.m. we are taking a break on the trail. Everyone is fatigued, dirty, hungry, and thirsty. Our hands hurt from gripping the litter rails. Our headlamp batteries are slowly dying.

And then the man perks up.

"I really appreciate you guys coming out this far so late at night, but I guess that's what you get paid for."

I see Lisa scowl; her headlamp lights up her face.

"No, actually," Lisa snaps. "We are all volunteers. We all have real jobs and we all have to be at work in the morning."

"We'll get down okay." I fudge the truth, not feeling confident we will get down without dropping the patient. "We do this all the time."

"We're almost there," says Brian, knowing we have another four hours to go.

Chapter Nine

Back into the Mountains

Two months after my near-death injury due to skiing, I went skiing.

My parents taught me to ski on a tiny ski hill called Summit Ski Area at Government Camp, Oregon, on Mount Hood's south side. Built in 1927, Summit is one of the oldest ski areas in continuous operation in the United States (Cooper Spur Mountain Resort on the north side of Mount Hood was established the same year. The oldest, Howelsen Hill Ski Area in Steamboat Springs, Colorado, opened in 1915.) Back then, Summit Ski Area had a T-bar, and when the bar came across my dad's knees, it hit me in the back so I had to struggle to stay on. I was five years old.

I grew up going on family ski trips all over the Western US, Canada, and Europe. In college, I spent a year in the Austrian Alps. I later taught my kids to ski and even took my daughters skiing at the legendary Ski Portillo in the Chilean Andes—not once, but twice.

Being divorced, I get only every other spring break with my girls. And with my kids getting closer to the time when they depart for college, I knew I only had a few more spring breaks left. I had to capitalize on this time, but I knew I couldn't jump for a grand adventure. I never had thoughts of getting back to skiing after my accident just to overcome the fear of skiing. In fact, I never had any fear of going back to skiing. I got in an accident, and I was healing. I simply wanted to ski, I wanted to take my kids on an adventure, and wanted to be with both family and friends.

So, when several of my Hood River friends planned a trip to Whistler, British Columbia, Canada, I asked my doctor.

"I want to ski. It is spring break and I want to take my girls to Whistler," I said in the office when she checked the healing incision on my abdomen. I should remind readers that Whistler is one of the largest and most challenging of all ski resorts in the world and I was about six weeks past my emergency surgery.

"Where?"

"Whistler. With my daughters. I'll be careful," I spit out in staccato nervousness.

"I think that's okay. Gently. Don't go crazy. It should be fine."

"I'll stick to groomed slopes," I said. I'm sure I had a gigantic smile.

The trip was fabulous. Spring at Whistler gave us great weather, great snow, and great friends. I skied groomers, very gently. A few times I passed on the steep mogul slopes when my daughters and our friends wanted more challenge than smooth blue-square runs. One afternoon, I did a short backcountry ski up a smooth, flat trail that is out of bounds in a canyon between Whistler and Blackcomb Resorts. Nothing exciting, but a chance to get into the backcountry and ski uphill away from crowds.

Once back home, a few months later, I have another challenge, a more daunting one: a mountain-rescue callout. Rescues have been quiet for several months. But when a text message hits my phone, I freeze for a moment.

I want to go.

First, I'm wondering if I should go, considering I'm still not quite 100 percent back to fitness and strength. Pretty close, but not quite. Second, I have two daughters to take care of, and risking my life in the night gives me pause. *What if it's a rope rescue? What if I have to lift patients? What if I have to climb a rock cliff or descend into a canyon, river, or waterfall?*

But, considering I have already been back to skiing, I am pretty sure I'll be fine. So I pack my gear.

The story will become all too familiar: two hikers lost. On Mount Defiance. In Warren Creek Canyon. At night.

The two hikers left the Starvation Creek Trailhead at noon to head up the 5-mile, 5,000-foot-elevation trail. Sometime around 3:30 p.m. they hit snow. The top thousand feet of Mount Defiance retains snow until June. If fact, gardeners in Hood River sometimes say they know when to plant tomatoes in their gardens when the snow is melted off Defiance. We go on rescues almost every spring for the same reason. The problem is that when hikers climb the 5,000-foot-high mountain, which is covered in thick groves of Douglas fir, they reach snow on the last 500 to 1,000 feet. But it's easy snow to hike on, being old, firm, and compacted from sun, rain, and temperature fluctuations. So people continue climbing to the summit of Defiance—you can walk right up on the snow wearing running shoes. The problem, then, becomes descent. When you turn around and hike down, it is nearly impossible to find the trail without a GPS or a map and compass. First, the forest all looks the same: thick groves of Douglas fir with no trail markers on the trees. Second, the snow all looks the same: littered with tree branches, wisps of old man's beard lichen, and dirt. Even boot prints someone just left in the snow are nearly impossible to find. But people generally just start walking downhill, not even thinking they need to look for a trail. So this couple, like many who get lost in this canyon, go down the fall line. But the fall line doesn't descend to either of the twin trails that reach the summit. Starvation Creek Trail runs up a ridge to the east and Mount Defiance Trail follows a ridge to the west. The two trails are separated by the mile-wide, thick, tangled mess of Warren Creek Canyon. And Warren Creek Canyon terminates in thick trees and then, once nearly down to the bottom, an impassible cliff.

The two hikers did exactly that: climbed up Mount Defiance Trail, bagged the summit, and then descended unknowingly into Warren Creek Canyon. At some point, they turned on their GPS but had trouble getting a signal when they were deep into the steep-walled, thickly treed canyon. Down they hiked and when they hit the cliff at 1,500 feet at dusk, they stopped and called 911. Fortunately, they had cell reception. Dispatch pinged their phone to get coordinates and the woman read the latitude and longitude from her phone. They matched. We know where they are.

Walter Burkhardt, Joe McCulloch, Dwayne Troxell, and I meet at the county yard, pile in the SAR truck, and drive 5 miles to the trailhead, Starvation Creek Rest Area, just off Interstate 84. Once there, we look at the map with the deputy on duty, find the couple's location, and ask the deputy to call them.

"They need to hike up, not down. They need to make their way slightly up and due west. Eventually they will hit the trail." We know this because of the numerous rescues we've done in this exact spot for this exact reason. A while back, Kevin Schlagel had used GPS to track a rescue in the same spot, marking an old logging road that traverses Warren Creek Canyon around 2,000 feet. If the couple can hike back uphill to this old road, they can follow it west to the trail.

The three of us set off up the trail in 55-degree temperatures and light rain. It is, of course, 7:30 p.m. Of course, it's night, once again.

This is one of the few times in two decades of mountain-rescue missions that I am a bit worried about myself. I've gone full-force with rehab. Once I heard you take the number of weeks you are out, and then double it for recovery time. I am three months deep into recovery, working hard to return to my fitness level. I'm feeling good, strong. Not 100 percent, but nearly so.

The couple follows instructions: They bushwhack upward and westward. They scramble and crawl over downed trees, rocks, and dirt. They reach the Mount Defiance Trail at 9:00 p.m., call the deputy, and start hiking down. As we ascend the trail, we meet them at 10:00 p.m. at 2,000 feet. We turn around and escort them home. We're back by 11:00 p.m. Straightforward—but never exactly simple or easy. I am a bit relieved.

Because I thrive on mountain rescue, I tend to gravitate to rescues. It may be, in part, because I've been a mountain rescuer and emergency physician for so long, it is familiar. It may be because I love helping people. It may be because I thrive on the adrenaline buzz. It's probably in a large part due to me being outside, constantly and daily. In fact, I seem to encounter rescues beyond the mountains, sometimes on my vacations.

Once I took my daughters on a kitesurfing trip to Mexico. Kitesurfing is a rigorous, demanding, hazardous sport. The sport uses a kite that ranges from 4 to 17 square meters, the shape of which is formed by inflatable bladders—the kite can produce tremendous force in a gust of wind. The kite is held aloft by four strong but thin 20-meter-long lines; if the lines get wrapped around an arm, leg, or finger, the traction of the kite can cause a debilitating injury. The kitesurfer steers with the lines being connected to a 20-inch-long control bar, which is then affixed to the kitesurfer via a harness—if you lose control of the kite, it can yank you abruptly and violently. Underfoot you ride one of several types of boards: a surfboard; a "twintip," which looks like a wakeboard or snowboard; or a hydrofoil that lifts the kiteboard 2 feet out of the water.

When my thirteen-year-old daughter said one day, "Dad I want to learn to kitesurf," I just couldn't say no. But one of the most dangerous adventure sports must be learned slowly, methodically, and with professional instruction. My daughter and I spent an entire summer learning to kitesurf together, safely and slowly and cautiously.

Our summer culminates in a family kitesurfing trip to Los Barilles, Baja California Sur, Mexico. We kitesurf most of the week-long trip. One day, after kitesurfing in the warm sun and moderate water, we relax on the beach before dinner. It being November, the sun drifts toward the horizon in early evening.

Then suddenly, we spy a kitesurfer who has apparently crashed and become tangled in his equipment. The wind has long since abated. All the kitesurfers are off the water, starting happy hour and packing up gear. I see the man floating in the ocean, adrift. He is not moving much—it looks like he is not even paddling in. Normally, he would be in self-rescue mode, floating on his kite and paddling toward shore. I quickly assume he can't paddle in, possibly because he is exhausted and hypothermic. Or maybe he doesn't know how to self-rescue. As the sun begins to set and the sky starts to darken, I grab a large stand-up paddle board, head for the water, and paddle out to the man. A kitesurfing instructor at the resort we are staying at has the same thought, and grabs another board.

We race out to the man adrift at sea: it takes ten minutes. When we reach the downed kitesurfer, we find him tangled in his gear, drifting. He is exhausted and barely staying afloat. The instructor and I go to work, together. I drag the man aboard my paddleboard, while the instructor untangles the gear from the man's legs. Once the man clutches my board unencumbered by the lines, the kite instructor deflates the kite, grabs the wadded mess of lines, and plops the whole thing on his board. We head for shore.

On the beach after the rescue, my daughters and I reflect on the important lessons. Their drive for excellence is essential and so is establishing a good foundation for safety and self-reliance. In this case, self-rescue skills are important and can only really be learned by practicing. Thereafter, my daughter and I practice self-rescue skills, which gives us both a foundation so that we are less likely to panic or fumble through the maneuvers if we actually need the skills.

This rescue business seems to happen to me repeatedly.

Once flying on an airplane to a ski mountaineering trip in the Alps, I am trying to sleep with my hood pulled over my head, ear plugs jammed in my ears, and an eye shade covering my face. I hear the overhead page by the flight attendant: *If there is a doctor or nurse on board, please ring your call button.* I sheepishly unravel my privacy garb, buzz the bell, and get escorted to the back of the airplane. I find a teenage girl bleeding from the mouth.

"Hi, I'm a doctor," I say. "What's the problem?"

"She's bleeding," says her mom, panicky, "from her mouth."

I take a quick look. An orthodontic appliance has come loose and lacerated the gum. The girl's mouth is oozing blood. I look through the flight first-aid kit, find some gauze, and roll it tightly into a tube the size of a breakfast sausage.

"Here, bite on this. Don't take it out for an hour," I say. "It will stop. If not, come find me." Everyone gives a sigh of relief and the flight attendant asks me to sign a form, my handwriting illegible.

On the return flight, after backcountry skiing for a week, I again try to sleep, and I again hear the overhead page: *If there is a doctor or nurse aboard . . .* This time I and a retired internist respond to a woman lying flat on her back in the galley.

"I'll defer to you, the ER doc, since I'm retired," he says after quick introductions.

The large, Russian-speaking woman is lying on her back sweating profusely. A friend is trying to translate with inadequate results.

"She feels bad," says the friend.

"Why?" I ask.

"She feels really bad," replies the friend.

The other doc hands me a blood-pressure cuff, and I find that the woman's blood pressure is sky high. I quickly listen to the woman's chest, heart, and abdomen; nothing seems amiss other than the blood pressure.

"She forgot to take her pills," says the friend. Bingo, we start getting somewhere. The friend pulls out a bag of medications in boxes and jars labeled in Russian. But I can tell enough from the generic names that one is a blood pressure pill and another is a benzodiazepine for anxiety.

"She has blood pressure problems?" I ask.

"Yes," says the friend, without confirming with the patient.

"She has anxiety?" I ask.

"Yes," says the friend.

"Any pain here or here?" I ask, point to the woman's chest and abdomen.

The friend says something in Russian to the patient, and then turns to me.

"No," she says.

"If she forgot to take her meds, she's probably having symptoms from high blood pressure and anxiety," I say to the internist. "Without chest pain, I would say we give her a dose of both medications and see how she does. We can give her an aspirin, too," I say. The retired doc agrees. The aspirin will help prevent heart damage if the patient is having a heart attack.

I've seen many patients in two decades of practicing emergency medicine. One of the first things I teach medical students and residents is that when you walk in to greet a patient, you immediately have to decide if this is a life-threatening emergency that needs immediate response, or an urgent situation that can't take a measured response. Part of this come from the first twenty seconds after you walk into a room and determine, without much data, how much distress a patient is in, by gathering just basic information like pulse, skin color and temperature, and respiratory rate. This woman was not in distress, so I felt okay watching and waiting.

The woman rests in the galley after taking her blood pressure and anxiety medicines. She feels better quickly and returns to her seat.

"Call if you need me again," I say to the flight attendant.

I go back to my seat, pull my hood over my head, insert foam ear plugs, and pull the eyeshade on. I need sleep.

On a surf trip to Sayulita, Mexico, I had to pull a swimmer from the water who was stuck in the undertow and unable to swim back in. He was panicking and splashing wildly—probably more hazardous activity than being caught in the undertow. I paddled up to him and had him hold onto the back of my stand-up paddle surfboard. I paddled him in.

Once, riding my mountain bike in the Post Canyon Trail near my house, I came across a man who was lying in the trail, unconscious. He'd crashed, hit his head, and was knocked out. I called 911, and of course, got a dispatcher I knew. She sent firefighters from the fire department, all of whom I also knew. The man woke up and was safely transported to the hospital to see the ER doc, also a friend. My ride was interrupted by forty-five minutes—no worry.

This is really in my blood, this rescuing business. It likely stems from watching Roy DeSoto and John Gage on the TV series *Emergency!* as a kid.

People occasionally ask me if I get worried about being sued. Lawsuits are something doctors think about constantly. We are, by nature, interested in helping people. Fortunately, a doc has never been sued for an airline emergency, and in America we have a Good Samaritan law that helps prevent lawsuits for airline emergencies. But laws don't necessarily prevent people from attempting to sue.

And Good Samaritan laws are somewhat tricky, since they vary by state or province in North America. Some laws are invalidated if you receive compensation—even a free T-shirt and free entrance to a music festival in exchange for working at a first-aid booth can be seen as compensation. Also, even if one has a duty to act, such as a volunteer firefighter who commits to responding to an incident, he or she may not be covered under a Good Samaritan law.

Fortunately, in Oregon, our Good Samaritan law covers doctors anywhere medicine is not usually practiced. In Washington, where we respond occasionally, the law covers first responders, who can make up to $500 for reimbursement for expenses like gas or broken equipment.

I'm also covered by Hood River County and Oregon State Office of Emergency Management, since we respond under the authority of the sheriff, and by the State of Oregon Office of Emergency Management.

I'm not too worried, though, because I've always used a system that has proven to be a good guide for my career: Practice good medicine, err on the side of caution with medical decisions, communicate, and be kind and compassionate.

The Warren Creek rescue of the couple wasn't a dramatic rescue. In fact, our main role in it was to give the couple directions via phone and then escort them down the trail. We tend to go to Warren Creek once a year, usually in the spring. Same story: hikers ascend the two steep trails (Defiance or Starvation Creek), reach snow near the top, lose the trail on the way down, hike straight down the fall line, and end up in Warren Creek Canyon stymied by thick brush and the cliff.

We went after a solo hiker in Warren Creek Canyon once. The call came in when I was working in the emergency department, deep in flu season, during my once-a-week, twenty-four-hour shift at an inner-city hospital. When the page came to my cell phone, I was momentarily transported to my other world far from the city and the hospital. Lost hiker. Alone. Mount Defiance.

I call Penny Hunting, the callout coordinator for this rescue.

"Can't go. At work." I say.

"All day, all night?" says Penny.

"Yep."

"We're sending Pricher with a crew out tonight, but I need to line up a few people for tomorrow's search."

"I can stop by on my way home. I can be at the trailhead at 8:30 a.m. But I don't have much gear."

Penny calls later and I make arrangements to meet two members of our team at the trailhead. I'll finish my twenty-four-hour shift at 7:00 a.m., grab coffee and breakfast at the Starbucks down the street, and drive an hour to the trailhead. I have the bare essentials in my car: a pack, headlamp, water bottle, a few granola bars, radio, raincoat, and my running clothes. My SAR ready pack is at home in the garage.

When I arrive at the trailhead, Todd Wells and Gavin Vanderpool have already set out up the Defiance Trail. The night before, Jeff Pricher had hiked up to around 3,000 feet but had no luck finding the guy. Mark Flaming is about an hour from arriving at the trailhead. I check in with the deputy at the staging area, and head up the Starvation Ridge trail in my running clothes. Because I'm solo and without much gear, I am just assigned to cover the lower trail. The two trails—Defiance and Starvation—intersect at 4,000 feet and 5 miles due south of the trailhead.

It's May, so snow still lingers on the peak. To stay warm, I jog up the trail. The soggy day, foggy and drizzly, is punctuated by the soggy soil and damp groundcover. Where the snow has melted, the trail is mud. The flora is soaked with dew, fog, and rain so that whenever I brush against a vine maple, Oregon grape, or broadleaf fern, I get a spritzing of mist.

Two hours later I reach snow. I'm only able to hike another thirty minutes, my running shoes luckily staying atop the snowpack. I follow the trail and a few sets of track that look to be a few days old. I reach a plateau with 3 feet of snow. I can't go any farther with running gear; I need boots and winter pants. Mark is forty-five minutes behind me heading up same trail, and he can keep going.

In addition, I have to turn back because I have a few commitments today. I have to give a 1:00 p.m. lecture to fifty wildland firefighters. My drop-dead turn-around time on Starvation Plateau is 11:00 a.m. because the hike down will take an hour. Since I have enough time to do some good, I scour the three-acre section of the plateau. Todd and Gavin are making their way up the Defiance Trail, covering the other exit. The only other way the guy could go was down the massive gully canyon in between Starvation Ridge and Mount Defiance trail: Warren Creek.

Which is, of course, where he is.

I make it back home, with time to spare. I take a hot shower, grab food on the run, give the lecture, and then meet up with my daughters after school.

The guy is found at dusk, I later hear. The fog lifted, so Joe Wampler was able to get in the search plane and located the guy in Warren Creek, deep in the thick, almost impassible brush. Todd and Gavin had already come down and Mark also had to go to work. Kevin Schlagel showed up late to the trailhead, about noon, and had to hike up to get the guy. They made it out at dusk because Kevin had found an old logging road that, although clogged with twenty-year-old trees, at least had the makings of a rudimentary trail that allowed an exit from the Warren Creek Drainage.

Thus, when we went back up after the missing couple, I remembered the old logging road exit from Warren Creek.

Every once in a while I feel a bit overcommitted. I have my new three-day-a-week job working in the clinic. I cover a few ER shifts a month. I have another job working ten shifts a season at the ski resort. I write books and magazine articles, and I lecture on wilderness and adventure travel medicine at medical conferences and adventure travel medical seminars. I work as an expert witness for outdoor cases. I volunteer in my daughters' school, at soccer, and of course with mountain rescue. And I tend to be obsessed about adventure sports: mountain biking, mountain running, backcountry skiing, ski mountaineering, snowboarding, road cycling, cyclocross racing, windsurfing turned kitesurfing, stand-up paddling, and occasionally outrigger canoe paddling. Usually, I do one sport a day, often two sports a day, along with at least one three-hour bike ride and one 10-mile run per week. After work I go kitesurfing on the river or spin a hot lap mountain biking in Post Canyon, the single-track trail network that is 2 miles from my house.

If I have to give up anything, I think I'll start working less and perhaps consolidating my life into fewer sports.

But I won't give up the rescuing, no matter how demanding it is. Mountain rescue volunteering is part of who I am, blending my career in medicine and my deep passion for the outdoors. In fact, my third love, writing, brings the three most important aspects of who I am as person together in these words.

I nearly died on the mountain. But I was not about to—I couldn't—give up either my love for the mountain or my love for mountain rescue.

So I'd accomplished two milestones in my rehabilitation: I'd returned to skiing with my family and I'd returned to mountain rescue.

Little did I know we were about to be called on another rescue. We again would hike halfway up Mount Defiance. We again would push through thick, tangled underbrush in the canyons. We again would rely on an old, decommissioned overgrown logging road to save someone.

Only the next rescue would send a chill up my spine: this time, it would be for a lost family.

CHAPTER TEN

Family Goes Deep, Falls Deeper

"There's a three-year-old. And they've been out all day," says Penn.

"What?" I ask incredulously.

"Yes, a family of four, and they've got a three-year-old."

At 9:30 p.m., I am already hunkered in for the night, just dozing off. I have patients to see the next day in the clinic, so when I hear the text buzz on my phone, I want to roll over and go back to sleep. Let the younger guys handle it, I think. I'm swamped with my daughters' school, soccer coaching, hospital duties, and a magazine story deadline.

Then, seconds later, I just can't help myself. I call Penny Hunting, the mission callout coordinator, and she says the words that make every parent shiver. Lost child. A family lost, especially a young child, is enough to jack me into high gear. My family, my two daughters Skylar and Avrie, are the most precious aspect of my varied and busy life.

On this dark, blustery night, four people are stuck deep in Wygant Creek Canyon.

The foursome had left their car that morning, trudged up a steep, windy trail to the top of Mitchell Point, and then kept going, toward the top of Mount Defiance. They were a young couple and their two kids, three and five years old. They got pretty far up an old decommissioned road or mountain bike trail or deer path when they hit two feet of dense, compacted snow, which was strewn with leaves, tree limbs, moss, lichen, and dirt from the blustery storms that had exploded through the thick Douglas fir forests that spring. They left nary a footprint in the hard, dirty snow. When the couple turned around to descend, they started walking straight down the fall line, without a second thought. Instantly, they became lost: everywhere they looked, the forest appeared the same. After several hours of hiking through thick brush, they could not find the trail. They walked directly down into the thickly tangled, super-steep void in between two ridges, and got stuck.

By nightfall, they were exhausted and stuck deep in a dense canyon with no real exit but to go back up. Even if retreating back up the steep, brush-covered slope was an option, finding their trail would be extremely difficult at night, on snow, with kids, without a map and compass and GPS. So they did the right thing: called 911 and stayed put.

"A three-year-old?" I clarify incredulously.

"Yup," Penny says. "And a five-year-old."

I drag myself out of bed. I grumble to myself, *What is the couple doing with these young kids on a mountainside anyway?* Yet deep down, I know the answer: taking my daughters into the outdoors is one of the most important aspects of my parenting life. In fact, I wrote a book called *Introducing Your Kids to the Outdoors* when my kids were quite young. I've taken them canoeing, backpacking, climbing, skiing, and biking since they were old enough to walk. They have surfed in Mexico, skied in Chile, and run through Europe.

And that is exactly why I leave the comfort of my warm bed to head into the bitter, black mountain wilderness: to save a family.

Fellow Crag Rats Jeff Pricher and John Inglis meet me at the Hood River County public works yard. John fires up the big motor in our truck, and we head down the freeway. On the way, I call the woman on her cell to ascertain their elevation is at 2,000 feet, based on the man's watch altimeter. "Stay put," I tell her. "No one's hurt?" I confirm. Jeff has the GPS coordinates from then-Sheriff Joe Wampler, who had flown over the canyon in the Piper Cub at dusk, sighted the family, and marked the location.

We set out on foot from Mitchell Creek Rest Area about 11:00 p.m., under a pitch-black sky and thick canopy of big-leaf maple, Douglas fir, and western red cedar. We briskly trot up the trail, but then slow as the trail becomes thick with brush and steepens. We make it up to the

2,400-foot elevation. After nearly two hours, we reach the spot where we need to leave the well-trodden trail and enter the thick, tangled brush of the canyon. Jeff marks the trail by tying bright yellow surveyor's tape on a tree limb.

Jeff and I take a time out.

"It's pretty thick brush," he says, wondering if it's too dangerous to duck off trail into Wygant Creek. "Maybe we should wait until morning?" It is dark, cold, and well past midnight. We become chilled instantly from a west wind and cooling air. Judging by the elevation, the GPS coordinates, and the condition of the off-trail terrain—which is thick with tangled brambles, downed logs, mud, and steepness—we estimate we are still an hour from the group.

"Let's hike for an hour. If we don't find them, we'll turn back," I suggest.

"Good plan," he says. "I'll mark the trail."

Heading off trail is dangerous, risky. But we decide to keep going because of the young kids. It is treacherous: bushwhacking through dense twists of vine maple, stepping over gargantuan, blown-down old-growth Douglas fir, clambering over slippery moss-covered basalt boulders, and traversing a hillside so steep we occasionally balance by resting a hand on the uphill slope while standing erect. While in the lead, Jeff flags the trail by tying surveyor's tape on vine maple and Douglas fir branches every 20 feet so we can retrace our path should we need to. Taking a sweep position, I periodically peer back to check the flagging: I can barely see the striped yellow-and-black strips flickering in the darkness, even with my high-power headlamp. The non-reflective tape seems to wiggle behind a branch out of sight, as if it were hiding behind the corner of a house in a game of hide and seek.

The route back out will be equally dangerous, I think.

As parents, we all ruminate, or some would say obsess, about safety when navigating the dynamics of a family. Good intentions sometimes go awry. Calculated risks are a key part of outdoor adventure, and of experiencing life beyond the "zone of safety": school, home, community, and friends. But, how do you find your family's equilibrium?

On that steep mountainside in the middle of a pitch-black night, I find myself contemplating this family and my own. As an emergency and mountain rescue doctor, I have had many chances to help families, peer into their lives, and provide them with a measure of comfort. This night I found myself trying to save a family from immediate harm when my own family had been recently rocked by my near-death accident.

Is taking risks with kids really all that important?

Yes, indeed.

Kids benefit in myriad ways from taking risks in the outdoors, which can be easily extrapolated to risk in all aspects of childhood. The obvious benefits are that the air is clean, the fun is wholesome, and the exercise is good for mental and physical health. It's also a healthy complement to the classroom: Kids will sleep better and perform better at school, and they learn a tremendous amount of life skills from outdoors recreation, sports, adventure travel, and wilderness exploration.

Kids benefit cognitively from taking risks, as well. They gain self-confidence, independence, and self-reliance. They gain skills in decision-making, leadership, and responsibility. In a world of social media, video games, and omnipresent tablets and smart phones, this is even more important. Taking outdoor risks helps foster respect and value for varied environments, teaches cultural heritage, and gives first-hand knowledge of the natural world. Outdoor adventures foster problem-solving in uncontrolled conditions and, hopefully, lifelong fitness.

In short, it builds character and smart, strong, physically and mentally healthy kids.

This applies to every facet of childhood. Kids need to take risks, with varying levels of supervision of course, in making new friends, trying new activities, attempting an art project, learning a musical instrument or language, picking out fashion, working at their first job, taking a difficult class at school, and, gulp, driving a car!

Lenore Skenazy spearheaded a movement that started with a 2008 story she wrote for the *New York Sun* titled "Why I Let My 9-Year-Old Ride the Subway Alone" and culminated in her bestselling book *Free Range Kids: How to Raise Safe, Self-Reliant Children (Without Going Nuts with Worry)*. She was once labeled "America's Worst Mom" by today's "helicopter parents," those constantly hovering and trying, often in vain, to remove all risks for their children. But we know now that Skenazy was spot on. Skenazy points out in her writings that our children are not constantly in danger, or the danger is often overstated by parents. Kids don't, in fact, need constant supervision. Au contraire, they need to take risks. When kids don't take risks, they don't develop independence, problem-solving skills, and passion to succeed. They actually become averse to exploration. With overcautious parents, kids may come to believe that fear is unfounded or exaggerated. In other words, if they don't learn how to fall and get back up, they can be less safe later in life.

Dr. Peter Gray, psychologist at Boston College and author of *Free to Learn: Why Unleashing the Instinct to Play Will Make Our Children Happier, More Self-Reliant, and Better Students for Life*, points out than when sheltered kids from risk-averse "helicopter" parents head to college, they have difficulty in that they expect someone else to solve their problems. "Less resilient and needy students have shaped the landscape for faculty in that they are expected to do more handholding, lower their academic standards and not challenge students too much," he writes. Young people who don't learn to solve their own problems are unable to take responsibility for challenges; they still expect someone else to solve their problems.

He puts the concept in a capsule: "Growth is achieved by striking the right balance between support and challenge. We need to reset the balance point."

Angela Lee Duckworth has made this concept particularly timely with the publication of *Grit: The Power of Passion and Perseverance*.

I have spent much time teaching my kids safety with regard to biking, canoeing, skiing, and international travel. Yet when people hear that my kids, from their earliest days, have skied in the Andes, snorkeled in the South Pacific, volunteered in poverty-riddled Haiti, and surfed in Mexico, I still get the question: "Isn't it dangerous?"

The quick answer is generally, no. Foul weather, injury from a fall, encountering a sea creature, and other adventure maladies can be offset by safety-conscious parents, who, of course, can strike a balance.

Give them the tools. Balance supervision with exploration. Foster independence with safety. Let them take risks that are appropriate for their age and their community. The tools are the same ones I discussed in Part I of this book: proper training and education, regular practice, starting safe and building to more complex adventures, using proper equipment, and employing good judgment. But these tools need to be tailored to kids.

When my kids were quite young, I bought a canoe from a nurse at work. It was a used red plastic Coleman 16-footer, originally sold at Costco for $400. It was indestructible! I lugged it around on my twenty-year-old gray Chevy Suburban affectionately called "the gorilla." We paddled the canoe extensively one summer, in the Columbia River a few miles from home to remote wilderness lakes. Once we took an overnight canoe-camping trip up the John Day River to a boat-in-only campground.

When I first got the canoe, I mandated life jackets. Then I realized that adults don't often use life jackets and that they are cumbersome to paddle with, especially in calm water. So, do I force my kids to wear them in completely flat, calm water, paddling 200 feet from shore?

A common myth when boating in cold water is that if one falls in, one will succumb to hypothermia instantly. The Columbia River ranges from a low of 45 degrees Fahrenheit in winter to over 70 degrees in the summer. But when people fall in, they don't get hypothermic instantly. In fact, they don't die from hypothermia very often.

The first big key for survival is to understand the cold-water gasp reflex. In cold water, you have a thirty- to sixty-second gasp reflex that, if you are aware of it, will pass while treading water. But if you are unaware, you can gasp, choke, inhale water, and drown. This is why people die instantly when they fall overboard: not because they freeze, but because they panic. If you're submersed, the gasp reflex is more dangerous because you need to hold your breath while the reflex is trying to make you gasp.

Then, after managing the first minute in cold water, say 50 degrees Fahrenheit, you have twenty to thirty minutes of usable energy before you become exhausted. In cold water, people die usually by drowning from exhaustion at this stage rather than hypothermia. This is why PFDs are so important, because they allow you to save your energy while keeping your head out of water when you are exhausted, not because you are cold. PFDs or not, you have a half hour to swim to your boat or to shore until you're exhausted. Then, at that point, the main goal is to keep your head out of water and minimize heat loss. The heat-escape-lessening position is the best way to do this. If wearing a PFD, you pull your arms and legs into a tight ball. If no PFD, you assume the face-down survival float. Interestingly, swimming causes one to both expend energy *and* lose heat because of the circulating cold water around clothes and skin. So if you are going to swim, do so immediately.

Then you wait for help. After energy is expended, you can last up to one to two hours until hypothermia sets in, as long as you can keep your head above water. This is why PFDs are important. You can last longer wearing a neoprene wetsuit, which varies from a burly 7-millimeter-thick survival suit with booties, gloves, and a hood to a thin 1- to 2-millimeter summer shirt. A word of caution: if it's not neoprene, it probably won't help keep you warm in cold water, even though there are lots of new water-sport fabrics out now.

So, knowing this survival information, I didn't want to take out the canoe with no training on survival. So one rainy early-fall morning I told my kids to put on their swimsuits so we could swim at the sports club.

"Put your suit on at home and wear your clothes over your suit," I said.

"Why? We always change at the sports club locker rooms," one of my daughters asked, head cocked quizzically to the side.

"I think the locker rooms are closed," I fibbed. "And wear your old shoes."

"Why?" again quizzical stare.

"There is problem with the pool," I said to a confused stare.

Walking across the edge of the pool to the locker rooms, I abruptly and suddenly pushed both my kids into the pool, fully clothed. They gasped and sputtered until I yanked them out of the pool. Their expressions of surprise and fear turned to scowls, and then erupted into laughter.

We then proceeded to jump, fully clothed and shoed, into the pool repeatedly over the next hour, accompanied by a great many laughs and giggles. They learned quickly that the first step was to remove heavy, water-logged shoes. Skylar found that nylon pants could be removed then inflated with an air bubble to float. Avrie learned that denim jeans soak up water, weigh you down, and become unruly to remove.

Thus, my simple exercise—teach them, then practice, then gain experience—gave them the tools for water survival. Over the following ten years, my daughters passed through their teenage years in our community, which is one of the world centers for windsurfing, kiteboarding, and stand-up paddling. Now, after a good many years teaching them to swim and survive in water, I let my kids head into the Columbia River, which is a mile wide and flows up to 6 miles per hour in the channel *without constantly wearing a life jacket*, depending on the situation. My daughter learned to kitesurf with a PFD, but when she could show me she could self-rescue, she stopped wearing one. My kids know the appropriate times to wear a PFD and know how to swim without one.

I find a similar decision-making problem with helmets. My girls and I wear one skiing, climbing, and cycling; but not when kitesurfing or surfing. Again, it is a balance: I ask myself about the likelihood of a head injury versus the difficulty of wearing a helmet. A helmet can hamper peripheral vision and hearing, be cumbersome to use, foster reliance on a safety device, and, theoretically, increase one's risk tolerance. If we really were staunch proponents of wearing a helmets to maximize safety and minimize injuries, we'd be wearing one in our cars—the most likely cause of head injury in kids and the cause of the highest lifetime risk of head injuries.

We never did capsize that summer. But we sure had fun.

After a half-hour of bushwhacking off trail, we reach a ridge above Wygant Creek, which puts us very close by GPS. In a half-hour we have traversed barely a thousand yards, a distance most people unencumbered can walk in five minutes. I blow my whistle and we pause, listening. We hear a faint chirp: a cry from the lost family.

Clambering down the mountainside, we bushwhack down to the 2,000-foot elevation contour. The grade is steep, making for very slow going, like walking down a staircase. We hold on to vine maple branches to scramble down some sections. After nearly every step we pause to climb over a boulder, forge through brambles, step over a log, or clomp through mud.

About 2:30 a.m., we find the foursome. The three-year-old is strapped in a backpack child carrier, asleep on the hillside. The five-year-old is in mom's arms.

"We have been holding back our supplies of food and water," says the man.

"Good work," I nod. "Go ahead now: eat and drink a little. We have a bit of a hike out. Do you have lights?"

"Yes," says the man. He pulls out their headlamps, which they had turned off to conserve batteries. I see the waves of relief pass over them, especially the mom clutching the five-year-old. The search is only part one of the mission, though. Now we have to extricate them.

Jeff rallies us immediately, since he and I both are due at work at 8:00 a.m. I can't help admiring this couple for taking their kids on such a burly climb. They set the stage for outdoor adventure. Unfortunately, they had probably picked a trail slightly too strenuous, and, of course, lost their way when descending. I too had dragged my kids out at a young age. My youngest, Skylar, first adventured up Eagle Creek Trail in the Columbia Gorge National Scenic Area when she was six months old, happily buckled in a child carrier backpack, munching on snacks or sucking on a bottle up the trail.

Tonight, after a bit of food and water, we climb out by hiking and crawling back up to the 2,500-foot elevation. It's 500 vertical feet, but takes an hour. The woman is now carrying the child-carrier backpack and the man carries the older child in his arms. John and I support them from behind should they fall over backward. Jeff leads the charge up the hill. When we reach 2,500 feet, we find our flagged trail and start following it back to the main trail. But we still can't walk in a straight line: we scramble over downed trees, boulders, and dirt, and plow through thick brambles and brush. At 1,600 feet, just as the sky starts glowing yellow, we arrive back at the Wygant Trail.

We take a few minutes to rest, then hike down the trail at dawn, with our headlamps off. The sun is about to pop up, so the sky is lightening. Both the coming daylight and the trail give us a sense of security. The couple is visibly relieved, joyous, and chatty as we hike down thick layers of soft and spongy forest duff. We rescuers are not talking: We are sleep-deprived and trying to make it to work on time.

Then, Jeff and I notice the couple stumbling. Jeff asks the couple if we can carry the two kids. No way, is the general sentiment. I understand the reluctance of letting your child go in a dangerous situation. It would be like being in a shipwreck, and letting your child go in someone else's lifeboat. Jeff and I are afraid that they will stumble and hit the ground with kids in tow. Then we might have a medical evacuation on our hands. After I trade concerned looks with Jeff, we level with the parents.

"Let us take these two, just for a few minutes," says Jeff. "We do this all the time; we know the trail. He's a doctor, I'm a paramedic. We see you stumbling."

"You're tired, hungry, and thirsty, and you've been out all night. I've got two young girls too, so I understand you want to carry your son. But for his safety and yours, I think you should let us carry the little guys for a while. You're going to fall and hurt your child."

"Come on, they know what they are doing," says the mom as she acquiesces. I pass my backpack to John and strap on the child-carrier backpack with the sleeping child; Jeff has the more difficult job of carrying the older child.

I've been there, too: turning over my kids to someone I need to trust. Once on a ski trip in Nelson, British Columbia, Avrie careened down a slope and hit her mouth with her ski pole. She crashed suddenly, ejected from both skis. Her helmet flew off and she face-planted into the slope. I thought she broke a tooth. She was oozing blood from her lip. She had a small but substantial cut in the corner of her mouth. I took her down to the ski patrol first-aid room, retrieved a suture kit from my car, and asked the patroller if I could sew her lip with his help.

"No problem, mate," he replied in a cheery Canadian accent. I put a single suture in her lip laceration with the help of the patroller, and then we went back to Nelson where we were staying at the home of our friends.

At 10:00 p.m., Avrie's neck was slightly swollen. I was almost certain there was nothing wrong, but I didn't want to be my own family's doctor, especially in a possible emergency. I took Avrie up to the emergency room. I wanted to make sure there was no blood clot that might block her airway.

The doctor was compassionate and understanding.

"Your daughter's fine. But I see why you brought her in, to make sure she has no airway compromise. I'm glad you brought her in."

After an hour of descending Wygant Trail, I decide it's a trail I'll never need to hike again. Not all that scenic. No big views. No specular waterfalls. No bubbling brook. Once down, all we have left is an easy, flat, half-mile walk on an old roadbed, the one that serviced the Bonneville Dam power lines. The woman insists on tending to her child in the backpack, which is still strapped to my back, which transforms a sleeping kid to a crying one. Then the man insists on changing a diaper, about fifteen minutes from the car. The two kids jolt awake, look startled, and then start bawling.

We take a break and wait for the couple to tend to their kids, right there in the middle of the power-line clearcut, a fifteen-minute hike from the awaiting deputy. Two sleeping kids became two crying kids in three seconds.

I can only smile: I've been there.

"Good work," I tell the couple. "You got them back safely."

Chapter Eleven

Resilience

For once, we get a callout to the Columbia Gorge in the morning. It's not night. There's no storm. It's not an hour's drive up the mountain. But conditions are not perfect: light rain showers are percolating in the canopy intermittently.

Unresponsive elderly man found down, Herman Creek, mile 5 reads the callout text on a drizzly, gray summer morning. We don't just go after families. Sometimes we get calls for those who are adventuring later in life. And these lost or injured hikers tend to be some of the most resilient. They tend to be prepared, smart, and logical. And they are survivors.

Earlier that day, far up Herman Creek Trail near Indian Mountain, a man was found down in the middle of the trail, unconscious. That's about all we know.

I jump in my truck and speed to the trailhead, where I meet a deputy and Crag Rat Jeff Pricher. His résumé includes Cascade Locks fire chief, paramedic, and wildland firefighter. He's a highly skilled wilderness responder. He and I are second to respond; a crew from Cascade Locks Fire Department has already started up the trail.

Jeff and I set off at a trot. This is no easy task considering it's a 5-mile climb uphill, and we are carrying heavy advanced life-support gear in addition to our personal gear. Jeff has a full advanced life support pack: airway equipment, intravenous fluids, and medications for heart attacks. I've got the bare essentials: equipment to intubate a person not breathing (putting a tube into their trachea), medications for a life-threatening allergic reaction or diabetic reaction, and wound supplies and pain medicine for major trauma.

At a fast clip, it's still well over an hour to our destination.

We find a man lying on the ground attended by a few volunteer firefighters who had just arrived with a litter. They are wrapping him in a blanket and about to lift him onto a wheeled stretcher.

"Hey, Doc. Hey, Chief," says one of the firefighters.

"What the story?" I ask.

"Found down. Unconscious." Jeff and I quickly team up to complete a quick exam of the patient. First, we attend to vital life functions following the ABCED mnemonic: airway, breathing, circulation, exposure, and disability.

His airway is clear and he's breathing, but barely. He's moving air in and out of his lungs in shallow sporadic breaths at five per minute, about half the normal rate. For circulation: his pulse is 50 and skin color is pink, so that's a clue he's able to pump blood and deliver oxygen to vital tissues—at least, for now. Exposure is a review of potential environmental stressors: cold and wet, the man is clearly hypothermic but we don't bother taking the actual temperature. Cascade Locks Firefighters are doing a fine job of initiating a hypothermia wrap with a blanket and tarp. Disability means neurologic exam: the man is obtunded, meaning unconscious and unresponsive.

So the differential diagnosis, the list of all possibilities that could have caused this, is lengthy: head injury, heart attack, stroke, allergic reaction, endocrine abnormality like low thyroid or diabetic reaction like too-low blood sugar, metabolic disorder, electrolyte disorder like low sodium or high potassium, dementia, overdose from drugs, overdose from toxic plants, or hypothermia. The list is so long, but doesn't really matter too much at this point. We're 5 miles up a trail; we need to get him down the trail before he stops breathing and his heart rate drops any lower. If we have to start cardiopulmonary resuscitation, we'll have an extremely difficult time. We can quickly try to identify the few things that might be treatable in the field.

While we gently place the man in the litter, Jeff uses a portable glucometer to check blood sugar: it's undetectable, meaning it's critically low. Normal blood sugar runs 60 to 100 milligrams of glucose per deciliter of blood. Sugar is vital to provide fuel to the brain. If the brain doesn't get enough sugar, it stops functioning. When blood sugar begins to dip below 50, people get agitated, dizzy, and light-headed—we've all been there. When it drops below 25, they become confused. When it approaches 10 or less, they lose consciousness. So, we've got the primary field diagnoses of hypoglycemia and hypothermia.

While I help the firefighters balance the litter, Jeff puts in an IV and shoves in an ampule of D50 (50 grams of dextrose in 100 milliliters of saline): a 170-calorie jolt of straight sugar. It's the only ampule he has. The guy moans a bit and arouses just slightly. But he does not wake up. We have to get down the trail.

It's rare that we find someone critically ill in mountain rescue. People are usually stable because it takes us so long to reach patients—the summons for help, the gathering of our gear, the mustering of our crew, the drive to the trailhead, the hike up the trail—that it's rare that we render lifesaving medications when someone is on the brink of death.

One of the firefighters astutely thinks to check the man's backpack for clues like medications. Nothing turns up, but I make an observation when I see the contents of the pack: the guy was prepared with a rain jacket, food, and water.

We start the long, two-hour extrication down the trail. Jeff calls SAR base.

"Can you have someone down there head up the trail with more D50?" More sugar—good thinking. An ambulance from Cascade Locks Fire Department is at the trailhead; they send a runner up with the medication. Halfway down we meet the runner, so Jeff injects more D50. The man moans again, and then falls back unconscious. Still breathing. Still has a pulse.

It takes two hours to get down.

Once down, we quickly transfer the man into an awaiting helicopter parked at the Herman Creek Trailhead. The man's core body temperature is 83.7 degrees. He has severe, life-threatening hypothermia, and his blood sugar is unreadable on the glucometer. He may not have survived a second night.

As readers know by now, many of those we rescue are prepared, and just have an accident. And it's not just families and athletes. Sometimes we search for and rescue folks who are exploring, exercising, and adventuring later in life. We've had our share of elderly patients, and, to my surprise, these are some of the most resilient. This man turned out to be having the first onset of a pituitary gland tumor. It was causing over-suppression of the hormones made in the thyroid and adrenal glands, which control metabolic functions throughout the body. The first presentation just happened to occur when he was out hiking.

He was not the first elderly gent or lady we've gone after, and would not be the last.

On the same trail a few months later, we rescue a seventy-year-old who was hiking, and then slipped and fell down a rocky scree field a half-mile up the trail, right where the spring dumps water on the trail year-round. His wife had scrambled down to help and got stuck too. We run up the trail, walk down the scree field, and find the man unable to walk. Maybe a hip fracture? Maybe a pelvis fracture? Maybe just banged up?

Meredith and Ron set up a basic rope belay for safety: this is a low-angle—about 45 degrees—extrication over a scree field about 50 feet below the trail. If he could walk, the couple might have been able to scramble on all fours back up to the trail. Two Cascade Locks firefighters, Mark Wiltz, and I package the patient in the litter. We have to balance the litter on the rocks and gently lift the man into it. Meredith and Ron start pulling on the rope as we carry him up the hill. Back to the trail, we attach the wheel to the bottom of the litter and head a mile down the trail. The ambulance transports the couple to the hospital. I later find out the hip is not fractured, just bruised badly.

The next day I realize we'd sent our custom backboard with the patient to the hospital. It's especially crafted to fit into the mountain rescue stretcher. So, that next weekend, I stop by American Medical Response ambulance headquarters in Portland on my way to my daughter's soccer game, bang on the door, and retrieve the backboard. More than two hundred backboards are lined up against a wall, from multiple first responder agencies in the Portland metropolis: fire departments, forest service units, ski patrols, lifeguards. The two hundred backboards are colored plastic, lined up according to agency, in a kaleidoscope of blues, greens, reds, yellows, and oranges. Ours stands out: it's the only one that's wood.

On the same trail, a few months later, a crew of us responds to an uninjured sixty-five-year-old woman who fell off the trail and landed on a ledge down a 50-foot slope, mired in poison oak. Jay Sherrerd goes over the edge on a rope, ties in the patient, and then scrambles up the steep incline while we drag him and the patient up the embankment. Note to team: wear long sleeve shirts, long pants, and gloves: poison oak is everywhere.

On rarely used Wygant Trail, the same one where we rescued the family of four, we once went after a seventy-year-old man who'd been hiking with a gaggle of his seventy-year-old compadres. During the hike, a boulder randomly peeled off a steep scree field and struck the man in the chest. It could have happened to anyone. We ran up the trail with Cascade Locks Fire Department and found the patient in the scree field with his friends. The man was calm, collected, and almost cheery. And, like many of the patients we find in the back country, he was very thankful. When I checked his chest I ran through the short list: Collapsed lung? Fractured ribs? Broken collar bone? Spleen or liver laceration? Not much we could do but haul him out—across a scree field, down a steep section of the trail, and out the thick overgrown trail. It took a dozen rescuers. It turned out that he had no major injuries, but was just pretty banged up.

Wes Baumann and I respond once to a sixty-three-year-old hiker who'd taken a day jaunt up Tanner Creek and was reported missing by her spouse. We get the call at 1:00 a.m. but don't know exactly where to search. Her car was found at Tanner Creek Trailhead, so at first light, Joe Wampler spots her in the airplane. She is walking back to the trailhead where her car is parked. Wes starts up the trail and finds the woman hiking down the trail. He reports she is in good spirits, uninjured, and "quite chatty," which is typical because people are relieved to be rescued. Cell phone, nope, doesn't have one. Backpack with food and water, yup, always. She wasn't really rescued. She lost her way, retraced her steps, found shelter under a log after dark, and hunkered in for the night. She woke the next morning, tired and hungry, and hiked out.

We have gone after lost elderly mushroom pickers more than once. A week after the Tanner Creek search we are called to assist a Skamania County, Washington, search for a missing ninety-year-old woman. She and her family were picking mushrooms in the fall to sell to Portland's high-end gourmet restaurants. She is slightly deaf. She is from one of the Pacific Islands and does not speak English. A big crew responds: Wind River Search and Rescue, a pair of equine rescuers, some human trackers, a 4x4 unit from a county to the north, and many ground teams. A Coast Guard helicopter comes in from Astoria, 200 miles away. (We are a bit shy on helicopter support. We rely on the Charlie Company 7th battalion 158th Aviation Regiment from the Army National Guard in Salem for Oregon searches or the Coast Guard in Astoria in Washington, even though for the latter we are 200 miles inland. A few times we've had the Navy helicopter from Whidbey Island up near Seattle come down. The MAST, Military Assistance to Safety and Traffic, in Yakima, Washington, sent helicopters to wars in Iraq and Afghanistan. The 304th Air Rescue Squadron from the Air Force Reserve lost their helicopters to the same wars.)

I am paired with a crew from South Puget Sound search and rescue to cover an area of heavily wooded section near search base. The trails are muddy and the sky is clear but cool. At one point I step across a dirt patch only to sink past my boot top in mud. After a morning of searching, I head home.

Later that night, I get word that the search is called off; the woman has been found by family members in a depression in the earth where she was covered by leaves and branches to stay warm. A quarter-mile from search base. Hundreds of rescuers walked right by her for three days.

Most recently, we were called to what would be a three-day search for a missing couple at North Lake. The man and his wife went off on a short hike around the lake; halfway through the hike, they walked off trail to a viewpoint. The view was spectacular, but when they hiked back to the trail, they went the wrong way and became lost. Three days we searched. No luck. Rescuers from Crag Rats, Pacific Northwest Search and Rescue ground team based in Portland, the Hood River Fire Department volunteer search and rescue team, the Mountain Wave search and rescue radio communications team, and many others. No luck.

I searched one of the three days with Todd Hanna, Penny Hunting, and Joe McCulloch. Our assignment was to hike a section of forest, using a grid pattern, between two old logging roads. The forest hike was not exactly a hike: it was bushwhacking. The forest was thick with trees; the understory was thick with vine maple, ferns, and miscellaneous shrubs; and downed logs and uneven ground made the search slow. We searched our areas by noon and headed home, back to family, household duties, work.

On day three, after two nights in the rugged backcountry, the couple walked out to North Lake, found some campers, borrowed a phone, and called in. No injury. Just tired, hungry, and thirsty. They later sent a nice note to the Crag Rats explaining that they had created makeshift shelters using tree limbs and logs and found water from a stream. And they sent a donation.

We always wonder about when to call off searches. The biggest factor is that we keep searching as long as we have volunteers and there's a reasonable probability we can find someone. Pressure from the family helps, too. My colleagues published a study a while back looking at Oregon search and rescue statistics, stating that fifty-one hours may be the cut-off point to stop searches. In other words, after two to three days, searches begin to become futile. I was a bit annoyed by that and wrote a letter to the editor—mostly because I looked at the data.

In 2006 in Oregon, we had two prolonged, high-profile searches, one successful. In November, a motorist and two children were found nine days after becoming lost in the Coast Range. This was the Kim rescue, noteworthy because it was the first in the nation to use reverse cell phone tracking data, and they were found by a helicopter hired by the motorist's family.

Survival stories readily available on Mount Hood date back to 1976, when teenagers Randy Knapp, Matt Meacham, and Gary Schneider were caught in a storm on Oregon's Mount Hood. They hunkered down in a snow cave and waited thirteen nights for the weather to clear. They walked out on day fourteen.

But the resilience is what interests me most. On August 24, 2007, a seventy-six-year-old woman was lost in Oregon's Wallowa Mountains and a search was called off after eight days. She was later found alive after spending thirteen days in the wilderness. On September 21, 2007, in Washington State, a thirty-one-year-old woman was found by a search helicopter after six days in the North Cascade National Park. And on September 28, 2007, in Washington state, a woman was found alive eight days after her car careened into a canyon; rescuers tracked her cell phone signal.

The best part of these data, in my view, is not the data on *how long* searches last but rather the *activity* of those who get lost. Of the 3,287 subjects in the study, 51 percent were hikers, hunters, and motorists. Only 127 were climbers (3.9 percent).

So, is it too late in life to head into the backcountry? Certainly not! Definitely, though, each individual has to pick activities commensurate with his or her experience, skill, and equipment, as well as take extra precautions. In many of these situations, people survived by using common sense: They created shelter, found water, and kept calm. Being hardy, fit, and prepared helps, too.

And, with the changing times, perhaps more people are heading into the backcountry. It's more accessible, perhaps. It becomes a popular low-cost activity when the economy takes a downturn. The outdoor retail industry heavily promotes recreation in our forests, mountains, rivers, and oceans. In 2015, for example, Recreational Equipment Inc., decided to close on Black Friday in an *Opt Outside* advertising campaign. The largest retailer of outdoor clothing and equipment in the world closed its doors on the biggest shopping day of the year. It worked: People went outside and then continued to buy outdoor gear. Modern technology—equipment and clothing—gives people more of a sense of safety, perhaps, also. Clothing is fabulous nowadays at warding off the elements. Telecommunications give people instant access to help (as long as they have a signal and battery power). And we have a proliferation of modern communication like blogs, chat rooms, social networking apps, and websites—this means hiking partners, route information, and weather data are readily accessible.

Add this all up, and we have more rescues.

Whatever the case, Crag Rats and our search-and-rescue colleagues will still need to go after people, young and old, prepared and unprepared, injured or just lost. Certainly, technology has changed how we function—namely: cell phones.

CHAPTER TWELVE

Great Storm King

Two guys a century ago set out to build a road, here in the steep-walled, thickly forested, deep canyon of the wild Columbia River.

The Historic Columbia Gorge Highway, or more commonly the *old highway*, is a pre-dam relic from yesteryear, a conduit that was the brainchild of legendary railroad tycoon and road builder Sam Hill, who teamed up with renowned Portland engineer Samuel Lancaster. They set their sights on constructing a bypass around the final segment of the Oregon Trail. At that time, pioneers caught a ferry down the treacherous Columbia River rapids of The Dalles and Cascade Locks. Or they tackled the bumpy Barlow Road bypass over the east and south passes of storm-riddled Mount Hood, which could be rife with snow, rain, mud, and deep ruts year-round.

For design, the duo turned to the famed mountain roads in Europe, which cut paths in burly jagged peaks. They modeled the highway after the Swiss Axenstrasse, which traverses the shores of Lake Uri. Construction commenced in 1913 and the section from Hood River to Portland opened in just two years on July 6, 1915. The whole shebang was finally paved from The Dalles to Portland by 1922. The cliff-side road, perched above the flood zone, served as an east-west connection between the fruit-growing valley of Hood River and the metropolis of Portland. Along the way motorists passed through tunnels carved through the basalt promontories, traversed bridges with spectacular views of bubbling streams and cascading waterfalls, and stopped at spectacular cliff-side panoramas of the great river. The greenery was much as it remains today: tall evergreen conifers with an understory of broadleaf ferns, Oregon grape, moss, old man's beard lichen, vine maples, and abundant wildflowers.

However, in the industrial age, infrastructure development moved quickly. With erection of Bonneville Dam beginning in 1933, the river backed up and created the Bonneville Pool, a large lake that slowed storm surges and minimized floods. Thus a smoother, straighter, river-level highway soon followed: US Highway 30 opened by 1947, which metamorphosed into Interstate 84 in 1969. Thus when bridges and tunnels collapsed and the pavement washed out from landslides and waterfalls on the old highway, little need existed to keep it functional. It fell into disrepair and was decommissioned.

Fast-forward to 1980: With the Columbia Gorge National Scenic Act, the National Park Service marked restoration of the old highway as a priority and began to rebuild sections of decaying bridges, tunnels, and roads. The project was championed by both Oregon State Parks (the bike/pedestrian sections) and Oregon Department of Transportation (the motor vehicle sections). On November 14, 2013, completion of the 1.6-mile section from Moffett Creek to John B. Yeon State Park (named after an original financer of the highway) linked Wyeth to Troutdale. We can now can ride, run, and drive westward on the highway once again alongside gurgling waterfalls, under columnar basalt cliffs, across old bridges, past rebuilt masonry walls, over moss-covered viaducts, and through antique tunnels, although part of the highway—from Cascade Locks to Ainsworth—is limited to bikes and pedestrians only. The section from Hood River to Mosier to the east has also been refurbished as a bike/ped path, commonly called the Twin Tunnels because the path passes through the basalt.

The crux of the problem with connecting the two sections is Mitchell Point, a 500-foot-high rocky outcrop that juts from the wall of the gorge into the river. A final 8-mile section from Wyeth to Hood River is slated for construction in the coming years, but is still stymied by Mitchell Point. The original access was a 385-foot-long tunnel drilled through the rock promontory known as Little Storm King by the Columbia River

Tribes (the sky was Great Storm King). The tunnel was decommissioned in 1955 and obliterated by dynamite in 1966 to make room for Interstate 84. It will take an engineering feat to redrill a tunnel or carve a road into the cliff to restore this section.

This spectacular highway—the unbelievably beautiful trails, waterfalls, canyons, creeks, and viewpoints—is the epicenter of our missions from May to September. Thousands of people come up to hike, bike, swim, and climb in what is the heart of the Columbia Gorge National Scenic Area. Our county reaches 20 miles west from Hood River to Eagle Creek. After Eagle Creek to Portland, another 20 miles, Multnomah County takes over, with richer resources for search and rescue (Pacific Northwest Search and Rescue, Mountain Wave, Portland Mountain Rescue, Northern Oregon Search and Rescue, and Multnomah County Sheriff's Office).

So now, guess what: another callout. Midsummer. At night. Two hikers had gone up a trail somewhere west of Mitchell Point after hiking along the paved bike/pedestrian section of the old highway. This flat, smooth track through lush forest is marked with an understory of hearty poison oak, laced with the urushiol oil that creates a nasty, itchy, red rash.

Two women went looking for a hike, and for some reason took an unmarked, unnamed trail from the road. The trail wasn't really a designated hiking trail but rather a rugged, barely maintained track used by workers to access the power line towers, which distribute power from nearby Bonneville Dam. It's little more than a narrow path that disappears into the woods, going uphill. The two hikers set off up the steep trail, reached the power lines, hiked for a while on the power-line clear cut, and then decided to hike directly downhill back to their car. They could hear Interstate 84 to the north, a half-mile and 1,000 feet below them.

The only problem is that although the fall line took them within a quarter mile of their car, the fall line follows a small drainage that ends at the brink of a cliff. And the cliff was substantial: 300 feet of sheer columnar basalt. The two were stymied almost within sight of the pavement. The second problem is that once they reached the cliff, they had unknowingly scrambled down an embankment so steep, they couldn't climb back up. They were stuck.

So at 10:00 p.m., Craig McCurdy, Stefan Gumperlein, Lisa Rust, Richard Hallman, and I set out to track down these two with then-Sheriff Joe Wampler leading the search. We stage at Mitchell Point and use GPS coordinates that dispatch acquired from the couple's phone. We know the two are stuck somewhere between the power-line bench and the parking lot. So we hike up a rocky, rooted, steep, narrow, overgrown path that ascends via switchbacks—it's not a known trail but a rudimentary path to access the power lines. We climb through thick brush and poison oak. The two trails split near the bench, so we take the west trail. Once we make it to the power lines, we scour the bench with no luck. We are very near the cliffed-out couple, but the wind lightly wrestling the tree branches makes yelling useless.

I call one of the women on her phone.

"Look to the west. Do you see the lights of the hotel sign?" I ask her because we have a clear view of Meredith Hotel's red neon sign, about a half-mile to the west.

"Yes," she says. That means the two are somewhere on the west side of the huge, rocky Mitchell Point monolith. I realize we are directly above the couple, probably only about 500 feet from the two, but we still can't find them.

After scouring the bench, we decide to head back down the trail to come back at daylight. A few minutes into our descent from the power-line bench, Craig finds a game trail and starts following it eastward just below the power-line bench, through thick brush. Craig and I stay in radio contact while he runs out the game trail for a while, then returns. Nothing. Nada. Zip. We bushwhack down the trail to regroup after two hours of searching. It's already 2:00 a.m. and the temperature won't drop below 60 degrees. The women will be fine for four hours until daylight comes.

Cell phones and GPS have changed the way we do rescues since the stories I collected in *Mountain Rescue Doctor* a decade ago. Back then, we had just begun using cell phones for tracking. The Kim rescue in 2002 was one of the first instances in the nation in which a cell phone was used to locate a missing woman and her children. A cell phone company employee figured out that by locating the last cell tower with which the Kims' phone had made a connection, they would know the approximate location and direction of the phone's last transmission. Since then, we've been pinging phones to locate them with variable but improving accuracy. It's better now with smart phones because almost all are GPS enabled, meaning one can locate the phone via the tower it pinged, but also get GPS data from the phone. The GPS data comes from the phone communicating with satellites, so a user can get the data without having cell service. But in order to transmit the data to a cell tower, one needs reception and the phone needs to be powered up. At one time, we had to get the information from the cell company. But new software allows the sheriff's office dispatch to ping the phone directly and usually to get instant results: this system is called "reverse 911."

When a person calls 911, the first question nowadays is, "Where is your emergency?" That's because cell phones often reach 911 centers that are not in the jurisdiction of the emergency. For example, if you call 911 from the Oregon side of the Columbia Gorge, you will likely get Skamania County, Washington, dispatch. They immediately forward the call to Hood River County, often without taking much information.

The 911 dispatcher has your phone number and the cell tower through which you're being routed. With a non-GPS phone, dispatch still gets approximate GPS coordinates by determining the tower, direction, and strength of the signal. With a smart phone, the GPS data, depending on the type of phone, is transmitted. A code division multiple access (CDMA) phone like those used by Sprint, Verizon, and US Cellular is very accurate—they yield coordinates that are within 50 meters 67 percent of the time and within 150 meters 95 percent of the time. That is excellent news for us rescuers. The Global System for Mobile communications (GSM) phones that AT&T and T-Mobile use are less accurate, within 100 and 300 meters respectively for the same percentages of accuracy.

Ideally, if someone can acquire the GPS data from his or her phone and call it in, that's probably the most accurate. Most smart phones, if you have location services turned on, easily have this capability, and those of you who use it for navigation through the city streets know it's quite accurate. On an iPhone, for example, if you pull up the compass app and your location services are turned on, you can read your GPS data directly. On some phones, you can "drop a pin" and mark your location on the map app. Another option that we have started using is to ask the lost person to text an image, which is usually marked with location information. Text messages sometimes can get through even when there's not a strong enough signal for a phone call. And of late, the new Text-to-911 cell program allows a person to send a text to 911 in certain locations.

The GPS coordinates system unfortunately is not exactly standard. My iPhone, for example, gives my latitude and longitude in the old-school notation of degrees-minutes-seconds. Aviation reports the coordinates often as degree-decimal-minutes. Ground SAR tries to use the Universal Transverse Mercator coordinate system. Fortunately, when a callout comes and I'm at home, I can plug any of the coordinate systems into my computer and locate the spot on the map. I can also do this with a GPS app on my phone or using a handheld GPS receiver. The biggest problem is remembering how to use all the functions of my GPS or GPS phone app.

An even better idea is for potential victims to download their own GPS app for use with their phones, which comes with a map, tracking, and even the ability to mark waypoints along a hike. GPS works well, provided one has a battery and is able to get satellite reception; thick clouds, deep canyons, tall trees, and low battery can all limit reception.

Sometimes, we need to coach smart phone users. Turn off your phone to save batteries, keep your phone warm so it functions, and if you have spotty reception or a low battery, send a text instead of a call. Keep location services, or better your entire phone, turned off until you need it.

Of late, in addition to a GPS receiver and a smart phone, hikers are also starting to carry personal locating beacon devices, aka PLBs, which use a GPS transmitter. Some of these PLBs must be registered with the Federal Communication Commission and used for emergencies only. When an accident occurs, the user can activate the beacon to send a distress call to a designated center, which then relays the coordinates to the local sheriff. This is just like an Emergency Position Indicating Radio Beacon on a ship.

Other devices are sold with a subscription service that offers real-time tracking so friends and family can follow one's progress on a hike. Some units come with several buttons for messages such as "Send help," or "I'm okay."

One such activation occurred on a Sunday evening. All we knew was that a fifty-five-year-old on a three-week hike of an Oregon section off the Pacific Crest Trail activated his emergency SOS button on his emergency beacon. We knew little else but the coordinates and his cell number. I was at home when I got the call and plugged the coordinates into my computer. He was at the junction of Huckleberry Mountain and Pacific Crest Trails, about 2 miles from Lost Lake Resort. As coordinator for that search, I mustered a hasty team to head up the trail. Injury? Don't know. Need a litter? Don't know. The hasty team has nearly completed the one-hour drive to Lost Lake when the stand-down page comes. The man had accidentally triggered the device. No emergency. Stand down. Turn around and drive home.

Every once in a while we have "the cell phone discussion" at our debrief meetings. On one hand, it's clear that we get more calls for help now compared to pre-cell-days, in which people would have to make their way down the trail or send someone out for help. Back then people needed to be more self-sufficient—this is particularly applicable to those with minor injuries who are still ambulatory or those who are not injured but just caught after dark in mild weather. Once daylight returned, the distressed party, in the "old" days, would have to find their way home or wait to be reported missing. Now, we get calls via cell phone and emergency requests via GPS locators immediately.

On the other hand, cell phones give us accurate information, which is a big boon. We can rapidly run up a trail knowing the victim's precise location. We know what gear to bring, how urgent the situation is, and sometimes, we learn whether the victims can easily survive the night. Subjects also tend to call us sooner rather than later, which can be good or bad. On one hand, sometimes we can respond at 4:00 p.m. to someone on a trail, instead of waiting until the middle of the night, when, as you already know, missions are more dangerous and situations are more dire. On the other hand, we get 911 calls from people who have a minor episode of panic because they momentarily lost their way or sustained a minor fall, but they are otherwise neither lost nor injured.

Cell phones and satellite locators are here to stay, so the discussion of whether they are good or bad is rather moot. The other, more pressing, question on my mind pertaining to risk is: Do people take more risks with cell phones? If someone knows they have constant communication with 911, do they go farther up the trail in bad weather, or go higher on the mountain when they are exhausted? I don't know the answer, but I suspect the answer for some folks is: yes. Cell phones, or communication in general, certainly give some people a sense of security, so that they likely take a bigger risk.

Or, expanding the consideration beyond cell phones: Do people take more risks—hike deeper, climb higher, ignore storm warnings—because *all* equipment is better nowadays? Our clothing is designed to withstand storms that would have been intolerable yesteryear: polyester fleece, polyester-filled puffy coats, nylon jackets treated with durable water-re-pellent coating, socks blended with strong acrylic and warm nylon, and boots made to be light and comfortable and weatherproof. This gear is so rugged and compact that even in a day pack, one can bring clothing to withstand a night in three seasons in the forests of the Columbia Gorge (the weather on Mount Hood is a totally different ball game).

Even our rescue gear is light years better than when the Crag Rats first used braided hemp ropes, alpenstocks, steel crampons, and waxed cotton coats. We've got high-strength lightweight ropes, crampons and ice axes built with aluminum, and skis and ski boots crafted with light, strong carbon fiber. Our main belay/rappel device is called an MPD, or multipurpose device, designed by CMC Rescue (California Mountain Company). The MPD is a single tool designed to raise and lower ropes, and can quickly convert between the two functions. It integrates both a pulley and a rope-grab mechanism. It's not necessarily lighter or less bulky than old-school prussic cords, carabiners, and pulleys, but it's faster to rig and simpler.

So, with telecommunications, it doesn't really matter. Smart phones are here to stay. GPS is here to stay. Both can be fabulous tools for safety and can help us coordinate rescues. So, we might as well just deal with it.

We might as well just take the good (better information) with the bad (a few calls for those not really requiring rescue).

We use GPS and cell phones on almost every rescue, with good success. One winter, we were called to Mount Defiance. At an elevation of 5,010 feet, it's the tallest peak in the gorge. Because the peak is only a few miles as the crow flies from the Columbia River, elevation 150 feet, the twin trails—Mount Defiance, 5 miles to the summit, and Starvation Creek, 7 miles—are among the steepest you'll find anywhere. Many mountaineers use them as spring training hikes to get in shape for climbing Mount Hood. Each trail traverses the edges of Warren Creek Canyon. You'll remember from earlier in the book that Mount Defiance Trail wraps to the west and Starvation Creek Trail wraps to the east. Both are steep and beautiful, and lead to the summit of Defiance. The summit, incidentally, is accessible by dirt road from the south, which is the main access for the radio towers perched on the peak.

We are called at 4:00 p.m. for a hiker who was ascending the Defiance Trail, took a side jaunt to an open snow-covered slope, lost her footing in the ice, and slid 1,000 feet into a gully. She was uninjured but felt like she didn't have the stamina, skills, and gear to hike back up the slope. When she called 911, she read coordinates from her GPS, probably the most accurate.

"She's on the scree field," says Brian Hukari when we gather at the trailhead. "About 4,500 feet, just below the summit."

"Stay put, we're coming," the sheriff's deputy tells the woman.

So we set out on the long hike up Defiance at 5:20 p.m. I plug the GPS coordinates into a GPS receiver we keep in our truck. On the trails, we can hike 2 to 4 miles an hour, depending on the terrain. But when the mountain steepens, we hike about 1,000 vertical feet an hour. This climb takes us three hours. First it's steep dirt with some mud. Then it turns to steep snow. And then ice—so hard we slow our pace and dig our boots in. We pass a tent with ice axes and crampons outside. We arouse the occupants.

"Hi, we're search and rescue. You guys see anyone come this way looking for help?" I ask.

"No. What's wrong?"

"Looking for someone," I say to keep it brief. We keep moving.

When we are out of earshot, I think about the gear outside the tent and the slippery ice.

"I thought about asking them if we could borrow their ice axes and crampons," I say.

"Me too," says Brian. "We may need them."

We reach the 4,400-foot level on the trail at 8:00 p.m. From there, we quickly find the scree field and start the 1,000-foot descent off trail, with snow covering all but the largest boulders. It's a bit dangerous. Sometimes the snow is ice-hard and slippery. In other places, we step through the snow and sink up to our knees in crevices created by the boulders. We make our way slowly, down and slightly traversing to a point where we can see the subject's headlamp. We find the woman huddled under a tree in a bivy sack, a one-person sleeping sack. When I'm 3 feet away, the GPS strapped to my chest pings: you have arrived at your destination.

"We're here," says Gavin.

"Dang, that's accurate," I say, knowing the accuracy but still amazed at this technology.

The ascent back up the snow- and ice-covered scree field and descent down the icy, steep trail takes us three hours.

Another time, we are called out to Indian Point, just down the road from Defiance, again at night. We have GPS coordinates from Joe Wampler, who, from the airplane, spotted three young men who are, like the Mitchell Point couple, stuck on a cliff. The men had been hiking up Herman Creek Trail when they took a side jaunt to Indian Point. Perhaps not exactly paying attention, they walked off trail down a steep slope to get to a viewpoint. They slid into Grays Creek drainage, adjacent to the more well-traveled Herman Creek drainage. Again, since it was too steep and dangerous and difficult to climb back up, they were stuck on a cliff.

At 11:15 p.m. Tom Rousseau, Todd Hanna, and I set off up the Herman Creek Trail. We pass the Indian Point Trail, and, after a quick recon, decide it's too dangerous in the dark and access looks easier by going down adjacent Grays Creek. So, we continue a bit up Herman Creek Trail, then start bushwhacking down Grays Creek, with the GPS pointing us in a straight line to the stranded hikers.

Unfortunately, Grays Creek is slow going. We initially scramble over downed logs and squeeze through tight thickets of vine maple on a moderate slope. Then after barely a quarter mile, Grays Creek steepens. The steep slope, mud, loose rocks and logs, and trickling streams make it impossible for us to find a safe route to get down Grays Creek to the ledge where the hikers are stranded. We try three different entrances to the steep section of the creek, which is the beginning of a narrow canyon that terminates in, you guessed it, a cliff. No luck. We decide shifting boulders and logs, muddy slopes, and steep terrain are not worth the risk.

At 3:00 a.m., after an hour in Grays Creek, we abort and hike back out. We are within a few hundred feet of the subjects, but can't quite get to them. We decide it's probably safer to access the stranded hikers via Indian Point Trail in the daylight. We get back to SAR base at 4:30 a.m. just as another crew of Crag Rats is rolling out of bed to continue the search. That morning, when everyone can see, a helicopter from the Army National Guard in Salem spots the two and plucks them off the cliff. And just because things are never simple, a potential disaster almost unfolded with the helicopter rescue. The two hikers had built a fire as they were perched on a rocky cliff. They failed to extinguish the fire, so when the helicopter flew in for the initial extrication, the force of the rotor wash hit the fire, causing it to spew flames and ashes. Fortunately, no wildfire was started and the hikers were uninjured.

We only recently used a portable small drone with a camera. On a rescue up Moffett Creek, a group of canyoneers descended a series of rappels through waterfalls. They had finished the entire descent when their rope got stuck. One of the group decided that, instead of coming back on another day, climbing back to the headwaters of Moffett Creek, and making the entire descent again to retrieve the rope, he would scale the 35-foot waterfall where the rope got stuck. Unfortunately, he got to the top of the waterfall free-solo climbing (without a rope), slipped, and fell above the waterfall. No one from the party could actually see the man, but it was presumed he died.

It is two hours before we can muster a team, drive to the trailhead, take an ATV up the access road, and get to the base of the waterfall. Once there, we see the stuck rope in the waterfall, above which is a deep, tight slot canyon. Meredith, Ron, Hugh, and I, along with two responders from Cascade Locks Fire, bushwhack up the scree field and gully to the west of the canyon. We try several attempts to traverse to the canyon but are stopped by the cliff. Finally, at 1,840 feet, we find path along a cliff edge to reach the slot canyon. We set up a belay station and Meredith lowers me to the edge of the cliff. I am still 200 feet above the floor of the canyon and the accident site. We need a longer rope. After a short huddle, we check the time. It is nearing 7:30 p.m. We don't want to be on the exposed cliff at dark and we don't want to be bushwhacking back to the trailhead at dark.

Luckily, someone at Cascade Locks Fire has a friend with a small personal drone. The friend brings the drone up to the bottom of the waterfall, flies it to the top of the falls and into the slot canyon, and spots the deceased. At least we have confirmed the fatality and location. The next day, we come back with 300-foot ropes to bring out the body.

But now, back at Mitchell Point, we have all but aborted the search for the two women stranded on the cliff. Then, Joe Wampler has a brilliant, old-school idea sometime after 2:00 a.m., tagging off my cell phone conversation with the woman about the hotel sign. Joe calls dispatch and asks for a deputy to go to the Meredith Hotel, which is about 2 miles to the east. The deputy then shines a spotlight across Interstate 84 directly to the east-facing rock wall of Mitchell Point. With the two women on the phone, Joe asks the subjects to let him know when they see the spotlight at its brightest.

Bingo. They see the light. He asks the hotel deputy to hold position.

"I got them," says the deputy into the radio.

There they are, right above us, a quarter mile away.

We hike up through thick brush to the base of the cliff in about 10 minutes. They are 300 feet directly above us, but the cliff is sheer and extends several hundred feet in both directions. We log the GPS coordinates. It's breezy so we can't really yell to them.

"We're not getting up that," says Craig.

"Nope."

So, we head back up around Mitchell Point, hike back up the trail and climb back to the power-line bench for the second time that night. We head out the deer trail that Craig had initially followed earlier that night—his instincts were perfect. After an hour, we find a short, steep gully leading from the bench down a steep ravine. After five minutes scrambling down the steep ravine, we make our way to where the ravine terminates in a cliff. From a small ledge above the couple, we find them in our headlamps, 50 feet below us.

Craig scrambles down the steep pitch over loose dirt, rocks, and downed tree limbs. Lisa and I rig up a safety rope—we set up a simple belay using a small maple to anchor the rope. We only have my basic rope-rescue gear: a piece of webbing, two carabiners, a harness, and a 20-meter 7-mm rope.

Lisa and I haul the hikers one by one up the 30-foot slope to the ledge. The two are uninjured, but dressed in shorts and tank tops, with no backpacks. But they do have a cell phone, which indeed makes our lives easier and harder. Better info, but more calls. It being midsummer, the couple would have survived the night okay, but it's doubtful they would have been able to safely scramble up the cliff and find their way home.

We then start the long walk out—back up the gully, across the bench, and down the trail.

And then, the intensity of the search passes. We are on the trail home, feeling much less anxious. The sky has given us respite for many of the missions in the Columbia Gorge. Night rescues continue to pummel us, but fortunately, few recently have been in nasty weather. The Great Storm King has reeled in the rain.

And then as I realize we're going to be back home safely soon, I notice the plants we are walking through: a robust bumper crop of waist-high poison oak.

CHAPTER THIRTEEN

The Culture of Responsibility

ALTHOUGH TECHNOLOGY HAS CHANGED IN THE LAST DECADE, RESPON-sibility has not—at least, not from my perspective.

One fall October Sunday, we get a callout, which is rare for this time of year. The hiking season is over and winter recreation has yet to begin.

The text comes in at 4:00 p.m. to fetch a 25-year-old guy who was hiking up a little-used, unnamed deer trail off the Herman Creek Trail. He and a friend were two hours into their hike when they encountered a mudslide on the trail. The mudslide was steep. If they had fallen, they would have careened a hundred feet below to the creek. If they landed in the creek, they would be unable to climb back out. With its steep walls, it might have been possible to hike down the creek to find an exit, if one survived the slide uninjured. In addition to the cold water and mud, large unstable logs and boulders could come crashing down the minute anyone tried to climb over them. And, the walls of the ravine were choked with thick brush.

The first man crossed the slide patch carefully, got halfway across to a large downed log, and froze. He was too petrified to move. Looking down the slide, he saw it was 100 feet down into the creek.

So they called a parent. A parent called 911. Dispatch called the sheriff. The sheriff called us. Fortunately, a nearby Forest Service ranger responded quickly, hiked up to the two, assessed the situation, and called for a rope-rescue team from Crag Rats.

Brian Hukari and I respond.

"I was hoping it was someone else," I joke with Brian. "I've done so many rescues with you this year, we have nothing left to talk about."

Brian smiles as he pulls our heavy SAR truck off the freeway into the Herman Creek ranger station. From there, the sheriff meets us and unlocks a gate to an access road, which allows us to drive on an old road that bypasses the lower 2 miles of the trail. Adam, a volunteer firefighter, joins us.

"Drive up the road," says the sheriff. "You'll see the Forest Service truck at the trailhead. The men are about a mile up the trail."

The swath of forest is thick and the road is rough: up and down hills, around embankments, across dry stream drainages, through ruts. It seems odd to me that this stretch of pristine forest is interrupted by the road, but this saves us at least a half-hour walk from the actual start of the trailhead down by Interstate 84. We find the ranger's truck after lumbering our heavy truck in four-wheel drive about 2 miles. We park and grab our gear.

"I've got a 20-meter rope and enough webbing to make a basic haul line."

"I've got a 20-meter line, too," says Brian. "I'll bring an extra harness."

Brian and I both carry basic rope-rescue gear, so we don't grab anything from the truck. We sling our packs and trot up the trail at a brisk pace. In twenty minutes we find the stranded young man, his friend, and the mudslide. The stranded hiker clings to a log about 10 feet across the mudslide.

"Hi, we are search and rescue. Any injuries?" I ask.

"No, he's not hurt," says the friend. "Just stuck. He went across the trail then was afraid of falling. He stopped at the log and got stuck," says the friend in somewhat pressured speech. Nervous, but somehow slightly relieved.

Brian quickly surveys the scene and makes a plan. I defer to him because his rope-rescue skills are superior to mine.

"I'll hike across and tie a hand line. If you can hike up the bank, tie a safety rope on a tree," he says, pointing to a giant Douglas fir about 20 feet above the mudslide, "we should be able to help him across with a hand line and a belay."

"Will do," I say, and go to work.

Brian ties his cord around a tree on our side of the mudslide and then expertly crosses the mudslide to reach the log with the stuck hiker. Once across, with grace and ease, Brian fastens the other end of the cord to the log to create a hand line that the young man can hold on to while crossing. He gently puts his climbing harness on the hiker.

Meanwhile, I clamber up the slope with Adam. We reach a point about 30 feet directly above Brian and the young man at the big Douglas fir.

"Can you tie the webbing around the tree with a water knot: wrap three, pull two?" I say, referring to making three wraps around the tree, tying the webbing in a loop with a water knot, and then pulling two of the tree wraps to clip onto a carabiner. The third wrap will lie snug against the tree trunk.

"I'm not quite sure I remember," he says. "It's been a long time." He's part of a group of volunteer firefighters starting to do search and rescue to augment the Crag Rats and mostly to contribute to the community, since firefighting doesn't keep them as busy as they used to be, given recent advances in fire suppression and fire safety. They are still training to learn basic skills, so I quickly set up the belay while talking him through it. Now is not exactly the time to teach him, but this is not a life-or-death emergency either. We have time for me to explain what I'm doing.

I wrap and tie a 20-foot piece of webbing around the trunk and clip a carabiner to the webbing. Then, I tie a double figure-eight knot on one end of the rope, and clip the rope to the carabiner. I tie into the rope with my harness and rappel a few feet below the big tree to a point where I am right on top of Brian and the hiker. I unclip myself from the rope and drop the free end down to Brian, 20 feet below me. He connects the free end of the rope to the harness that he's put on the young man. So, the stuck hiker is tied into the safety rope and has the second cord to use as a hand line to cross the mudslide.

Adam and I scramble back to the trail.

"Ready!" I yell to Brian.

"Okay, here we come," he says. In about five seconds, the young man scrambles and crawls his way 20 feet across the mudslide. Brian escorts him to the edge of the washed-out trail where Adam and I grab him.

Short, simple. No injury. We are a half-mile from the truck, 2 miles down the dirt road to the trailhead, and 10 miles from home. The rescues don't get much simpler.

In Oregon, we have more than 1,000 SAR missions annually. In 2014, 1,135 missions accounted for 19,506 hours for paid personnel, 131,031 volunteer hours, and 4,778 hours for transportation. This excludes hours of administration and training. In addition to all of our trainings and rescues, the Crag Rats participate in the monthly meetings of Mount Hood Search and Rescue Council, the regular meetings and certifications of Oregon Mountain Rescue Council, meetings with the Forest Service about our special use permit on Cloud Cap Inn, meetings with the Sheriff's Office, completing tasks related to owning the Crag Rat Hut in Pine Grove, and the accounting, record keeping, and archiving the history of our non-profit club.

No one keeps national stats, but including the National Park Service and US Coast Guard, the United States probably has 100,000 SAR missions a year.

In *Mountain Rescue Doctor* I wrote about responsibility for search and rescue and the controversy of who should foot the bill. Even these simple rescues—excluding volunteer time—are costly in terms of a paid sheriff's deputy and the equipment and training credentials we maintain. In 1995, Oregon was the first state to enact an SAR cost recovery law, allowing sheriff's departments to send a bill to those rescued. Several other states followed suit. The Oregon law was instigated by a group of college students who were climbing Mount Hood and became caught in a storm. Lawmakers did not feel taxpayers should pay for "those jokers on the mountain," referring to the climbers. Paradoxically, the climbers hiked down on their own after waiting out the storm. One Oregon sheriff did collect in 1996, when a group of rafters knowingly floated past closed-river signs and warning bystanders, and then required rescue. But for the most part, people don't pay for search and rescue in Oregon, or elsewhere in the United States and Canada.

Several states do have the ability to charge for SAR. Most noticeably, New Hampshire has billed approximately sixty individuals or parties and recovered $70,000 for negligence; the state even collected a fee from one victim who took his case to the state supreme court and lost. Colorado and Vermont can send a bill to those who ventured out of bounds from a ski resort. Idaho can send a bill to those entering areas closed to the public. Utah counties can charge, and Grand and Wayne Counties in the red rock country do regularly. Their SAR gets quite expensive, up to $200,000 per year. The rationale is that their small tax base of 10,000 people supports SAR mostly for visitors. It's simply too expensive for the county taxpayers to foot the bill. And some county fire agencies are now sending bills to patients when fire and rescue responds to calls out of their tax jurisdiction.

On one hand, many people feel search and rescue falls under the public-safety doctrine. Some feel SAR ought to be paid by tax funds, just like fire and police departments. A supporting argument, which has not been validated, is that if people know they could get a bill, they may be hesitant to call and then wait until late in the day, when rescues are more dangerous and the person's condition is more dire.

On the other hand, some people feel that those who are irresponsible should pay for their own mistakes. As you can tell from reading the chapters of this book, more people than not herein were not being irresponsible, but just had accidents. Most were not doing anything foolish or breaking any laws. Many were prepared. And yes, some people went out in foul weather and some went out with little more than the clothes on their backs. Nevertheless, good, responsible people can still get into trouble.

Look at this another way: We live in a country where one-third of the population is overweight and a quarter is morbidly obese. Many more tax dollars are taking care of obesity-related disease compared to SAR. Perhaps penalizing people for getting outside isn't the best overall savings.

Other ways, besides charging victims, have been used to lessen search and rescue costs and time commitments.

One technique is to close recreation areas to prevent people from getting hurt. Nobody really wants access limited, but when areas are too dangerous, or too many people get into trouble, sometimes limiting access is the only way to manage areas.

Another technique that is moderately successful in defraying costs is to charge up-front access fees for some locations. For example, individuals must buy permits to climb Mount St. Helens, Mount Adams, and Mount Rainier. These funds go, in part, to ranger services to mark trails, patrol lands, and provide search-and-rescue services. Mount Hood does not have a climbing fee, although revenue would help offset the climbing ranger and SAR programs indeed, with some 10,000 climbing per year. But climbers are the least of our worries. In Oregon most searches are for hikers, motorists, wanderers (such as children, the mentally ill, or elderly people), non-power boaters, and hunters. Some years, hikers top the list, sometimes motorists, but climbers are not even in the top five—ever.

Some states, spearheaded by Colorado, have a voluntary SAR Fee. In Colorado, for $3 per year or $12 per five, a person can buy a Colorado Outdoor Recreation Search and Rescue Card. The card isn't insurance. It doesn't do anything. It's just a volunteer donation for hikers, in good faith, to help defray the cost of SAR before they need SAR, or even if they never utilize SAR. Some other states have followed suit. New Hampshire has a Hike Safe Card for $25 and Utah has an SAR Assistance Card for $25 per person or $35 per family.

Insurance is an option, too. The American Alpine Club offers insurance to their members to reimburse up to $10,000 for SAR. The annual cost for membership is $70.

Another technique is education. Public safety campaigns have definitely shown to be useful, such as avalanche safety courses, caution signs at ski resorts and popular hiking trails, and of late, social media info. After a rash of cliff jumpings over several years at Punchbowl Falls on Eagle Creek, Oregon, lawmakers passed a law to levy a fine on cliff jumpers and erected caution signs around the waterfall. The waterfall jumpers decreased and rescues declined—in part due to the law, but also possibly due to the signage. The mountain climbing program on Denali also showed the effectiveness of education: Accidents on Denali decreased after the Park Service instituted a mandatory safety briefing for climbers before they are issued permits. My colleagues at Teton County SAR have started a "Backcountry Zero" campaign to eliminate fatalities through utilizing safety resources and public education on preparedness.

But forget about who pays or how we fund SAR for the time being. The guy rescued from the mudslide wasn't really being irresponsible. He wasn't necessarily self-reliant, but still, he was out enjoying the backcountry when he simply got stuck.

The Crag Rats are going to respond with our own time and our own gear if we have to. We are passionate about the outdoors and passionate about helping people in trouble.

Although I am not in favor of limiting access, I am in favor of use fees and permits in certain areas that require extra patrols, signs, and route markings, such as high-use mountains and rivers. The fees and permits not only defray SAR costs, but also create an extra step that people have to complete before heading into the wilderness. This extra step alone—stop, think, fill out a form, pay a fee, get a permit—may cause people to think twice about what they are doing and if they are prepared.

That said, I'm more interested in the culture of responsibility, regardless of who pays.

A year after my accident, long after I'd returned to skiing, I booked a trip. I'm a life-long skier and adventure junkie; skiing and adventure travel are in my blood. I wrote a backcountry ski and snowboard guidebook to Oregon in 2000, and revised it in 2011. Both before and during the writing of that book, I skied most major backcountry routes from Mount Rainier in Washington to Mount Shasta in Northern California. I went beyond the Northwest, skiing in Canada and Europe. I took my daughters on one of the most sought-after ski trips in the history of skiing: Portillo, Chile, a resort nestled at 12,000 feet in the Andes. Although for some people this is a trip of a lifetime, we went again, a second time. I don't have a new car. I don't have an RV. I don't have a hot tub. I have a modest house. I work hard but live a bit frugally, except when it comes to good equipment and world-class adventures.

So I decided to choose the pinnacle of backcountry ski trips a year after my accident: The Haute Route. It was my first big backcountry trip after my accident, so I knew I had to be careful. The classic seven-day ski mountaineering traverse begins in the outdoor capital of the world, Chamonix, France. We skied over seven days from high mountain hut to high mountain hut. In the huts, we'd typically arrive midafternoon after skiing all day across glaciers. At the huts, we got dinner, a bunk, and breakfast. A few had showers. A few had solar charging stations for our phones. All had blankets and pillows, so we just had to carry a small sleeping sack in addition to our day ski backpacks. The tour terminates in glitzy Zermatt, Switzerland—where we skied around and under the Matterhorn, then down through the ski resort. This is still one of my favorite trips of all time, of nearly one hundred countries in the world I've visited. I signed up cold with a guide and ended up being paired up with three Oregonians who became such good friends we later did a second trip to the Ortler region of Italy and a third trip to the Hokkaido volcanoes in Japan. We also had six from Juneau Mountain Rescue with our group. Everything lined up: good group, great weather, safe guides, and spectacular skiing. Part of my newfound perspective after my accident: I didn't want to wait to continue adventuring. But I knew I had to be careful.

On this journey, my goal was not to reach the top of a challenging, dangerous mountain. Instead, my goal was to ski great snow, and to immerse myself in the Alpine ski culture of Switzerland, France, and Italy (the latter we skied through for about four hours on one day).

But what fascinates me with regard to risk is the different perspective on responsibility that skiers take in the Alps. They not only have a culture of self-sufficiency, but also know that if they need to be rescued, they most likely need to pay for it. So they buy mountain-rescue insurance. When we bought a lift ticket at Grand Monets ski area to start our seven-day traverse by jumpstarting with a tram ride, for a few Euros extra we got backcountry rescue insurance for the day we'd be in France. Before I left home, I bought Swiss helicopter rescue membership for $30 that covered me for eighteen months to cover the portions we were in Switzerland (we did duck into Italy when traversing a glacier for a few hours). In other words, in the Alps you assume it's your responsibility to pay for rescue and buy insurance accordingly. If you don't have insurance and it is not a life-or-death emergency, you'll likely have to pay for calling a helicopter.

Similarly, on a trip to Kilimanjaro in Tanzania, my team witnessed a man being evacuated by helicopter. He was at high camp Barafu at 15,239 feet when he bent over and dislocated his artificial hip joint. At the time he dislocated his hip, we were readying ourselves for a summit bid and were unaware of the accident. Our team had myself as the emergency doctor, my orthopedic-surgeon climbing partner, and his son, who was a medical student. We certainly would have tried to reduce the dislocated hip, but unbeknownst to us, the man was evacuated by his team. We summited that morning and made the long trek down the mountain to the final camp Mweke at 12,500 feet. From there, we watched the man being helicoptered from camp by Nairobi's Flying Doctors. They took him to the hospital in Arusha because they couldn't fly him to Nairobi without a passport and credit card. In other words, if you play and get hurt, you have to pay for it.

This seems to be the norm in Europe as well as in developing countries in Asia and Africa. As I mentioned earlier, I trekked to Everest Base Camp the year of the devastating ice avalanche that killed sixteen Nepalese "ice doctors," guides responsible for setting up the route through the Western Cwm seracs. We landed in Kathmandu on the day of the accident, and along our ten-day trek to Everest Base Camp we spied hundreds of helicopters evacuating climbers, film-makers, and trekkers, including those trapped at high camps. All of it was for a fee. The Nepali helicopter companies and pilots make a good living rescuing western climbers. If you climb Mount Everest or even trek to Everest Base Camp and need a helicopter, you pay for it. In fact, at the end of our fourteen-day trip, we were fogged in at Lukla for three days. No airplane flights got in or out, so helicopter flights finally brought us back to Kathmandu—for $500, of course. Luckily, most people in our group had travel insurance that covered their flight cost.

In some areas of the world, you may not find any formal rescue services. I was in Fiji teaching a wilderness medicine seminar to a group of doctors; my oldest daughter came along. We arrived the night before the devastating Cyclone Winston that killed forty-two and leveled many villages, especially on the north island. On some of those islands, like Bequ Island where we were stationed, we expected neither free search and rescue nor paid search and rescue. In fact, there are many places in the world with no SAR. With limited resources, many communities make do with whoever can pitch in to help.

During four trips to Haiti, I found the same situation: There was no organized SAR and only a very basic ambulance system. My first trip, our group brought down a two-piece, ultralight search-and-rescue litter for the Centre Medical Dumarsais Estimé hospital in Verrettes. I found the ambulance one day parked out back next to rusted fifty-gallon drums burning hospital waste. The ambulance was a diesel 4x4 Land Cruiser with a non-medical driver and an empty cargo space in the back. No paramedics. No firefighters. No advanced life support equipment. No basic life support equipment. No first aid kit. When the ambulance goes into the hills to bring in a cholera victim from the remote hills around Verrettes, the driver can do little more than load up the patient with whatever help is available, and bring him or her to the hospital.

So what does all this mean with regard to risk? I'm less interested in who foots the bill or how much the climbing fee costs on Mount Rainier. I'm more interested in why, when we take risks in some societies, we think that someone else is responsible and rescue is guaranteed. In Europe, you expect to pay. As a result, they have well-funded, highly trained emergency medical services helicopter teams. Many emergency medical services helicopters in the Alps have mountain-rescue doctors on board. In other places in the world there simply are no resources. You're largely on your own until someone can piece together an SAR response, if they can at all.

So what all this means is that certain places in the world have nothing, others have highly developed SAR systems and people understand they have to help pay, and others, like ours in the United States, is part of the public safety doctrine with no charge, except for a few situations.

Fortunately, most people we rescue understand that we are all volunteers. We usually feel greatly appreciated. We get many thank-you notes and small donations after rescues. Most thank-you notes say things like, "Thanks you for putting your lives on the line," and "Thank you for returning us safely." And that, for us, is enough.

CHAPTER FOURTEEN

Into the Abyss

THINGS DON'T EVER SETTLE DOWN IN MOUNTAIN RESCUE.

We have trainings, gear maintenance, cleaning parties at our hut, and work parties at the cabin. We have meetings with the Forest Service and Sheriff's Office. We have to go to Portland to retrieve our backboard or buy parts for Cloud Cap Inn, like high-altitude mantles for the gas-powered lanterns. We have recertification and record keeping. We even have social functions, too.

And we have a constant flow of callouts. The Sheriff's Office responds to one hundred calls per year, only a fraction of which involve us, the mountain rescue team. A marine unit patrols the Columbia River in the summer. A forest patrol deputy, covered jointly by the county and Forest Service, monitors the trails and back roads in the summer. The aviation unit uses the Piper Super Cub for SAR and other tasks. The off-road vehicle unit patrols the motorcycle and ATV trails. Aside from the Sheriff's Office, the local fire departments—particularly in Cascade Locks, the town located 20 miles downstream at the west edge of our county—does dozens of trail rescues every year.

And of late, the Crag Rats have found themselves getting some basic plans together for large-scale natural disasters—namely, the Cascadia Subduction Zone mega-earthquake and subsequent tsunami. An 8.0 to 9.0 earthquake is predicted to occur offshore in the Pacific Northwest along the 800-mile fault between the North American Plate and the Explorer, Juan de Fuca, and Gorda plates. The big one apparently strikes every two hundred to five hundred years. Recently scientists speculate a large earthquake occurred sometime around four hundred years ago. This has people predicting an impending earthquake—the whole state of Oregon is focused on it. The Cascadia Subduction Zone is 200 miles offshore, so the coast and Willamette Valley cities, including Portland, could be hit hard.

Although Hood River is a few hundred miles inland and might be spared major damage, we may be isolated from help and quite low on the list for federal and state assistance compared to the metropolitan areas in the Willamette Valley: Portland, Salem, Eugene. The Columbia Gorge, which runs 90 miles through basalt with up to 4,000-foot-high walls, has two river-level roads: Interstate 84 in Oregon and Highway 14 in Washington, along with corresponding train tracks. If not taken out by mudslides, which occur every few years, the roads have dozens of smaller bridges that span the creeks crossing under the roads. The bridges could be washed out or damaged. The Hood River Toll Bridge, spanning the Columbia River between Hood River and White Salmon, Washington, would not take much of a hit to render it unsafe. Even the small bridge across the Hood River, which connects downtown with the east side neighborhoods, could be impassable. Our road to the south, Highway 35, connects us to Bend and Portland, by traveling along the east and south side of Mount Hood and then turning west to Portland. That is a twisty, narrow mountain road that could also easily be clobbered by mudslides and landslides. We do have one road that leads east, Interstate 84, which theoretically may be preserved since the mountains, and thus risk for landslides and treefall, lessen east of Hood River.

One day, Sheriff Matt English comes to a Crag Rats meeting to discuss how we may help in such a disaster. He says Hood River County should be prepared to be self-sufficient for up to three weeks in the event of a natural disaster like the Cascadia Subduction Zone earthquake. We decide, as a group, to get a basic emergency cache together.

So I make another list. Water and water purification is probably most important, along with being able to shelter in place with food, spare radios, flashlights and spare batteries, candles, a camp stove and fuel, and other such equipment. We should think about carrying emergency kits in our cars, too. And then, we'll need mass causality SAR gear to be able to respond to patients. Right now, our SAR truck is set up to extricate two injured people or several uninjured people. If we have a large-scale callout—people trapped in buildings, stuck in cars, or stranded on a road with bridges washed out—we will need extra gear. We consider stockpiling equipment at our hut in Pine Grove: spare litters, extra medical supplies, extra rope-rescue gear, more radios, a slew of headlamps, sleeping bags. Maybe a generator and solar power system. And a big stash of batteries.

So, we go about preparing our homes and possibly our Crag Rat Hut with some gear. I ask the local hospital for a donation. I ask the county Emergency Services Coordinator and the Hood River City Fire Chief for help with grants. I talk to my daughters about what to do in such an emergency, especially because my oldest is headed off to college. Shelter in place, seek out water and food, and try to get home. The first day of a natural disaster, not much happens: you protect yourself and protect your family. Then, as resources begin to muster, help out where you can.

The girls and I are chit-chatting at a local golf course restaurant that is removed from the bustle and busyness of downtown—it has outside tables, an in-your-face view of Mount Hood, and good burgers. I worked all day at the hospital, but got out at lunch for a short run, and then had gone kitesurfing that evening after work for an hour. Sometimes I ride my mountain bike on the Post Canyon Trail System, 2 miles west of town after work. This is an integral part of our life and lifestyle. Play hard, work hard. Balance.

Like my day of work and play, my colleagues were similarly working hard and playing hard. Hugh was just coming off a Mount Defiance hike. Cully was cleaning his bike preparing for a mountain biking and rock climbing road trip to Canada. Brian was working in his orchard, getting ready to harvest blueberries. Gary was also back from a bike ride. We were all in the normal swing of a Wednesday evening.

Then, in the small summer vacation town of Hood River, you guessed it, amid eating dinner with my daughters and planning for a large-scale Cascadia Subduction Zone mass causality event, my phone vibrates in my pocket.

I know it's not my daughters; they are right here. I doubt it's my parents; they are out of town. Possibly a friend is texting me to see if I want to go on a mountain bike ride tomorrow. But knowing it is Sunday evening in the middle of the summer, I instantly guess, before I pull my phone out of my pocket, who's texting me.

HRSO Dispatch.

Sunrise Falls. Female with a head injury and possible broken ankle about 4.5 miles up from trailhead. Dog.

And then:

Injured girl in pool after fall—need as many Rats as we can get.

And then:

Exact location is unknown.

I look at my daughters.

"What's your plan tonight?" I ask, wanting to spend the evening with my two girls but also feeling the adrenaline starting to boil in my blood. I don't want to miss a rare and precious evening with my girls. I don't want to miss a rescue.

"Hanging with friends," says one.

"Going to a party," says the other. "Why?"

"Crag Rat callout," I say. I don't really need to say anything else; they are quite familiar with the procedure.

"Oh, you should go," says my oldest.

"Whose party?" I ask, trying to look stern-faced.

"You don't know him," says my youngest.

"I'm going, too," says my oldest.

"Try me," I say. Then we spend two minutes sorting out the details of the party and I give the short teenage safety talk—the one I've given a thousand times before.

Then, I switch gears.

"I need to pay the bill and get home." My mind is already moving at rocket speed, clicking through the gear list.

Is she in the water? I'll need a life jacket and wetsuit. *Is she down a cliff?* We'll need rope gear. *Is she ambulatory?* If not, we'll need to bring the stretcher and wheel. *And a dog?* Getting a stretcher up and down that section of trail alone is difficult and dangerous. Adding in the water-rescue factor is doubly so.

I race home, grab my pack, and quickly change into rescue gear: lightweight nylon pants to protect against this year's waist-high crop of poison oak, my lime-green Crag Rats rescue shirt, and boots. While trading texts and phone calls with coordinator Todd Hanna, I grab a few things not in my pack: my 1,000-lumen mountain-biking headlamp, which I'd forgotten to charge from last week's Ruckel Ridge mission, an old battered wetsuit that I keep for SAR, a life jacket, and a bottle of water.

I meet Hugh, Brian, Stefan, and Gary at the county yard, and we jump into the new Sheriff's Department SAR truck, a Ford F-350 quad-cab, long-bed pickup. We head down the road. A few others are meeting us at the trailhead. With our lights flashing, people move out of our way as Stefan gets in the fast lane and floors it. This truck still has that new-car smell.

At the trailhead, we meet a patrol deputy. SAR Deputy Bob Stewart is en route with the Com Rig. The report is that a girl is in the water at Sunrise Falls, 5 miles up the trail. No, wait: she might be out of the water but down a cliff. Not sure. Someone has made it down to her. No, wait: someone has maybe either made it down to her or was able to get her some clothes. Not sure.

Nothing, in fact, is exactly clear about the situation. It's a cell phone blackout area. Apparently, SAR was notified by bystanders walking down the trail and via Spot messenger, a type of GPS emergency locator beacon that provides coordinates and a "need help" signal but not much more. A reporting party coming down the trail was able to give the basics: Stuck on a ledge or cliff, in the water or waterfall, arm and head injury, or maybe leg and head injury. Possibly out of the water. Not really sure.

"In the water?" I ask.

"Not sure," says the deputy.

"Injured?"

"Report of head and ankle or knee, but we don't have any clear information yet." Although it seems repetitious, that's the way it happens: everyone asks the same questions, repeatedly, to try for clarity.

Two teams are already headed up the trail. Team 1 is composed of two Cascade Locks Fire Department firefighters: they are toting the litter and rope-rescue gear. Team 2 is composed of two backcountry paramedics from American Medical Response Reach and Treat Team. We are Team 3.

"Team 1 from Team 3," I call on the radio.

"Team 1," is the reply.

"This is Crag Rats, about to head up the trail, wondering if you have ropes and a litter," I ask.

"We've got a 150-foooter and a 200-footer. We have an MPD and slings and webbing. We have a litter," I hear.

"Do you have a bridle for the litter?" I ask, knowing the CLFD litter is designed for trail rescues, and not rope extrication. Our litter has a bridle tied on in four points, with an adjustable pulley system. This allows us to quickly clip a rope to the bridle to haul a litter up a cliff.

"No bridle, but we have enough webbing and cord to make one."

"Team 3 from Team 2," crackles the radio. The AMR paramedic hears the radio chatter and calls in.

"Team 3," I reply.

"We've got a 150-foot rope, carabiners, belay/rappel gear, cord, and webbing," the AMR paramedic says.

"Okay, Team 3 is departing the trailhead. We'll go light," I reply, thinking we don't need any additional gear. Brian, Gary, and I pack wetsuits. I take out my life jacket and toss it in the truck. Then, at the last minute, I grab my life jacket and strap it back on the outside of my pack.

We set off for a one-and-a-half-hour hike up the trail. At dusk, of course. Brian and I prefer not to turn on our headlamps to preserve our night vision. Gary has a red bulb on his headlamp. There's no moon, but a bit of glow in the fading daylight. We keep a brisk pace uphill. When we get to a section of trail that's washed out from a mudslide, we need the lights. We have to leave the trail, climb down into the streambed, scramble over large boulders and giant logs, and then climb back out of the stream to rejoin the trail. We communicate with the other teams, but after a while, we have mostly static when we try to talk to SAR base. The canyon is so steep, windy, and heavily wooded that communication is difficult.

All three teams converge at 10:30 p.m. at Millennium Camp, marked by a backpack sitting on the trail. This small backpacking camp is on a cliff about 50 feet above the creek, which lies in a slot canyon below a pair of unnamed waterfalls. Earlier that day a family of four plus two extra kids had been taking a photo at the upper falls. One of the boys, not a girl as the initial call reported, maybe thirteen years old, slipped and fell. The rocks were as slippery as a Zambonied ice rink since they were covered with water and moss. He was sucked over the first 20-foot waterfall, fell into the boiling plunge pool, and came up uninjured and breathing. After shucking his pack, the boy swam in ice-cold water to a ledge that was about 3 by 3 feet and covered with slippery moss, but just out of the water. Had he been sucked down the creek, the current would have likely drawn him over another waterfall, over rocks and logs, and into the slot canyon that lies below the waterfalls. Into the abyss.

The boy dragged himself onto the ledge and stayed put, unable to go anywhere as the cliff above him was sheer and if he tried to stand, the wet moss was so slippery he'd end up back in the water. He had been cowering on the ledge, getting buffeted by the waterfall spray, for at least five hours, half of which were in the dark. Some bystanders came by and had been able to drop a Mylar space blanket and a bottle of water. Since he was walking up the trail in the warm summer sun that day, he was wearing only shorts and a T-shirt.

By the time we get to the cliff, it is dark. The cliff is a thick tangle of vine maple and dense shrubbery. Underfoot are slippery roots, mud, and rocks, soaked constantly from the spray of the waterfall. We now have ten SAR responders, all searching the cliff. We can barely hear our radios because of the cascading water. Richard Hallman, a Crag Rat and former nurse turned photographer, shouts, "We should put on harnesses!"

"Good idea," I say. I stop, set my pack down in the mud, pull out my harness and helmet.

The AMR crew asks if we have life jackets.

"I have one, and a wetsuit," I say. "Gary and Brian both brought wetsuits." I'm the only one with a life jacket.

"You'll be the first responder," he says. I will by default be the point person to go over the cliff.

After about five minutes of searching a twenty-foot section of cliff—for which we need to scramble through thick clusters of vine maple, peer over the edge, and point our lights down into the dark abyss of the plunge pool—something sparkles in my light.

"I got him," I yell when I spotted the sparkly orange Mylar blanket. The boy is perched on a ledge barely out of the water, tucked into the cliff. I can only see the top of his space blanket when I lean out dangerously over the edge of the cliff.

So, we go to work.

One of the AMR paramedics, Trevin, quickly outlines the tasks required.

"Let's set up a rappel team to access the patient and a second team to set up a haul system." Divide and conquer. Since we have ten people, a third team of two people heads down a trail below the second waterfall, to see if the boy is reachable by walking up the riverbank.

Gary sets up a rappel line by wrapping the rope around a thick Douglas fir. I want to clip to the rope before I look over the edge.

"Let me dress the knot, then you are good to go," says Gary, referring to making sure the knot is clean without being jumbled or twisted. And then, "You are good to go." At the same time, the Cascade Locks firefighters are constructing a separate rope-raising system independent of the rappel line. Hugh, Richard, and one of the AMR paramedics followed a trail downriver to see if they could reach the patient from below—no luck.

"I'm not going over the cliff yet, just going to the edge to take a look," I yell to Gary and Brian Hukari. I have my harness, helmet, and life vest on. I tie into the rappel line. From the edge of the cliff, while tied into the rope, I see the boy just 40 feet below me. He's on a small ledge out of the water, getting buffeted by the wind and spray from the falls. Just inches below the ledge, I see the boiling strong hydraulics of the cauldron. Just below the cauldron lies a second waterfall, the slot canyon, and the abyss.

I'm not thinking, *What could go wrong?* but rather, *What are the hazards?* Falling into the water and drowning is the biggest risk. I walk away from the edge, and then look at Brian and Trevin.

"He's right below us. About 40 feet. There's a good spot to haul him up just to my right. There's a secondary ledge halfway down."

Then, it dawns on me: In addition to the chance of falling into the creek, I may be with the patient for a while, smack in the middle of the spray of the waterfall. I'll get soaked instantly. I'll get cold.

"I'm going to put on my wetsuit," I yell to Brian and Gary.

I go through the laborious task of untying from the rope and doffing my life vest, harness, boots, and pants. I pull on my wetsuit, and then put the rest of the gear back on. I pull on gloves. I leave my pack on the edge of the cliff. I tuck my radio into the life vest, hoping it will stay dry. To my harness, I clip a second harness to use to *pick off*, or secure, the patient. I have three prussic cords, two carabiners, and a 20-foot piece of webbing. This is the bare minimum.

I'm about to drop over the edge, when I decide to put my jacket on too. So I take off my life vest, pull on my jacket, and then put the life vest back on. Then, I decide my headlamp isn't secure on my helmet. So I take off my helmet, secure the headlamp on the helmet using clips designed for this, and then strap it back on my head. If I drop the light, I'll be screwed. I tuck the radio in my life jacket. If I drop the radio, I'll be screwed. I have a quick pause, a time-out, to make sure everything is secured. Brian checks my harness and knots.

I am about to drop over the edge when Brian tells me to stop.

"Where are you going over?"

"Just here to my right," I point.

"Let me reroute the rope," he says. "It will have too much side tension." Being the expert at rope systems, he knows that spending two minutes to reroute the rope will make it safer. The rope angle, as it comes from the tree to the cliff edge through thick brush, needs to be as straight as possible. So I untie from the rope again, and Brian quickly reroutes all 150 feet of rope through the thick tangle of greenery.

I have a moment of emotion, fleeting. It's not fear, exactly. It's caution. But oddly enough, I have a sensation of trust. I trust Brian and Gary to set up the rappel line. I trust the Cascade Locks crew to set up the haul system. I trust the redundancy of the rope strength. I trust the life jacket and, perhaps overdressed, the wetsuit and jacket.

I drop over the edge.

I slide down the wet rope. We're using a strong 13-mm line and I'm sliding down the rope using a rappel device and also tied to the rope prussic knot as a backup, in case my hand were to slip off the belay device. Everything is overkill in the name of safety. As I'm coming down the rope, I land on top of the boy, pulverizing him with my headlamp and hitting him with my feet.

"Don't move!" I yell. My feet hit the ledge as I drop behind the boy. Immediately I find the moss- and water-covered ledge is so slippery I can barely stand. I'm still tied to the rope so I use the tension of the rope to hold me up.

"Don't move!" I yell again. "Everything is going to be okay! Don't move."

"I'm cold. I'm scared. I can't move it is so slippery," he says.

"Don't move. Do exactly what I say!" I shout. I'm still locked into the rappel line, and crouching over the patient, squatting right behind him. He's sitting cross-legged, with the space blanket around his shoulders. My headlamp is piercing the darkness, but reflects in sparkles on the spray from the waterfall a bit like a disco ball. It's disorienting. The boiling plunge pool is a few inches away, the water lapping the edge of the rock ledge. Waterfall spray is pelting me; I'm soaked instantly but I'm warm in my wetsuit and life vest. I unclip the patient harness from my belt, and gently put it on the patient, which is a chore and dangerous, because he has to move on the slippery ledge, which could cause him to slide right into the pool. I yell at him to extend his legs, and then I help him slip on the harness.

First he wiggles into the waist belt and leg loops from a sitting position and pulls the harness up to his thighs. Then, he must get the harness over his hips to his waist by lifting his butt off the rocks and sliding the harness, a maneuver that could cause him to slide right into the water. I'm holding his torso and trying not to slip myself. But considering the darkness, the wet clothing, the spray from the waterfall, and the moss and water on the rocks, I don't exactly have a firm grip.

Once the harness is on, I cinch the straps around his waist and legs as tight as possible, but he's a small kid so the harness barely fits. Then I unclip a cord from my belt, tie a prussic knot to secure the cord to my rappel line, and then use a carabiner to clip the cord to the patient's harness. That completes step one: the pick off. The patient is safely tied into the rope.

The radio crackles, "I'm about to come down," says Trevin, the AMR paramedic. He has a backpack full of advanced life support gear.

"There's no room on the ledge," I shout back into the radio, hoping he can hear me.

I do a quick survey: the boy has an ankle injury, but it's not deformed. It is still in his boot. He seems to be otherwise uninjured.

After only a few moments, the first haul rope comes down. The rope is weighted with a knot at the end; the knot drops in the water and disappears into the blackness. I lean out from the ledge, stretch my arms, and grab the rope. I quickly clip the patient into the knot with a carabiner. The second rope comes down; I retrieve it with a stretch, and clip the patient in again. The patient is tied into both ropes, for safety redundancy, and the rappel line. I unclip him from the rappel line. I hear the radio crackle so I retrieve it from my life vest.

"Repeat that," I yell, then hold the radio up to my ear.

"Ready to haul?" I hear.

"Stand by, need to tie myself in."

I am still tied into the rappel line with a prussic knot, but need to tie myself into both haul lines, so I can come up the cliff with the patient. I use two remaining cords and tie one cord using a prussic knot into each of the haul lines and clip the cords to a carabiner on my harness. I'm above the patient so we will both go up together. Then I untie from the rappel line.

"Ready to go?" I yell to the patient. "You'll feel the rope pull you up. Stand up and put your feet against the wall. Don't fight it." I'm yelling above the noise of the waterfall.

"Ready to go," I yell into the radio. The water and wind are still pummeling me and my headlamp dims a notch, running low on power. I'm warm, though, in my wetsuit, jacket, life vest, and boots. Up above, a 3:1 mechanical advantage using the MPD (multipurpose device) has been set up using a tree as an anchor.

Four rescuers above me start pulling rope.

Up we go.

As we make the 40-foot ascent, I'm constantly yelling at the patient to keep his feet against the wall. The natural instinct is for one to bear hug the wall with arms and knees. But raising goes more smoothly if you can get your feet against the wall and lean on the rope in a sitting position. He can't figure this out—he's scared and likely has never done this before. So, the boy is basically dragged 20 feet up to a small ledge halfway up the cliff.

"Hold," I say into the radio. And then when we are both standing on the ledge, after catching our breath for a second, I say into the radio, "Resume hauling."

Then, just minutes later, we are at the top of the cliff. Trevin and Brian are there to help us untie from the rope and escort the patient away from the cliff to a log. I doff all my gear and put my shirt and pants back on.

There is still a flurry of activity at the campsite away from the cliff, but everyone is more relaxed and relieved. The boy is sitting on a log where Trevin and Richard are checking him. I do a quick exam: He's okay. Someone gets him a dry shirt and feeds him a peanut butter and jelly sandwich, so his shivering stops. The parents are hovering and relieved. The rest of the rescuers are breaking down the two rope systems—the rappel line and the twin-rope haul system.

We will, in the forthcoming days, debrief the rescue: The patient pick-off harness we keep in the truck does not fit kids too well. We need more batteries for the SAR truck—headlamps kept dying during the night. Stefan carried the telescopic antenna, which worked well when we were deep in the canyon. Bob Stewart, deputy at the trailhead, had erected the high-gain antenna on top of Com Rig, which also helped. Craig McCurdy, who came late, stationed himself as human repeater halfway up the trail, which helped relay radio transmissions. Tom Rousseau later gets permission to program our radios with the Forest Service repeater on Indian Mountain, making SAR communication much better in this canyon.

When I talked to the *Hood River News*, I didn't discuss any specifics. But I did comment on our rescues in general. More than half the time, people are not taking great risks, but slip and fall due to footwear, lapse of attention, or difficult trail conditions. Occasionally people are doing something foolhardy, but not as often as you'd think. Yes, people call us more often with cell phones. No, phones don't always work.

We will go into these trails many times and have many issues to discuss at meetings.

At our meeting, we usually find something to laugh about—not at the expense of any victims, but as a coping mechanism that enables us to continue to get out of bed at zero dark storm and rescue people.

That night, at Sunrise Falls with the young boy, we are packing up, anxious to start down the trail—and anxious to head home, which will be a two-hour hike down and a half-hour drive home. Home for a shower to scrub skin to eliminate the poison oak oil. Home to scarf food and guzzle water. Home to dry and repack gear, charge radios and headlamps. Find extra batteries. Order a smaller harness. Write a brief report.

After my first decade in mountain rescue, I wrote a book about wilderness medicine and balancing life, out of pure love for adventure, adventure travel, mountain rescue, and the indoor, solitary task of writing. After my second decade in mountain rescue, I find myself more interested in risk—why it's important in mountain rescue, in outdoor recreation, and, for that matter, all aspects of life. In the coming decade, now that I'm fifty, I will continue to collect mountain rescue stories. Things may change: rules, rescue techniques, access issues, equipment, technology. Risks will change and perspectives perhaps too. One thing I'm certain will remain largely unchanged: the Crag Rats. We'll still keep getting calls for help and the Crag Rats—ninety years deep—will continue to respond.

Just before we hike down the trail—patient fed and warmed, rope systems broken down, gear stuffed in backpacks, rescuers all accounted for—I look at my watch, and have a singular thought: *Possibly, I can be in bed by 1:00 a.m.*

CODA

Haiti in the Time of Cholera

IN THE MONTHS AFTER MY ACCIDENT, I HAD ONE FINAL CHALLENGE IN my recovery. I'd been on my first SAR mission since my accident. Not only was it quite simple—the uninjured couple who made their way out of Warren Creek Canyon—but I had some control. At any time, I could have excused myself from a portion, or all, of the rescue. I'd also already been back skiing, on the Whistler trip with my daughters. Again, I had some control: I could stop skiing or dial back the speed, intensity, and terrain at any time.

But I had one more hurdle: I didn't want to miss a trip I had planned before my accident. It wasn't just that I needed to prove a point to myself. It was driven by passion.

But it is not just any trip, not just any type of adventure.

I am going to Haiti.

Among other risks in Haiti—civil unrest, tropical infectious disease, and car accidents on substandard roads, with fast drivers, in older cars, with a substandard emergency medical system—if I contracted malaria, I could die. The spleen is vital to warding off malaria; I have no spleen. This would be a control challenge.

But this passion I have for adventure travel runs deep. It began a long, long time ago. I traveled all over the world as a kid. Dad and Mom participated in an organization started by Jimmy and Rosalynn Carter called the Friendship Force. This program was designed to arrange home stays between two countries so families could foster friendships across borders. By the time I'd graduated from high school, I'd been to a dozen far-flung places. In South Korea we stayed with a family in Seoul and took a trip to the Panmunjom Demilitarized Zone. We went in the single building that sat smack on the border of North and South Korea. Inside it had a large conference table with a line painted on the wall, ceiling, floor and table—delineating the two countries. It was like something I did as a child to separate my half of the Lego table from my brother's. We took a walk around the table, so for ten seconds I strolled into North Korea.

In Egypt, they told us not to talk religion or politics; we stayed with a Coptic family and talked religion and politics every evening. We hit it off so well we stayed for a few days in their summer villa in Alexandria before heading on a Nile cruise. My main memory of Alexandria: The cockroaches were as large as rats and crawled in our bed, on the ceiling, on the walls. My main memory from the Abu Simbel to Luxor Nile cruise: The eerie feeling that I was James Bond in the Valley of the Kings when a guard caught my brother and me taking illegal photos of the tombs, tried to confiscate our camera, and let us go, after much arguing and hand waving, with film intact.

In Oulu, Finland, we connected so well with our family that we spent an impromptu weekend camping and cloudberry picking with them in the forests before traveling up to the Arctic Circle. My parents, nearly four decades later, still stay in touch with our Finnish family.

We went to the Soviet Union, without a homestay, via train from Helsinki to St. Petersburg (then Leningrad) and then via Aeroflot to Moscow, way before the fall of the Berlin Wall caused the demise of the Eastern Bloc. And much later, when I was attending college in Salzburg, Austria, for a year, I met my parents for a homestay outside of Vienna, where I remember drinking sturm, the tart, milky, slightly fermented wine that comes during harvest, and twenty-year-old mushroom schnapps, both of which I've never drunk, nor wanted to drink, again.

One of the most poignant trips was to Ecuador, on a medical and dental trip with my father. He and Mom, in addition to the Friendship Force, participated in relief missions with Christian Medical and Dental Society. Dad is a retired orthodontist who did relief work pulling diseased and decayed teeth. In Ecuador I scrubbed in for surgeries on cleft palates, helped pull teeth, and dispensed medications in the makeshift pharmacy. When I came home, I felt like a rock star. People who found out I went to

Ecuador thought I was a saint. But I began to wonder, despite obviously personally benefitting greatly, if I'd actually helped people in Ecuador. I wondered if I'd made any difference to their health and quality of life. I entered medical school, enrolled in an evening informal travel medicine elective, and eventually wrote a research paper that was published a decade after my trip, *Attitudes Toward Medical Relief to Developing Countries*. In the hundred people I surveyed in my research, nearly all commented that they personally benefited greatly, but very few felt that they helped the indigenous people. Most just were not sure how much good they did.

So I continued to travel, but not for humanitarian relief. I lived in the Austrian Alps for a year in college, spent four months circumnavigating the earth by ship, and explored the coasts of six continents by skiing, hiking, cycling, windsurfing, surfing, kitesurfing, and eventually stand-up paddling. I learned to scuba dive. I taught adventure travel medical seminars around the world, and even did a stint as a cruise ship physician, in hopes of laying the groundwork for joining an Antarctica expedition. And I kept backcountry skiing: Chile, Europe, Japan. Eventually I logged nearly one hundred countries on six continents.

But I'd yet to go back to humanitarian relief.

Until I got a call to go to Haiti.

It is a way, I suppose, of merging my two separate lives. I have one as a medical doctor in a hospital and a clinic. I have another as an adventurer, traveling around the world seeking out the best surf breaks, powder runs, mountain ascents, and mountain bike trails. Haiti, I suppose, would bring it all together, medicine and adventure, twenty-five years after the Ecuador trip.

My longtime friend and mentor, Bill "Doc" Forgey, who's quite famous in wilderness and travel medicine circles, teaches medical students in Indiana. A year after the 2009 earthquake, Doc took a group of medical students to Haiti under the umbrella of a religious group. Let's just say they had challenges beyond those in Haiti while trying to work under the auspices of a religious group. So Doc started his own nonprofit, Medical Student Missions, now called Health Corps Haiti, developed both to provide medical care to Haiti and to educate medical students on international health. When Doc called to ask me to lead an education trip in 2012 and wanted me to make a reconnaissance trip in spring 2011, I dropped everything to arrange the trip.

Then I had my accident.

I really wanted to go. I wanted to help and I wanted the adventure. I talked to my doctor. She gave me clearance. And so I went to Haiti. Partly I helped teach a wilderness first responder course, but mostly I worked in the local hospital, seeing around five hundred patients with medical students in the five days I was in country. I was indeed careful, from mosquito precautions, to motor vehicles, to walking on the street, to the trail hike to a mountain-top medical outpost. Haiti was remote, rugged, taxing. I was careful.

I ended up returning to Haiti four times. On my third trip, I bought my oldest daughter, Skylar, when she was fifteen.

"Can I bring a friend?" she asked, like a typical teenager during the planning stages.

"Only if they bring a parent," I said. Haiti requires one-to-one parenting, even with teenagers. I ended up taking five teenage girls (with corresponding parents), all of whom worked just as hard as anyone. We were barely in Haiti for twenty-four hours when Skylar whispered to me one evening, "I never thought people could be this poor." She'd imagined Haiti would be like rural Mexico and Chile, but nothing quite compares to one of the poorest countries in the world.

On my fourth trip, at the peak of the Chikungunya epidemic, I take an inflatable stand-up paddle board. It rolls up and fits, with a collapsible paddle and pump, in a duffel bag. Because I travel with a carry-on, the paddle board is my only checked bag. It looks like just a duffel bag full of clothes. After the first long day working in the hospital, my interpreter Sonson, whom I'd known from three prior trips, hires a motorcycle taxi. With a driver, Sonson, me, and a giant duffel bag, we barely fit on the motorcycle. I tell Doc that I am headed to surf the Artibonite River. He shakes his head.

"Take a Cipro," he says referring to the medication that helps prevent cholera. "That river's full of cholera." Indeed, a tributary of the Artibonite River near Verrettes was the epicenter of the epidemic. Fortunately, we are in the dry season. Because some houses have no latrines or human waste system, the human waste sits in the ravines and gullies until a rain storm washes the waste, and cholera, into the river and irrigation canals. An hour later, I am paddling the stand-up paddle board in the cholera-infested Artibonite River. After a short paddle, I give Sonson a ride on the back of the board.

The next morning, he asks to go back so that he might try. We load up the motorcycle taxi and go back to the river. I find a small irrigation ditch with a gentle current. Sonson strips to his underwear, jumps on the board, and paddles up and down the small creek. His smile is so huge and is laughter so infectious, the motorcycle taxi driver suddenly jumps off the parked motorcycle, strips off his clothes, and takes a turn paddling.

"You changed my life, Doctor Christopher," says Sonson later, never having been exposed to such an odd and unique form of recreation.

So medical relief in Haiti, much like mountain rescue, is unpaid, risky, and arduous work. But it's also marked with great reward and enjoyment.

Which brings me to the final issue, which might be quite obvious by now: Why do we do this business, spending all night rescuing someone from a slot canyon, climbing a mountain to save lost skiers, and traveling to far-flung locations in austere conditions to help others? Why do we take this risk when the probability of mishap is moderate to high and the consequences are higher?

The reason, I suppose, is partly to gain a sense of giving to the community: humanitarianism. We are driven to help others in need. But I won't lie—a good bit of selfishness is another motivating factor. We have a deep passion for the outdoors and a passion for helping people. It is a very rare opportunity we have, using our skills to save lives. It's rewarding. It develops camaraderie. And it is, sometimes, pure fun, especially when we see the mountains and forests from such a different perspective, at night, in a storm, at zero dark thirty. We love outdoor recreation and adventure travel. But mountain-rescue missions give that adventure deeper meaning: a sense of urgency, importance. Similar to our experiences in providing medical relief to developing countries, we get an enormous sense of satisfaction after a successful rescue mission.

I just wish so many missions were not at night.

Postscript

Not long after I finished the manuscript for this book, my youngest daughter asked me to take her up Mount St. Helens. She had been thinking about climbing and skiing the volcano for a year, given that she watches me pack up my truck, pile in a few friends, and ski it every spring. I did not push the idea of my daughter skiing the peak. As most parents know, some things we need to insist our kids learn—like swimming, for example. But, mountaineering, or more specifically, ski mountaineering, is not necessarily something we need to teach our kids. They have to want to learn this sport.

So, one Friday evening, we pack our gear, buy a permit online, and drive an hour to the trailhead. The next morning at 4:30 a.m., after sleeping in the back of my truck, we start the climb. The first few minutes on the trail Avrie is nauseated and has a headache. We are hiking by headlamp, with heavy ski boots and skis strapped to our packs. It's not a situation where anyone feels good—my back hurts and I am tired from sleeping in the back of my truck. Avrie looks awful, as if she's about to cry.

But as the sky lightens with the coming of dawn, Avrie eventually gets her hiking mojo. After four hours of hiking—flat trail, scrambling up basalt lava, and climbing on snow—we reach the top. The glorious sunny summit has spectacular views of Mounts Adams, Rainier, and Hood and the steaming cauldron of the crater. After a few photos and gawking at the panorama, we ski down in half the time it took us to climb. We make turns in the smooth, soft, spring snow back to the truck.

A few days later, barely recovered, Avrie asks me to take her up Mount Hood, a much more technical climb than Mount St. Helens. Normally, the safest time to climb the safest route, the South Climb, is in April or May. Spring provides good weather and safer snow conditions; cooler weather is mandatory to keep the snow firm for climbing, to minimize the rock and ice fall, and to keep the crevasses closed. But, she asks me in July.

"I'm not climbing all night," I say to Avrie. Climbers who do attempt the route in summer often leave the parking lot at midnight and climb before the heat of the morning. "We have plenty of time to climb it next year in the spring when we can climb during the day." I'm downright sick of doing rescues at night.

"I want to climb all three mountains in one summer," she says.

It is impossible to ignore her motivation. I check climbing conditions and notice that the second week in July has an unusually cool stretch of weather. So, being compulsive, I call my friends and fellow Crag Rats.

"Oh, it's ideal. Not one speck of rock or icefall," says Richard Hallman, veteran of dozens of climbs of the mountain. "We caught the last chair yesterday to be on the summit for sunset. Excellent conditions."

"Taking first chair is perfect; let the snow warm up for the ski down," says Wes Baumann, Mount Hood Climbing Ranger.

"You should do it," says Paul Klein, ski patroller.

Due to a stretch of cool weather, the snow had been freezing at night and not warming up too much. The crevasses were open but visible and easily avoidable. A few spats of new snow the past month kept the route smooth and free from "sun cups," depressions caused by solar heating. And a light wind kept the snow cold to minimize rock and ice fall. Add that all up: relatively excellent (read: safe) climbing conditions.

So, Avrie and I pack our gear, wake up at 4:30 a.m., drive an hour to Timberline Lodge, buy a one-ride climber's lift ticket, sign in at climber's registration, fill out a free permit, and catch the 7:00 a.m. Magic Mile and Palmer chairlifts. We look quite out of place with our mountaineering packs loaded with crampons and ice axes and wearing climbing harnesses over our ski pants. We stand in line with two hundred ski racers bedecked in spandex race suits and bulky race helmets with face guards and mirrored-lens goggles (The ski area, as I mentioned earlier in the book, is open all summer on Palmer Glacier for young ski racers at training camps and national teams for off-season training.)

We ride up in forty-degree temperatures under a cloudless, clear blue sky. To the west, I can see a thick marine layer of clouds covering

Portland and encroaching on the mountains. I will watch the cloud layer all day. At the top of Palmer Chairlift at 8:00 a.m. we start hiking, at 8,000 feet. After an hour, with Avrie slipping in her alpine ski boots and getting frustrated, we strap on crampons. We continue to climb toward Hogsback Ridge, at 10,000 feet. We have a conversation about turning back. In fact, it's later in the day than I expected, due to our methodical but slow pace and the chairlift line. I'm planning on turning back. But the air is still cool and the light wind is keeping the snow firm (as in, safe). And the biggest risk of climbing in July has been eliminated: crowds. We've see only two other climbing parties on their way down (without skis, they climbed all night, and didn't need to wait for the snow to soften for descent as skiers do).

I'm about to call off the climb, when at Hogsback Ridge we meet another couple. I briefly discuss the route conditions, and instantly I can tell the man is quite skilled at climbing Mount Hood and find out we have mutual mountaineering friends.

"Snow seems firm. Wind keeping ice frozen. No rockfall apparent."

"We're taking the safer route, up Old Chute."

"Good idea. We are, too."

So Avrie and I dump our skis at Hogsback. Although the conditions are ideal to ski from the summit, I want to go light to make sure we bag the top. We walk up the narrow ridge of snow, and reach three large crevasses called a *bergschrund*, where the glacier peels away from the rocky headwall. We continue around the bergschrund and then traverse a steep slope to the west. The winter route—when the crevasses are closed and you can walk right over them—goes directly up a chute called Pearly Gates. But if we were to slip in Pearly Gates today, we'd fall right into the crevasse. So we divert about twenty minutes to the north to climb the safer, crevasse-free Old Chute.

I give Avrie instructions on how to use the ice ax right there on the spot and tell her to keep three points in the snow at all times—referring to the ice axe in one hand, ski pole in the other, and both crampon-strapped boots. I give her instructions on how to avoid a falling rock or ice chunks. We traverse the slope, get good purchase on the softening snow, and then climb up a wide, steep snowfield.

The final pitch, Old Chute, is a steep, 50-degree, 150-foot-long chute. The snow is just soft enough to get good traction with crampons, but not so soft that we *posthole*, or sink up to our knees. Up we go, like climbing a staircase: my neck gets sore from looking up, but I want to watch for rock and ice fall.

Halfway up Old Chute, I think to myself, *This is really steep.* If Avrie has a minor slip, the snow is soft enough she should be able to stop her fall. If she falls backward, though, she could tumble head-over-heels. I climb fast to reach the summit, pound in a picket (a snow stake to provide an anchor to attach my rope), and pull out my rope. I am just about to toss down the safety rope.

"I'm tossing down a rope for you to tie into," I yell.

"I'm okay, I don't need it," she says confidently.

A few seconds later we're standing on the summit of Mount Hood.

It's noon. And some climbers might think that's very late to be on the summit in July. Indeed. But the snow is just barely softening and the wind is still keeping the ice on the cliffs frozen. We spend only ten minutes at the summit, despite it being crystal clear and warm, as I am attentive to possible rock and ice fall with warming temperatures. We spy the core of the Cascade Volcanoes: Mounts Adams, Rainier, and St. Helens to the north, and Mounts Jefferson, Three Sisters, and Broken Top to the south.

I belay Avrie on a rope down Old Chute, but she doesn't really need it. We climb down the expansive slope and traverse the exposed bowl over to Hogsback ridge with no rock fall whatsoever and no post-holing. After retrieving our skis, doffing crampons, and having a quick bite of food and drink of water, we ski.

The 3,000-foot descent below Hogsback Ridge and the large Crater is superb: creamy soft, smooth snow; it's just soft enough to ski but not warm enough to turn the snow to slush, which surprises me for July. Back through Timberline ski area, the ski racers are gone because the race course is too slushy by midday. The freestyle snowboarders and skiers are out in force in the terrain park. The ski area maintains one 40-foot-wide ribbon of snow in a gully so that we can ski all the way to Timberline Lodge. We are back to the car at 2:30 p.m.

Two down. The most gnarly, Mount Hood, is in the bag.

Finally, Avrie asks about the third in the trifecta of volcanoes. Mount Adams in Washington, like Mount St. Helens, is a non-technical climb. But it's a long climb: 6,000 vertical feet from car to summit via trail, then rocks, then snow. Just six days after the Hood summit, we drive an hour to the trailhead on short notice when the weather and our schedules line up. We stop at the ranger station for a permit, and then drive up to the trailhead, which is 11 miles down a gravel road and 5 miles down a rough, unmaintained dirt road filled with potholes. At the trailhead, we don our packs loaded with ski gear, to join what will be more than eight hundred people climbing the mountain that weekend. We make the three-hour climb to Lunch Counter by 8:00 p.m., pitch our tent, and boil snow for drinking water and a small cup of hot chocolate.

The next morning, fairly rested from a windless night, we continue up the snowfields, wearing crampons and carrying skis. At the false summit, the hardest pitch on the mountain, we have a problem. We are tired. Avrie and I had climbed Mount Hood six days earlier. For soccer training, we'd also gone on two 6-mile runs that week. And Avrie had to work that evening in Hood River, so she was a little worried about taking too much time. And the skiing was downright difficult: frozen suncups.

"I want to summit because I don't want to have to come back," she says.

"Sometimes you have to make the decision to bail on the climb. Getting up is optional. Getting home is mandatory. It's okay to turn around," I say.

And then, knowing the indecision of my teenager and the struggle to want to achieve the summit despite my warning to the contrary, I make the decision for us, just as a guide or a mountain rescuer might.

"We are going down," I say, matter of fact. "It's fine." We bail on the climb before reaching the summit. But I can see Avrie is relieved and thankful that she didn't have to make the decision. On the way down I reflect on the many mountains on which I've turned around.

Once, twenty-five years ago, during my first attempt at this very mountain, my group turned around thirty minutes from the summit due to clouds. I was on a group climb with the Washington State University outdoor club during my first year of medical school. It was a small group of students with the outdoor club adviser as the group leader. He made the decision and we all followed it.

On a trip backcountry snowboarding the remote Steens Mountain in southeast Oregon, I turned around fifteen minutes shy of the summit because a warm front moved in, the snow softened to slush, and Matt, Jay, and I were post-holing up a gully, sinking to our knees. We descended without reaching the top.

Same thing on Mount Jefferson: I planned a weekend climb, drove to the trailhead, hiked in to high camp, and woke the next morning to knee-deep slush at 9,000 feet. Post-holing to our knees equals danger. Matt, Jay, and I again turned around.

Years later, on Mount Shasta via the Hotlum-Bolam Ridge, I got concerned about avalanche and snow conditions, and bailed on the climb an hour and 1,000 feet from the summit.

Alas, when you spend time in the mountains, you are always at risk. I don't know how much more at risk I am in the mountains than I am driving my car to the city or riding my bike on the 2-mile commute down May Street to work. I am at risk every time I run, ride, ski, climb, surf, and paddle. I am at risk in the mountains and forests and rivers and oceans of the world. But, just as I try to explore the nature of risk, the measure of something so intangible as comparing time spent outside in human-, gravity-, ocean-, wind-, and river-powered adventures, I understand I gain tremendous enjoyment from being outside—spiritual, physical, and mental. It is, indeed, the most favorite and cherished part of the day and what makes me function.

Before my accident, I was reserved and cautious. After my accident I was reserved, perhaps slightly more so. I realized, in fact, that the great enjoyment I get from being in the mountains is the journey, more so than the goal.

So after climbing with Avrie that summer and working feverishly to finish this manuscript, I had a few thoughts sparked by the aborted Mount Adams summit bid with Avrie and the Haiti trip with Skylar. My daughters may become Crag Rats. If they are to become members of this relatively elite group, what exactly would I tell them? How would I pass on my infinite wisdom as their father? Or, for that matter, even if my daughters do not become Crag Rats, what have I learned from my mentors and colleagues, my experiences on the mountain, and my life in medicine and rescue, that I can pass on to my girls? What would the list of lessons be? And would the list be useful beyond ski mountaineering and mountain rescue? And would it be useful to anyone besides my daughters?

I love lists. I have to-do lists for work and home, for sure. But my more favored list is the one about upcoming adventure travels and the one about those I'm still investigating (stand-up paddle surfing and backcountry skiing Morocco, mountain biking in Iceland, kitesurfing in Cuba—you get the idea).

One of my early books developed from a list. *Backcountry Ski and Snowboard Oregon*, a guidebook originally published in 2000, then revised in 2011, started from a list of all my backcountry ski and ski mountaineering trips in Oregon and Washington. *Adrenaline Junkie's Bucket List: 100 Extreme Outdoor Adventures to Do Before You Die* metamorphosed from a list of grander adventures around the world.

So now I have another list: A list of how to take positive risks in the wildernesses of the world and come out with a low probability of accident and a low probability of consequences.

The lessons aren't earth shattering, and they are mine and mine alone, collected from experience and mentors you have only barely heard of, like Jim Wells, Brian Hukari, Bernie Wells, Bill Pattison, Rick Ragan, and Doc Forgey. Hopefully my daughters, my family, future Crag Rats, and you, dear reader, will identify with these. Maybe some lessons can be adapted for other places in life: work, home, family, romance, friendships. Maybe we can indeed step out of the known world into the backcountry of the world's mountains, forests, rivers, oceans, beaches. And do so safely. So, here you go:

- Take a bit of risk to gain rich reward.

- Get outside; it will make you feel good.

- Balance your life: Work hard, but play hard, too. Take a risk, but not too much.

- Spend time with yourself, your family, your friends, and your colleagues. Develop relationships. These relationships may save your life one day.

- Keep your overhead low and your backpack tidy. But take a chance now and then outside your comfort zone.

- Don't be afraid to be a leader—the world needs more.

- Your safety is first priority: Stay fit, eat right, drink enough water, moderate vices, and get enough sleep. Mental fitness is important, too: be clear-headed when you have an important job at hand.

- Take care of your team.

- Accidents can happen to anyone at any time; don't judge or blame. Laughing is important, but save it until after the mission is done and everyone is home safely.

- Quality experiences are better than quantity. Search out deep powder snow, a clean wave, and a beautiful trail. Don't stress if you don't make the summit.

- Be smart. Good judgment is the foundation for safety.

- Be prepared. Buy good equipment, hone your skills, and seek experience.

- Learn a skill, and then practice 10,000 times.

- Go with partners who have three qualities: You can trust them, learn from them, and teach them.

- Take your kids outside and take your parents outside. Just be attentive to supervision and adjust adventures accordingly.

- Be cautious of groups: Sometimes going against the group is difficult, but necessary. Surround yourself with kindred souls.

- Be cautious of distractions; multitasking, the adrenaline buzz, and fatigue should be identified and guarded against.

- If a mission or project becomes too complex, revert back to the basics.

- Embrace technology. A cell phone is an excellent tool. Learn how to use the GPS app.
- Be careful of the extremes: severe terrain, difficult conditions, and high-risk activities. Make sure the risk doesn't outweigh the benefit.
- It's okay to turn around. The mountains will be here tomorrow. Going up is optional; getting down is not.
- It's okay not to go. Don't climb mountains if you don't want to. Don't be a Crag Rat if you don't want to. Choose something else in the vast array of possibility and opportunity in this life.
- Take responsibility for your actions—sometimes that just means saying thank you. Write thank-you notes.
- Ask for help when you need it.
- Trust those who help you, but don't be afraid to ask questions.
- Give back when you can. If you want to be a Crag Rat: *berg heil*, or greetings at the top. If you want to contribute to your community in some other way, that's just as honorable.
- Find your passion and act on it.

About the Author

Christopher Van Tilburg studied science communication at the University of Portland and medicine at University of Washington. He has worked for two decades as an emergency physician. He is currently staff physician at Providence Hood River Memorial Hospital in Oregon, where he serves as medical director of Occupational and Travel Medicine, staff physician in the emergency department, and ski resort doctor at Mountain Clinic at Mount Hood Meadows. He also works as a cruise ship doctor, a medical relief team leader in Haiti, a wilderness medicine instructor, an expert witness, and a mountain rescue doctor.

A frequent contributor to medical and non-medical publications, Dr. Van Tilburg is editor emeritus of *Wilderness Medicine* and editor-in-chief of *Travel Medicine News*. He is an active member of Crag Rats mountain rescue team and serves as chair of Mountain Rescue Association Medical Committee.

He has published eleven books. His memoir, *Mountain Rescue Doctor: Wilderness Medicine in the Extremes of Nature*, was a finalist for Oregon Book Awards and Banff Festival of Mountain Books and was a *Reader's Digest* Editors' Pick. *Adrenaline Junkie's Bucket List: 100 Extreme Outdoor Adventures to Do Before You Die* was awarded the Far West Ski Association's Bill Berry Award. For his editing and volunteering, Dr. Van Tilburg has been honored three times by the Wilderness Medical Society with the Dian Simpkins Award for Service in 2011, the Haiti Humanitarian Research Award in 2013, and the Wilderness Medical Society Ice Axe Award for Service in 2014.

For more information, visit www.christophervantilburg.com.